THiNK

TEACHER'S BOOK 4 B2

Brian Hart, Herbert Puchta, Jeff Stranks & Peter Lewis-Jones

CAMBRIDGE
UNIVERSITY PRESS

Acknowledgements

The publishers are grateful to the following contributors:
Blooberry: text design and layouts
Claire Parson: cover design
Vicky Saumell: author of *Using the Digital Resources*

CAMBRIDGE
UNIVERSITY PRESS

University Printing House, Cambridge CB2 8BS, United Kingdom

Cambridge University Press is part of the University of Cambridge.

It furthers the University's mission by disseminating knowledge in the pursuit of
education, learning and research at the highest international levels of excellence.

www.cambridge.org
Information on this title: www.cambridge.org/think

First published 2016
Printed in Italy by Rotolito Lombarda S.p.A.

A catalogue record for this publication is available from the British Library

ISBN 978-1-107-57328-4 Student's Book Level 4
ISBN 978-1-107-57325-3 Student's Book with Online Workbook and Online Practice Level 4
ISBN 978-1-107-57369-7 Workbook with Online Practice Level 4
ISBN 978-1-107-57416-8 Teacher's Book Level 4
ISBN 978-1-107-57423-6 Class Audio CDs Level 4
ISBN 978-1-107-57428-1 Video DVD Level 4
ISBN 978-1-107-57432-8 Presentation Plus DVD-ROM Level 4

Additional resources for this publication at www.cambridge.org/think

CONTENTS

MAP OF THE STUDENT'S BOOK

Welcome p 4   **A** A lucky pilot; Descriptive verbs; Phrasal verbs; Childhood memories; Elements of a story; Talking about past routines   **B** Future plans; Life plans; Future continuous; Future perfect; Being emphatic: *so* and *such*; Extreme adjectives   **C** Conversations; Personality; Using *should*; Career paths; Decisions; Permission   **D** A change of lifestyle?; Reporting verbs; Negative adjectives; Another country; Changes; Regrets: *I wish … / If only …*

	FUNCTIONS & SPEAKING	GRAMMAR	VOCABULARY
Unit 1 **Survival** p 12	Issuing and accepting a challenge Discussing situations and your emotional reactions to them	Verbs followed by infinitive or gerund Verbs which take gerund and infinitive with different meanings: *remember, try, stop, regret, forget*	Verbs of movement Adjectives to describe uncomfortable feelings **Wordwise:** Expressions with *right*
Unit 2 **Going places** p 20	Expressing surprise Discussing nomadic peoples	Relative clauses (review) *which* to refer to a whole clause Omitting relative pronouns Reduced relative clauses	Groups of people Phrasal verbs (1)
Review Units 1 & 2 pages 28–29			
Unit 3 **The next generation** p 30	Emphasising Discussing the Tiger mum style of parenting	Quantifiers *so* and *such* (review) *do* and *did* for emphasis	Costumes and uniforms Bringing up children
Unit 4 **Thinking outside the box** p 38	Expressing frustration Guessing game to practise personality adjectives	*be / get used to (doing)* vs. *used to (do)* Adverbs and adverbial phrases	Personality adjectives Common adverbial phrases **Wordwise:** Expressions with *good*
Review Units 3 & 4 pages 46–47			
Unit 5 **Screen time** p 48	Advice and obligation Talking about technology	Obligation, permission and prohibition (review) Necessity: *didn't need to / needn't have* Ability in the past (*could, was / were able to, managed to, succeeded in*)	Technology (nouns) Technology (verbs)
Unit 6 **Bringing people together** p 56	Using intensifying comparatives Discussing the use of the Internet for doing good Role play: Stuck in a lift	Comparatives Linkers of contrast	Ways of speaking Love and relationships
Review Units 5 & 6 pages 64–65			
Unit 7 **Always look on the bright side** p 66	Cheering someone up *Silver linings* game: – thinking of optimistic solutions	Ways of referring to the future (review) Future continuous Future perfect	Phrases to talk about the future: *about to, off to, on the point of* Feelings about future events **Wordwise:** Expressions with *so*
Unit 8 **Making lists** p 74	Saying 'Yes' and adding conditions Discussing wonders of the world	Conditionals (review) Mixed conditionals	Phrasal verbs (2) Alternatives to *if: suppose, provided, as long as, otherwise, unless*
Review Units 7 & 8 pages 82–83			
Unit 9 **Be your own life coach** p 84	Asking someone politely to change their behaviour Discussing further education and work experience	*I wish* and *If only* *I would prefer to / it if, It's time, I'd rather / sooner*	Life's ups and downs Work and education
Unit 10 **Spreading the news** p 92	Making a point Introducing news Interviewing a well-known person Discussing the ethics of journalism	Reported speech (review) Reported questions and requests	Sharing news Reporting verbs **Wordwise:** Expressions with *way*
Review Units 9 & 10 pages 100–101			
Unit 11 **Space and beyond** p 102	Sympathising about past situations Discussing the greatest films Discussing life in space	Speculating (past, present and future) Cause and effect linkers	Space idioms Adjectives commonly used to describe films
Unit 12 **More to explore** p 110	Speaking persuasively Giving a presentation about human activity and the natural world	Passive report structures The passive: verbs with two objects	Geographical features Verb + noun collocations
Review Units 11 & 12 pages 118–119			

Pronunciation   pages 120–121   **Get it right!**   pages 122–126   **Speaking activities**   pages 127–128

PRONUNCIATION	THINK	SKILLS	
Dipthongs: alternative spellings	**Train to Think:** Thinking rationally **Self-esteem:** How adventurous are you?	Reading	Article: Sacrifice for survival? Article: The ultimate survivor Photostory: The challenge
		Writing	An email about an experience
		Listening	Radio show: *Desperate Measures*
Phrasal verb stress	**Train to Think:** Distinguishing fact from opinion **Values:** Learning from other cultures	Reading	Article: Refugees bring new life to a village Blog: From London to Lyon Culture: Nomadic people
		Writing	An informal email
		Listening	Radio interview about migration in nature
Adding emphasis	**Train to Think:** Changing your opinions **Self-esteem:** Developing independence	Reading	Blog: An embarrassing dad Book blurb and reviews: For and against – Tiger Mums Literature: *About a Boy* by Nick Hornby
		Writing	An essay about bringing up children
		Listening	Radio show about bringing up children in different cultures
Pronouncing words with *gh*	**Train to Think:** Lateral thinking **Values:** Appreciating creative solutions	Reading	Article: Lion lights Web post: A problem on Answers4U Photostory: Writer's block
		Writing	A story ending: *'Thanks, you saved my life!'*
		Listening	Talking heads – being imaginative
The schwa sound	**Train to Think:** The PMI strategy **Self-esteem:** Learning from elderly people	Reading	Texts: Smart screens? Article: Great success for teenage teachers: When silver surfers get connected Culture: When pictures learnt to walk and talk: the history of film
		Writing	Instructions
		Listening	A conversation about watching too much TV
Linked words with /dʒ/ and /tʃ/	**Train to Think:** Exaggeration **Values:** Doing good	Reading	Blog: The day people started talking Article: An Ice Cold Summer Literature: *A kind of loving* by Stan Barstow
		Writing	An essay about social media
		Listening	Radio show: *Radio romances*
Encouraging someone	**Train to Think:** Learning to see things from a different perspective **Self-esteem:** What cheers me up	Reading	Blog: Me, Myself and My take on the World Website page: QUOTATIONSforWORRIERS Photostory: The competition
		Writing	A short story ending: 'Every cloud has a silver lining'
		Listening	Radio show: *Silver Linings*
Weak forms with conditionals	**Train to Think:** The 'goal setting' checklist **Values:** Lists	Reading	Book review: *The Checklist Manifesto* by Atul Gawande Blog: Adrian's list blog Culture: The New Seven Wonders of the World
		Writing	An essay: A Modern Wonder of the World
		Listening	An interview about why we make lists
Linking: Intrusive /w/ and /j/	**Train to Think:** Jumping to a hasty conclusion **Self-esteem:** Being diplomatic	Reading	Presentation: Life and how to live it Quiz: Are you in control? Literature: *The Remains of the Day* by Kazuo Ishiguro
		Writing	An article for the school magazine
		Listening	A radio programme about life choices
Linking: Omission of the /h/ sound	**Train to Think:** Identifying the source of a piece of news **Values:** News or not?	Reading	Magazine article: Everybody's Tweeting Article: Bad news Photostory: The news clip
		Writing	A magazine article about an interview with a well-known person
		Listening	An interview with a foreign correspondent
Stress on modal verbs for speculation	**Train to Think:** Spotting flawed arguments **Self-esteem:** Who we are	Reading	Article: They might not come in peace … Blog: My all-time favourite films about space Culture: Real Humans
		Writing	A report about a problem on a school trip
		Listening	A talk about the Voyager mission
Linking: Intrusive /r/	**Train to Think:** Exploring hidden messages **Values:** Human activity and the natural world	Reading	Article: Our undiscovered world Article: Explorers: a friend to the native people Cândido Rondon Literature: *The Lost World* by Arthur Conan Doyle
		Writing	A short biography
		Listening	A talk about discovering new species

COURSE METHODOLOGY

Solid skills and language work

Think is a six-level course for adolescents and teenagers from A1 to C1 levels of the Common European Framework of Reference (CEFR). Based on a carefully crafted skills and language syllabus, the course helps students develop their receptive and productive language skills and strategies, and provides a systematic approach to competence training to help them prepare for their Cambridge English exams.

The authors have put great emphasis on the continuous extension of students' lexical knowledge by including two vocabulary sections within each unit, together with WordWise activities in every other unit. WordWise aims to develop awareness of and competence in using high-frequency words and chunks of language, important collocations, and phrasal verbs, as well as increasing fluency. In addition, an entertaining and thought-provoking teen photostory offers natural contexts for the presentation and practice of phrases for fluency. These are high-frequency lexico-grammatical chunks of language used in spoken communication.

Students are guided through the grammar via inductive exercises, which support them in their grasp of both form and meaning. The structures are then practised through a sequence of exercises in which students learn how to apply them in motivating and communicative activities.

Adolescents and teenagers do not always find it easy to participate in speaking activities, especially when they are asked to say what they think and feel. *Think* takes this concern seriously. Based on research in teenage classrooms in many different countries, the authors of *Think* have found that adolescents and teens generally find it easier to engage in thinking activities if they are embedded in the framework of topics and texts that they can emotionally connect with, and especially those that are far from their day-to-day realities. This remoteness gives students the opportunity to look outwards rather than inwards, and in so doing feel less self-conscious. So in the first few levels of the course, units often start somewhat removed from students' own lives, presenting stories of extremes, set in faraway places and cultures but whose protagonists – the heroes and heroines of these stories – young people can identify with. This helps them to get in closer touch with inspirational human qualities such as creativity, courage, perseverance, passion and care, and makes it easier for them to get involved in the speaking activities leading into or following the texts; this in turn makes their learning much easier, quicker and more pleasant.

Based on educational principles

Piaget (1981:3) asserts that all learning involves states of 'pleasure, disappointment, eagerness, as well as feelings of fatigue, effort, boredom'. The transition period from adolescence to early adulthood offers its own additional emotional challenges, as it is characterised by the individual's struggle for identity. During this period, many teens are overwhelmed by their emotions, and these can exert a strong influence – both positive and negative – on their behaviour and their attitudes. The integration of both emotional qualities and cognitive processes is key to the successful development of students' cognition, their understanding of the world, and their development towards becoming responsible human beings.

Think supports you as a teacher in helping your students integrate their emotional reactions and cognitive processes. It achieves this through an invaluable and comprehensive support system aimed at systematically developing your students' thinking skills, their awareness of values and their self-esteem, whilst at the same time building their language skills and competencies. This in turn will increase students' awareness of the issues that are important to their present and future lives, deepen their understanding of important social and global issues, and enable them to become more caring and thoughtful young adults.

TRAIN TO THiNK

At the lower levels, *Think* focuses on building basic cognitive tools, i.e. capabilities that are required for the development of so-called higher order thinking skills that will be addressed later on in your students' English language development. Examples of such basic thinking skills include Comparing and Contrasting, Categorising, Sequencing, Focusing Attention, Exploring Space, Time and Numbers, and Understanding Cause and Effect.

The higher levels of *Think* focus on the development of more advanced thinking skills. The B2 and C1 levels guide students in developing critical thinking skills. According to Cottrell (2011), these include such things as ascertaining the extent to which we believe what we see or hear, determining whether something is true, arguing one's case, identifying when further information is required and selecting information for a given purpose.

The activities in the books have been carefully designed to offer an appropriate level of challenge, taking into account the fact that students are tackling/approaching them in a language they are still learning and not in their own.

THiNK VALUES

Values are what we need to guide us through our life and to inform the way in which we interact with others. They are crucial for young people. Parents, teachers, schools and societies have an obligation to convey positive values to the next generation.

Teaching values is undoubtedly a challenging task. Telling teens how they should or should not behave is rarely the most efficient way of inculcating the right values in your students. It might be more promising for you to model the behaviour you want to evoke in your students. So, for example, if we want our students to become empathetic listeners, we need to demonstrate what it means to be a good listener; we ourselves need to listen to them empathetically. Other important elements in promoting positive values in the classroom are: a supportive and encouraging learning atmosphere; and a positive rapport between you and your students. Moreover, exposure to emotionally engaging content (stories) and motivating activities that involve the exploration of important universal values and making them their own, further enables students to increase their awareness of and understand the importance of values, and ultimately, adapt their behaviour accordingly. This is where *Think* offers you significant support, as it gives your students many opportunities to reflect on and discuss a wide range of important values, including ethical, environmental, health-oriented and artistic ones.

▬ THiNK SELF-ESTEEM ▬

As many teachers have noticed, a lack of self-esteem and self-worth can lead to an attitude of defensiveness in teenage students. This frequently observed pattern can lead to serious behavioural issues that are usually very difficult to deal with, such as students failing to take responsibility for their own actions, bullying and threatening others, withdrawing from work, daydreaming, or even giving up study altogether.

Studies show that attempts to try and help students build their self-esteem by repeating affirmations, for example, tend to fail or even result in the exact opposite. Goodman (2013) claims that 'the quest for greater self-esteem can leave people feeling empty and dissatisfied' (*op cit*, p. 27) and stresses (*op cit*, p. 28) that 'a far better way to bolster your sense of self-worth is, ironically, to think about yourself less. Compassion toward others and yourself, along with a less self-centred perspective on your situation, can motivate you to achieve your goals while helping you weather bad news, learn from your mistakes and fortify your friendships.'

And this is exactly what the activities in *Think* labelled *Think Self-Esteem* are for. They help students reflect on their role in society, their attitudes and those of others. It encourages them to learn from their mistakes, and develop an insight into their own thinking (meta-cognition) – all important stepping-stones towards building a strong sense of self-worth and self-esteem.

Sources:

Cottrell, S. (2011) *Critical Thinking Skills*, Basingstoke: Palgrave Macmillan

Domasio, A. (1994) *Descartes' Error: Emotion, Reason, and the Human Brain*, New York: Penguin Putnam

Goodman, A. (2013) 'Letting go of self-esteem', *Scientific American Mind*, October

Shaver, J.J.P. and Strong, W., 'Values in education and education in values', in Halstead, J.M. and Taylor, M.J. (eds) (1976) *Facing Value Decisions: Rationale-building for Teachers*, Belmont

Le Doux, J. (1998) *The Emotional Brain: The Mysterious Underpinnings of Emotional Life*, New York: Simon & Schuster

Piaget, J. (1981) 'Intelligence and Affectivity: Their Relationship during Child Development', Palo Alto: Annual Reviews

Puchta, H. and Williams, M. (2011) *Teaching Young Learners to Think*, Helbling Languages and Cambridge University Press

Unit and Topic area	Critical Thinking	Values	Self-esteem
1 Survival	Thinking rationally [Choosing relevant facts to make decisions]		How adventurous are you? [A sense of purpose: assessing positive and negative effects of trying new things]
2 Going places	Distinguishing fact from opinion [Asking questions to make the distinction]	Learning from other cultures [Personal values: the benefits of understanding other cultures]	
3 The next generation	Changing your opinions [Checking the evidence that your opinion is based on]		Developing independence [A sense of identity: the extent to which we make our own decisions]
4 Thinking outside the box	Lateral thinking [Finding alternative ways of looking at a problem]	Appreciating creative solutions [Social values: how people can solve problems in a variety of ways]	
5 Screen time	The PMI Strategy [A way of making decisions through brainstorming]		Learning from elderly people [A sense of purpose: seeing how others can help you develop]
6 Bringing people together	Exaggeration [Understanding what someone is really saying, despite exaggeration]	Doing good [Social values: Fundraising for good causes]	
7 Always look on the bright side	Learning to see things from a different perspective [Taking an optimistic viewpoint]		What cheers me up [A sense of identity: how to overcome negative feelings]
8 Making lists	The 'goal-setting' checklist [Deciding what you want to achieve and how to go about it]	Lists [Personal values: assessing the value of list-making]	
9 Be your own life coach	Jumping to a hasty conclusion [Spotting over-generalisations]		Being diplomatic [A sense of purpose: not upsetting other people unnecessarily]
10 Spreading the news	Identifying the source of a piece of news [Whether you can trust a source of news]	News or not? [Social values: the worth of publishing a story]	
11 Space and beyond	Spotting flawed arguments [Detecting lack of evidence in arguments]		Who we are [A sense of identity: choosing things that represent us]
12 More to explore	Exploring hidden messages [Understanding what people really mean]	Human activity and the natural world [Social values: assessing the effects of what we do on the world around us]	

The first reading sets the scene for the unit …

4 THINKING OUTSIDE THE BOX

OBJECTIVES

FUNCTIONS: expressing frustration
GRAMMAR: be / get used to (doing) vs. used to (do); adverbs and adverbial phrases
VOCABULARY: personality adjectives; common adverbial phrases

> **Objectives,** focusing on skills and language, are clearly displayed. These signal to you and your students what you can expect to achieve by the end of the unit.

> **Reading** texts are about contemporary topics that teens can relate to. They span a range of genres from magazine articles and blogs to webchats and product reviews.

> Pre-reading activities activate students' prior knowledge, get them interested in the topic of the text and provide a tool for pre-teaching key vocabulary.

READING

1 Look at the photos. Match the photos with these words:
- lions
- cattle
- a scarecrow
- a light bulb
- a battery
- a solar panel

2 SPEAKING Work in pairs or small groups. There are people in a tribe in Africa who want to stop lions killing their cows. Think of ways they could do this using the items in the photos.

3 Read the article and match summaries A–F with the sections 1–5. There is one extra summary.

A The lions are finally fooled ☐
B An accidental light on the problem ☐
C Some success with scarecrows ☐
D The dilemma of the Masai people ☐
E The outcomes for animals and the inventor ☐
F An idea that didn't quite work ☐

4 Read the article again. Seven sentences have been removed. Choose from A–H the sentence which fits each gap (1–7). There is one extra sentence.

A But that didn't work at all – in fact, it seemed that the fire actually lit up the cowsheds and made life easier for the lions.
B After a night or two, they got used to seeing this motionless thing and realised it posed no danger.
C Richard's creativity also led to him winning a scholarship at one of the top schools in Kenya.
D The lions kept well away.
E He connected everything up to some light bulbs, which he then put outside the cowshed.
F They went in to kill the cattle.
G Richard, a responsible young man, felt terrible about it and decided he had to do something to keep the lions out without killing them.
H It has also given him the pleasure of seeing people and cattle and lions living together without the conflict that used to exist in the past.

5 ◼ 3.21 Listen and check your answers to Exercise 4. Were your predictions in Exercise 2 right?

6 SPEAKING In pairs or small groups, do the following.

1 On a scale of 1–5 agree on how impressive you think Richard's invention is. (1 = not impressive at all, 5 = brilliant!) Say why your group has given this score.
2 Richard gave a talk about his invention. Imagine you were in the audience. Think of two questions you would ask him at the end of his talk.

> The reading text is also available for students to listen to. This provides you with greater flexibility in how you approach the text. The audio also helps to focus students' attention on the sounds of the language.

4 THINKING OUTSIDE THE BOX

His next idea was to use a scarecrow. Richard hoped that he could trick the lions into thinking that there was a person there, but lions are pretty clever. ³_____. And then they went in to attack the farm animals.

Then one night, Richard spent hours walking around in the cowshed with a torch. That night, no lions came, so he work_____ of the_____ imag_____

Richa_____ who _____ to se_____ learne_____ gadge_____ a batt_____ to cha_____ an indicator box from an old motorcycle – the box that makes a light blink, to show if the biker is turning left or right. ⁴_____. The bulbs flashed throughout the night, and the lions thought that someone was walking around inside the

on the basis that lions were probably scared of fire. ²_____. So Richard had to come up with something else.

more cattle to lion attacks. And now Richard's idea is being used in many different places, to keep lions, leopards and elephants away from farms and homes for good. ⁶_____. He was also invited to talk at a conference in the USA. ⁷_____.

> Each sequence of exercises helps students to unlock the text. First, learners read either for gist or to check predictions. Then they re-read for more detailed understanding.

> **Train to Think** focuses on improving students' critical thinking skills by extending the topic of the reading text. The aim is to exploit a topic that students have already engaged with in order to develop a skill that they will use across their whole curriculum.

◼ TRAIN TO THINK ◼

Lateral thinking

1 Read the example.

'Lateral thinking' means solving problems by thinking in a creative way. It means not following the obvious line of thinking. Here is an example.

A woman is driving down a city street at 25 miles per hour. The speed limit is 30 miles per hour. She passes three cars that are travelling at 20 miles per hour. A police officer stops her and gives her a £100 fine. Why?

If we think too much about the speed, we may not get the answer. What does the situation NOT tell us? It doesn't tell us, for example, what time of day it is – so a possible reason for the £100 fine is that it is night time and the woman is driving with no lights on her car. Or another possible reason for the fine is that the street is one-way, and the woman is driving the wrong way.

2 SPEAKING Work in pairs or small groups. Here are more situations. See if you can find possible answers.

1 A father and son are in a bad car crash. They are both taken to hospital. The son is taken into the operating theatre. The doctor there looks at the boy and says: 'That's my son!' *How is this possible?*
2 A woman is lying awake in bed. She dials a number on the phone, says nothing, puts the phone down and then goes to sleep. *Why?*
3 A man lives on the twelfth floor of a building. Every morning, he takes the lift down to the entrance and leaves the building. In the evening, he gets into the lift, and, if there is someone else in the lift, he goes directly to the twelfth floor. If the lift is empty, he goes to the tenth floor and walks up two flights of stairs to his apartment. *Why?*

39

... before exploring core language and developing listening skills.

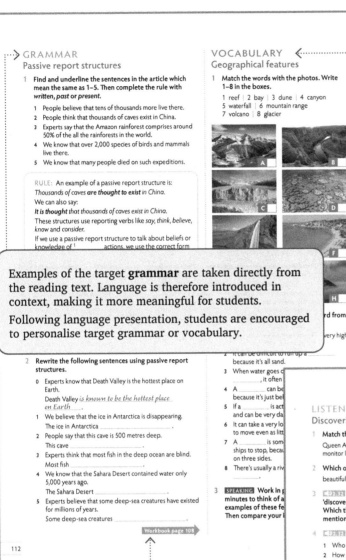

GRAMMAR
Passive report structures

1 **Find and underline the sentences in the article which mean the same as 1–5. Then complete the rule with *written, past* or *present*.**

1 People believe that tens of thousands more live there.
2 People think that thousands of caves exist in China.
3 Experts say that the Amazon rainforest comprises around 50% of all the rainforests in the world.
4 We know that over 2,000 species of birds and mammals live there.
5 We know that many people died on such expeditions.

RULE: An example of a passive report structure is:
Thousands of caves are thought to exist in China.
We can also say:
It is thought that thousands of caves exist in China.
These structures use reporting verbs like *say, think, believe, know* and *consider*.
If we use a passive report structure to talk about beliefs or knowledge of [1]   actions, we use the correct form

2 **Rewrite the following sentences using passive report structures.**

0 Experts know that Death Valley is the hottest place on Earth.
Death Valley *is known to be the hottest place on Earth*.
1 We believe that the ice in Antarctica is disappearing.
The ice in Antarctica   .
2 People say that this cave is 500 metres deep.
This cave   .
3 Experts think that most fish in the deep ocean are blind.
Most fish   .
4 We know that the Sahara Desert contained water only 5,000 years ago.
The Sahara Desert   .
5 Experts believe that some deep-sea creatures have existed for millions of years.
Some deep-sea creatures   .

Workbook page 108

112

VOCABULARY
Geographical features

1 **Match the words with the photos. Write 1–8 in the boxes.**

1 reef | 2 bay | 3 dune | 4 canyon
5 waterfall | 6 mountain range
7 volcano | 8 glacier

A   B   C   D   F   H

...rd from

...very high

...It can be difficult to run up a
because it's all sand.
3 When water goes d
              , it often
4 A   can be
because it's just bel
5 If a   is act
and can be very da
6 It can take a very lo
to move even as litt
7 A   is som
ships to stop, becau
on three sides.
8 There's usually a riv

3 **SPEAKING** Work in p
minutes to think of a
examples of these fe
Then compare your i

---

12 MORE TO EXPLORE

LISTENING
Discovering new species

1 **Match the photos and the names.**

Queen Alexandra's butterfly | honeyeater
monitor lizard | rainbow fish | tree frog | river shark

2 **Which of the creatures do you think are:**
beautiful?, poisonous?, endangered?, dangerous?

3 **02.17 Listen to someone giving a talk about 'discovering new species' in Papua New Guinea. Which three creatures in the photos are mentioned?**

4 **02.17 Listen again and answer the questions.**

1 Who does the speaker work for?
2 How many new species were found in Papua New Guinea between 1998 and 2008?
3 Why wasn't the honeyeater found earlier?
4 What does the speaker say is the 'good news'?
5 She says: 'It's human beings who are doing it.' Doing what?

FUNCTIONS
Speaking persuasively

1 **02.18 Listen again to the end of the talk. Complete the text.**

'... and so these animals find it harder and harder to live. The [1]   of this will be more and more animals becoming extinct – and that's a [2]   thought. If we [3]   now, to stop habitats being destroyed, many animals will disappear and future generations will only see them in books. I think it's [4]   for humans to find ways to live well and without harming other living creatures, [5]   ?

2 **In the extract from the text in Exercise 1, find:**
1 adjectives and adverbs used to make a point strongly
2 a question tag
3 a conditional clause to show urgency

3 **Write two or three sentences from a speech where someone wants to persuade listeners that:**
1 traffic has to be reduced in a town
2 having a new supermarket in a town is a bad idea
3 a leisure centre is needed in a town

Pronunciation
Linking: Intrusive /r/
Go to page 121.

▮ THiNK VALUES ▮
Human activity and the natural world

1 **Read what the speaker says at the end of her talk. Then think about the questions. Make a note of your ideas.**

'... forests are being turned into fields to grow food, and trees are being cut down to get wood, and rivers are being used by more and more boats, and so these animals find it harder and harder to live.'

1 Can you give any real life examples of what she's describing?
2 What other problems can human activity cause (not just problems for animals)?
3 Do you think there might be problems if people explore the deep ocean? Or caves? What kind of problems?

2 **SPEAKING** Work in pairs or small groups.
1 Use your notes from Exercise 1. Decide on which question you are most interested in.
2 Together, prepare a two-minute presentation

Callout boxes:

Lexical sets are presented with clear visuals to support immediate understanding of new **vocabulary** items.

Each unit includes two **vocabulary** sections in addition to two **grammar** sections. Lexical sets are related to the topic of the unit and so can be understood, practised and applied in a meaningful context.

Examples of the target **grammar** are taken directly from the reading text. Language is therefore introduced in context, making it more meaningful for students.
Following language presentation, students are encouraged to personalise target grammar or vocabulary.

The **listening** section follows established procedure: a pre-listening activity, a listen-for-gist task and an activity which tests understanding at a deeper level.

Cross-references indicate where in the **Workbook** you can find further practice of the grammar and vocabulary covered on this page.

Practice exercises for key **pronunciation** points are available at the back of the book. These relate to the language of the unit and are accompanied by audio material. Cross-references on the Student's Book page indicate the most appropriate point in the unit to exploit the relevant **Pronunciation** section.

Regular opportunities for personalisation, for developing students' spoken fluency and for promoting collaboration between students through pair and group work appear throughout the unit. Look for **SPEAKING**.

The second reading text introduces a new language focus.

Students are guided through the established **reading** skills procedure of predicting (Exercise 1), reading for gist (Exercise 2) and reading for detailed understanding (Exercise 3).

Photos and illustrations act as a visual hook for teens. They also provide a springboard into the text itself: motivating students to read the text, getting them to predict content and often illustrating meaning of key vocabulary.

READING

1 Look at the photo and answer the questions.
   1 What are the people doing?
   2 Why do you think they are doing it?

2 Read the article and check your ideas. Explain the play on words in the last sentence.

3 Read the article again and mark the sentences T (true), F (false) or DS (doesn't say).
   1 Pete Frates wanted to play professional baseball. ☐
   2 He was diagnosed with an illness called ALS in 2014. ☐
   3 If you did the Ice Bucket Challenge you didn't have to pay any money. ☐
   4 You had to film yourself doing the challenge. ☐
   5 Barack Obama refused to give any money to the charity. ☐
   6 Some people felt the Ice Bucket Challenge was a bit dangerous. ☐
   7 Nearly 10% of the UK population donated money through the Ice Bucket Challenge. ☐
   8 Some people thought it gave the wrong message about water. ☐

An Ice Cold Summer

In the summer of 2014, a weird and wonderful craze swept across the world. Everywhere you looked people were pouring buckets of freezing water over their heads. The craze soon had a name – 'The Ice Bucket Challenge' and the idea behind it was to raise money for charity. Despite the popularity of the challenge, not many people knew where it had come from. In fact it was the idea of an American called Pete Frates. He had been a promising colle_ seemed to have a bright future with the Boston Red Sox. Ho_ cut short when he fell ill with a disease called amyotrophic l_ for short). ALS attacks the nervous system and can cause sp_ paralysis. It can also kill. Frates wanted to do something to r_ awareness to help sufferers of ALS. He had a simple but bril_

The idea was that you chose a couple of friends and challen_ bucket of freezing water over their heads. If they did this the_ the charity. If they refused, they paid $100. To prove they ha_ 24 hours to post a video of their challenge online. Then it wa_ nominate two more people and challenge them.

Soon it had gone viral with plenty of celebrities worldwide jo_ Bolt, Lady Gaga, Oprah Winfrey, Taylor Swift, Cristiano Ronal_ US president George W. Bush. The US President Barack Oba_ Minister David Cameron were also challenged although they_

media to raise money for charity?

who you talk to.

Nevertheless, for a few hot months of summer back in 2014_ Challenge brought millions of people from all over the plane_ 'cool' cause.

60

Students can discover the rule for themselves, via an inductive approach to learning **grammar**, with the help of scaffolding.

This supported approach continues through to the grammar practice stage, which always begins with a controlled task.

GRAMMAR
Linkers of contrast

1 Read the example sentences about the article and use them to complete the rule.
   1 Most people thought the Ice Bucket Challenge was brilliant. **However**, there were people who disagreed.
   2 **Despite** its popularity, many people didn't know where the idea had come from.
   3 Pete Frates found the time to raise money for charity **in spite of** being quite ill.
   4 **Although** he was challenged, Barack Obama decided not to pour water over his head.
   5 I didn't do the challenge **even though** four of my friends nominated me.
   6 Many people did the challenge without donating. **Nevertheless**, the charity still made a lot of money.

RULE: To contrast ideas and facts, we use these linking words: *although, even though, however, despite, in spite of* and *nevertheless.*
   1 *Despite* and _____ are followed by a noun phrase or a gerund. They can be used at the beginning or in the middle of a sentence.
   2 *Although* and _____ are followed by a full clause. They can be used at the beginning or in the middle of a sentence.
   3 *However* and _____ introduce the contrasting idea and come at the beginning of a new sentence. They are followed by a comma.

2 Rewrite the sentences using the word in brackets.
   0 I didn't know anyone at the party but I still had a good time. (in spite of)
   In spite of not knowing anyone at the party, I still had a good time.
   1 I studied hard for the test. I failed it. (despite)
   2 He doesn't earn a lot of money. He gives a lot of it to charity. (However)
   3 I'd seen the film before. I still really enjoyed it. (although)
   4 I started to eat less. I didn't lose any weight. (in spite of)
   5 It wasn't very warm. We had a good time at the beach. (Nevertheless)
   6 I don't speak a word of Chinese. I understood what he said. (even though)

3 Rewrite this idea using each of the linkers from the rule box.
   I felt really tired. I stayed up till midnight to celebrate the new year.

   Workbook page 55 ➤

Think Values invites students to consider their broader opinions and values through reflection on the reading text. Expressing opinions in pairs/groups provides support, while also offering extra fluency practice.

▶ THINK VALUES
Doing good

1 Work in groups of four. You are going to run an internet fundraising challenge for a charity. Use the points below to help you organise your ideas.
   1 Decide on a charity.
      • Why are you choosing this charity?
      • What will the charity use this money for?
   2 Decide on a challenge
      • What is the challenge?
      • How are people chosen for the challenge?
      • What do you have to do if you refuse to do it?
   3 Think of a famous person to get involved.
      • Why this person?
      • What do you want them to do?
   4 Extras
      • What other things can you do to help your campaign? (T-shirts, write a song, etc.)

2 SPEAKING Present your ideas to the class. Each student in your group should talk about one of the points above.

61

 Be aware of common errors related to verb patterns. Go to Get it right! on Student's Book page 122.

These cross-references, which appear in the **Teacher's Book**, indicate appropriate points in the unit to exploit the **Get it right!** section at the back of the Student's Book. Get it right! provides exercises to help students avoid common errors as identified in the **Cambridge English Learner Corpus**.

The **Cambridge English Corpus** is a multi-billion word collection of real-life written and spoken English. It includes the **Cambridge Learner Corpus**, the world's largest collection of learner writing, comprising more than 50 million words of exam answers written by students taking Cambridge English exams. We carefully check each exam script and highlight all errors made by students. We then use this information to see which words and structures are easy and difficult for learners of English, and ultimately, work out how best to support and develop students.

In units 1, 4, 7 and 10 you'll find the photostory ...

> Each episode of the **photostory** involves the same four British teens but is a complete story in itself.

> Each story begins with several photos and accompanying text. Students can also listen as they read.

> The four friends from left to right: Liam, Emma, Nicole, Justin.

PHOTOSTORY: episode 2

Writer's block

1 Look at the photos and answer the questions.

1 Look at what the teacher has written on the board. What do you think the homework is?
2 How does Emma feel about the homework?
3 Do you think Justin is being helpful?

2 ⬛ 01.25 Now read and listen to the photostory. Check your ideas.

Thanks, you saved my life!

> Students predict the ending of the story before they watch. This increases motivation and makes understanding easier.

> See how the story concludes in the video found on DVD or class presentation software. The video picks up precisely where the photostory ends.

TEACHER OK, everyone, so this is what I want you to do by Friday, OK? A short story, of five hundred words.
EMMA Five hundred words!? She can't be serious!
TEACHER ... and the story has to end with the words, 'Thanks, you saved my life!'
EMMA What? This is awful. I can't do that. I'm hopeless at writing stories.
TEACHER It h...
stories and
want some
creative! C

EMMA And she
tomorrow. I
An original
LIAM Sounds li
NICOLE Liam h

> Further comprehension questions guide students through the story at a deeper level before target language embedded within it is explored.

JUSTIN Well, I'
got to do is t
you've seen
EMMA No, no, t
LIAM Well, the
EMMA You don
book, seen c
JUSTIN Why do
got to write
idea and the
The hero co
NICOLE Give it

EMMA OK, well this isn't getting me anywhere. And I've got to go home. I'm off – I'll see you lot later. And thanks for all the help, Justin! You're a real pal – not.
JUSTIN Hey, what did I do?
LIAM Well, you were a bit out of order, Justin. You can see that Emma's stressed out already, and you didn't exactly hel

> **Phrases for fluency** focuses on authentic language that students can use in conversation to make them sound more natural and fluent. They see these phrases in context and at a level graded for them in the photostory.

44

DEVELOPING SPEAKING

3 Work in pairs. Discuss what happens next in the story. Write down your ideas.
We think Emma watches a film and gets an idea.

4 ⬛ EP2 Watch to find out how the story continues.

5 Match the sentence beginnings and endings.

1 Emma sees a woman who
2 The woman works for
3 The woman is desperate because
4 Emma tries to help
5 When Emma gets an idea
6 Emma gets the keys out
7 Emma's really happy about

a but she can't get the keys out.
b the last thing the woman says.
c is looking for something.
d using something she got at a shop.
e the owner of an art gallery.
f she goes to a shop nearby.
g she hasn't got a spare set of keys.

PHRASES FOR FLUENCY

1 Find these expressions in the photostory. them? How do you say them in your lang

1 (She) can't be serious.
2 (What's the ending) again?
3 Calm down.
4 That's just it.
5 Give it a rest.
6 (You were a bit) out of order.

2 Use the expressions in Exercise 1 to complete the sentences.

1 I know you told me before, but what's your name _____ ?
2 A Let's go for a walk in the park.
  B A walk in the park? You _____ ! It's raining!
3 A Come on, we're late!
  B _____ , we're not late at all, we've got another fifteen minutes.
4 A Your hair looks really stupid!
  B Oh, _____ , Michelle. I'm tired of how you criticise me all the time. You're really _____ , you know?
5 A I don't feel like going out. Let's stay here and watch TV.
  B _____ . You never want to go out.

WordWise
Expressions with *good*

1 Use the phrases in the list to complete these

> **WordWise** takes a word or phrase which has a number of different meanings in English and provides analysis and practice using them.

5 _____ Emma's such a nice person.

> Key phrases for a particular speaking function are explored in the **Functions** section. Students have the opportunity to practise these in the context of a communicative task.

FUNCTIONS
Expressing frustration

1 Read the photostory again. Which of these things does Emma not say? What do all the sentences have in common?

1 I can't (do that).
2 I'm hopeless (at ...)
3 This is hopeless!
4 No chance.
5 I give up.
6 I'll never (come up with anything).
7 This is pointless.

2 Think about the woman who loses her keys. Write three things she might have thought using the expressions in Exercise 1.

I'll never get the keys out.

WRITING
A story

Write a story. The story must end with the words:
'Thanks, you saved my life!'
Write 120–150 words.

45

... and in units 2, 5, 8 and 11, a culture text.

The focus of the **Culture** section is on getting students to think and talk about life in other countries and how it compares with their own.

This reading is also available for students to listen to.

Here, students have the opportunity to develop their ability to deduce meaning from context and increase their receptive vocabulary.

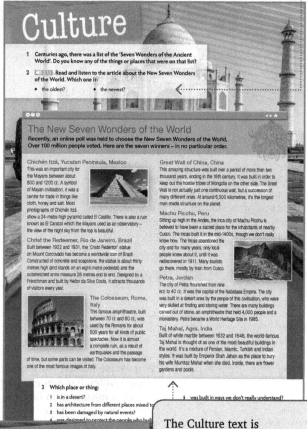

Culture

1 **Centuries ago, there was a list of the 'Seven Wonders of the Ancient World'. Do you know any of the things or places that were on that list?**

2 **Read and listen to the article about the New Seven Wonders of the World. Which one is:**

- the oldest?
- the newest?

The New Seven Wonders of the World

Recently, an online poll was held to choose the New Seven Wonders of the World. Over 100 million people voted. Here are the seven winners – in no particular order.

Chichén Itzá, Yucatan Peninsula, Mexico

This was an important city for the Mayans between about 800 and 1200 CE. A symbol of Mayan civilisation, it was a centre for trade in things like cloth, honey and salt. Most photographs of Chichén Itzá show a 24-metre high pyramid called El Castillo. There is also a ruin known as El Caracol which the Mayans used as an observatory – the view of the night sky from the top is beautiful.

Christ the Redeemer, Rio de Janeiro, Brazil

Built between 1922 and 1931, the 'Cristo Redentor' statue on Mount Corcovado has become a worldwide icon of Brazil. Constructed of concrete and soapstone, the statue is about thirty metres high (and stands on an eight-metre pedestal) and the outstretched arms measure 28 metres end to end. Designed by a Frenchman and built by Heitor da Silva Costa, it attracts thousands of visitors every year.

The Colosseum, Rome, Italy

This famous amphitheatre, built between 70 CE and 80 CE, was used by the Romans for about 500 years for all kinds of public spectacles. Now it is almost a complete ruin, as a result of earthquakes and the passage of time, but some parts can be visited. The Colosseum has become one of the most famous images of Italy.

Great Wall of China, China

This amazing structure was built over a period of more than two thousand years, ending in the 16th century. It was built in order to keep out the hostile tribes of Mongolia on the other side. The Great Wall is not actually just one continuous wall, but a succession of many different ones. At around 6,500 kilometres, it's the longest man-made structure on the planet.

Machu Picchu, Peru

Sitting up high in the Andes, the Inca city of Machu Picchu is believed to have been a sacred place for the inhabitants of nearby Cusco. The Incas built it in the mid-1400s, though we don't really know how. The Incas abandoned the city and for many years, only local people knew about it, until it was rediscovered in 1911. Many tourists go there, mostly by train from Cusco.

Petra, Jordan

The city of Petra flourished from nine BCE to 40 CE. It was the capital of the Nabataea Empire. The city was built in a desert area by the people of this civilisation, who were very skilled at finding and storing water. There are many buildings carved out of stone, an amphitheatre that held 4,000 people and a monastery. Petra became a World Heritage Site in 1985.

Taj Mahal, Agra, India

Built of white marble between 1632 and 1648, the world-famous Taj Mahal is thought of as one of the most beautiful buildings in the world. It's a mixture of Persian, Islamic, Turkish and Indian styles. It was built by Emperor Shah Jahan as the place to bury his wife Mumtaz Mahal when she died. Inside, there are flower gardens and pools.

3 **Which place or thing:**

1 is in a desert?
2 has architecture from different places mixed to
3 has been damaged by natural events?
4 was designed to protect the people who buil
5 was built in ways we don't really understand?

The Culture text is primarily exploited for its informative rather than linguistic content. Students are encouraged to respond to the text and relate it to their own experiences and cultures.

4 VOCABULARY **Match the highlighted words in the article to the definitions.**

1 left the place for ever and never went back
2 put something into a hole in the ground
3 grew, developed very successfully
4 unfriendly and aggressive, wanting to attack
5 a famous thing or person that represents a group or country
6 exciting public shows or events
7 one thing coming after another
8 made by cutting

SPEAKING

Discuss in pairs or small groups.

1 Imagine you could choose one of the seven wonders to go and see. Which one would it be and why?
2 Think of two things from your country that you could campaign to be included in a list of seven wonders of the world. Give reasons to support your choice.

WRITING

Essay

1 **Read Javed's essay. Why does he think the Simplon Tunnel is a modern wonder of the world?**

2 **Read the essay again. Ten things are underlined. Five of the things are mistakes, the other five are correct. Find an example of:**

- a spelling mistake ☐
- a mistake with the verb tense ☐
- a mistake with the wrong choice of connecting word ☐
- a preposition mistake ☐
- a mistake which is a missing word ☐

3 **Correct the mistakes in Javed's writing.**

4 **Look again at the list of kinds of mistakes in Exercise 2.**

1 Are there other kinds of mistakes that people make in writing? What are they? (e.g. punctuation, ...)
2 Does the list in Exercise 2 show the kinds of mistakes that you have sometimes made in your writing so far using this book? If you've made other kinds of mistake, what were they?
3 Make a checklist for yourself of 'Mistakes I should try not to make when I write in English'.

5 **You're going to write an essay entitled: 'A Modern Wonder of the World'.**

1 Look at question 2 in the Speaking exercise above. Choose one of the things that you discussed there.
2 Make notes about why you think this thing is a good choice for a modern wonder of the world.

6 **Write your essay in 150–200 words.**

- Make sure you state clearly what your choice is, and say where and what it is.
- Give reasons for your choice being a 'wonder of the world'.
- When you have written your text, read it through again and use your checklist of personal mistakes (Exercise 4.3) to make as sure as possible that there are no mistakes in your writing.

A Modern Wonder of the World: The Simplon Tunnel

My choice for a modern wonder of the world is the Simplon Tunnel [1] at Switzerland. It's actually two tunnels – railway tracks run through both of them. They're each almost twenty kilometres long, so they're not [2] ... longest tunnels in the world now, but they were when they were built, back in the beginning [3] of the twentieth century. The first one was started in 1898 and opened in 1906. The other one was started in 1912 and was opened in 1921, so each one [4] has taken about eight years to construct.

The first tunnel was built by drilling in both directions – when the two drill-holes met in 1905, they were only two centimetres out of alignment. In those days, that was a fantastic achievement.

While it [5] was being built, about 3,000 people worked on the construction every day. The working conditions weren't very good – for example, it was often very hot inside – and more than sixty people died [6] while the building of the tunnel.

The tunnel joins Switzerland and Italy, [7] and it has helped to make [8] ... travel between the two countries a lot easier [9] then it was before. Now, people can put their car on the train and take it through the tunnel, and so they don't have to drive over the Simplon Pass.

I think this was a great thing to build all those years ago and it has made a big difference to the [10] whole of that part of Europe.

This *extended* **writing** section, designed to guide students step-by-step through the writing process, also appears in even-numbered units. A *writing task* is set in all units.

Students are presented with a model text for analysis of task purpose, and for presentation and practice of useful language before they move on to produce their own compositions. The final task is closely modelled on the type of tasks which appear in the Cambridge English: First writing test.

Literature

1 **Look at the photo and then read the introduction to the extrac about his relationship with his mum?**

2 **Read and listen to the extract and check your ideas.**

About a Boy by Nick Hornby

Marcus is a schoolboy who lives with his mum, who is depressed. Marcu bullied quite a lot, especially because of the clothes his mum makes him w man who makes friends with Marcus and buys him new trainers.

Here, Marcus and his mum are going home after visiting Will at his flat.

'You're not going round there again,' she said on the way home.

Marcus knew she'd say it, and he also knew that he'd take no notice, but he argued anyway.

'Why not?'

'If you've got anything to say, you say it to me. If you want new clothes, I'll get them.'

'But you don't know what I need.'

'So tell me.'

'I don't know what I need. Only Will knows what I need.'

'Don't be ridiculous.'

'It's true. He knows what things kids wear.'

'Kids wear what they put on in the mornings.'

'You know what I mean.'

'You mean that he thinks he's trendy, and that [...] he knows which trainers are fashionable, even though he doesn't know the first thing about anything else.'

That was exactly what he meant. That was what Will was good at, and Marcus thought he was lucky to have found him.

'We don't need that kind of person. We're doing all right our way.'

Marcus looked out of the bus window and thought about whether this was true, and decided it wasn't, that neither of them were doing all right, whichever way you looked at it.

'If you are having trouble it's nothing to do with what shoes you wear, I can tell you that for nothing.'

'No, I know, but –'

'Marcus, trust me, OK? I've been your mother for twelve years. I haven't made too bad a job of it. I do think about it. I know what I'm doing.'

Marcus had never thought of his mother in that way before, as someone who knew what she was doing. He had never thought that she didn't have a clue either; it was just that what she did with him (for him? to him?) didn't appear to be anything like that. He had always looked on being a mother as straightforward, something like, say, driving: most people could do it, and you could mess it up by doing something really obvious, by driving your car into a bus, or not telling your kid to say please and thank you and sorry (there were loads of kids at school, he reckoned, kids who stole and swore too much and bullied other kids, whose mums and dads had a lot to answer for). If you looked at it that way, there wasn't an awful lot to think about. But his mum seemed to be saying that there was more to it than that. She was telling him she had a plan.

If she had a plan, then he had a choice. He could trust her, believe her when she said she knew what she was doing [...] Or he could decide that, actually, she was off her head [...] Either way it was scary. He didn't want to put up with things as they were, but the other choice meant he'd have to be his own mother, and how could you be your own mother when you were only twelve? He could tell himself to say please and thank you and sorry, that was easy, but he didn't know where to start with the rest of it. He didn't even know what the rest of it was. He hadn't even known until today that there was a rest of it.

36

This extract from a novel gives you the opportunity to introduce your students to authentic English-language material. Comprehension questions and follow-up discussion questions help students to understand and engage with the text.

Literature appears in units 3, 6, 9 and 12.

Exam practice and review consolidates content from each pair of units.

Cross-references indicate where in the **Workbook** you can find further practice of these Cambridge English exam task-types as well as useful exam tips.

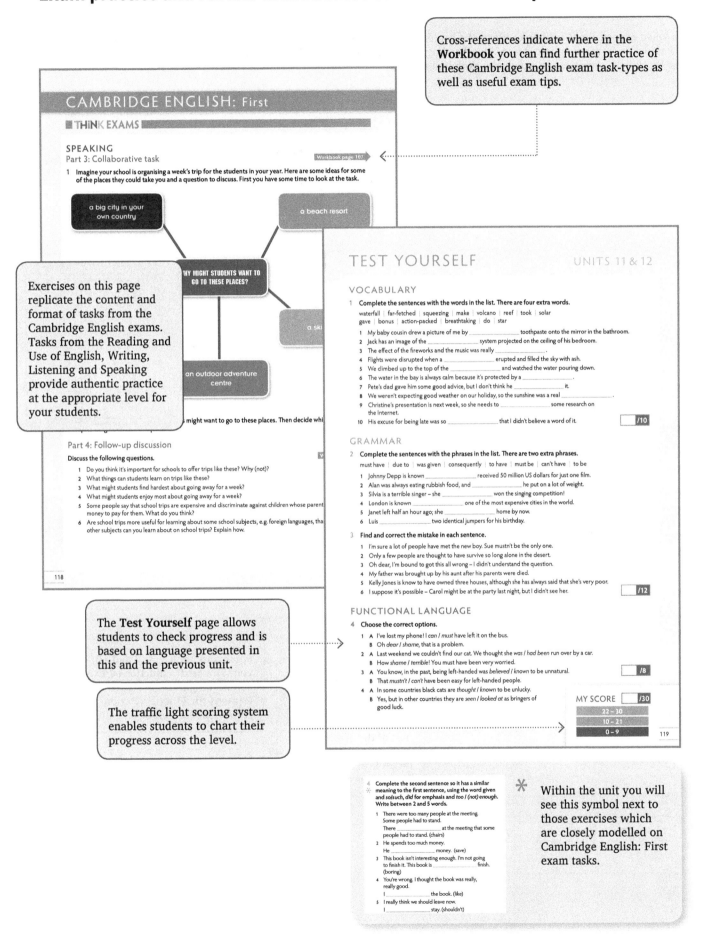

CAMBRIDGE ENGLISH: First

THINK EXAMS

SPEAKING
Part 3: Collaborative task

Workbook page 107

1 Imagine your school is organising a week's trip for the students in your year. Here are some ideas for some of the places they could take you and a question to discuss. First you have some time to look at the task.

- a big city in your own country
- a beach resort
- WHY MIGHT STUDENTS WANT TO GO TO THESE PLACES?
- a ski
- an outdoor adventure centre

might want to go to these places. Then decide whi

Part 4: Follow-up discussion

Discuss the following questions.

1 Do you think it's important for schools to offer trips like these? Why (not)?
2 What things can students learn on trips like these?
3 What might students find hardest about going away for a week?
4 What might students enjoy most about going away for a week?
5 Some people say that school trips are expensive and discriminate against children whose parent money to pay for them. What do you think?
6 Are school trips more useful for learning about some school subjects, e.g. foreign languages, tha other subjects can you learn about on school trips? Explain how.

118

Exercises on this page replicate the content and format of tasks from the Cambridge English exams. Tasks from the Reading and Use of English, Writing, Listening and Speaking provide authentic practice at the appropriate level for your students.

TEST YOURSELF

UNITS 11 & 12

VOCABULARY

1 **Complete the sentences with the words in the list. There are four extra words.**

waterfall | far-fetched | squeezing | make | volcano | reef | took | solar
gave | bonus | action-packed | breathtaking | do | star

1 My baby cousin drew a picture of me by _____ toothpaste onto the mirror in the bathroom.
2 Jack has an image of the _____ system projected on the ceiling of his bedroom.
3 The effect of the fireworks and the music was really _____.
4 Flights were disrupted when a _____ erupted and filled the sky with ash.
5 We climbed up to the top of the _____ and watched the water pouring down.
6 The water in the bay is always calm because it's protected by a _____.
7 Pete's dad gave him some good advice, but I don't think he _____ it.
8 We weren't expecting good weather on our holiday, so the sunshine was a real _____.
9 Christine's presentation is next week, so she needs to _____ some research on the Internet.
10 His excuse for being late was so _____ that I didn't believe a word of it.

/10

GRAMMAR

2 **Complete the sentences with the phrases in the list. There are two extra phrases.**

must have | due to | was given | consequently | to have | must be | can't have | to be

1 Johnny Depp is known _____ received 50 million US dollars for just one film.
2 Alan was always eating rubbish food, and _____ he put on a lot of weight.
3 Silvia is a terrible singer – she _____ won the singing competition!
4 London is known _____ one of the most expensive cities in the world.
5 Janet left half an hour ago; she _____ home by now.
6 Luis _____ two identical jumpers for his birthday.

3 **Find and correct the mistake in each sentence.**

1 I'm sure a lot of people have met the new boy. Sue mustn't be the only one.
2 Only a few people are thought to have survive so long alone in the desert.
3 Oh dear, I'm bound to got this all wrong – I didn't understand the question.
4 My father was brought up by his aunt after his parents were died.
5 Kelly Jones is know to have owned three houses, although she has always said that she's very poor.
6 I suppose it's possible – Carol might be at the party last night, but I didn't see her.

/12

FUNCTIONAL LANGUAGE

4 **Choose the correct options.**

1 A I've lost my phone! I *can / must* have left it on the bus.
  B Oh *dear / shame*, that is a problem.
2 A Last weekend we couldn't find our cat. We thought she *was / had been* run over by a car.
  B How *shame / terrible*! You must have been very worried.
3 A You know, in the past, being left-handed was *believed / known* to be unnatural.
  B That *mustn't / can't* have been easy for left-handed people.
4 A In some countries black cats are *thought / known* to be unlucky.
  B Yes, but in other countries they are *seen / looked at* as bringers of good luck.

/8

MY SCORE /30

| 22 – 30 |
| 10 – 21 |
| 0 – 9 |

119

The **Test Yourself** page allows students to check progress and is based on language presented in this and the previous unit.

The traffic light scoring system enables students to chart their progress across the level.

4 Complete the second sentence so it has a similar meaning to the first sentence, using the word given and *so/such*, *did* for emphasis and *too / (not) enough*. Write between 2 and 5 words.

1 There were too many people at the meeting. Some people had to stand.
There _____ at the meeting that some people had to stand. (chairs)
2 He spends too much money.
He _____ money. (save)
3 This book isn't interesting enough. I'm not going to finish it. This book is _____ finish. (boring)
4 You're wrong. I thought the book was really, really good.
I _____ the book.. (like)
5 I really think we should leave now.
I _____ stay. (shouldn't)

✳ Within the unit you will see this symbol next to those exercises which are closely modelled on Cambridge English: First exam tasks.

As you'd expect, the **Workbook** reflects the content of the Student's Book, providing extra practice of language (grammar, vocabulary and pronunciation) and skills (reading, writing, listening and Train to think). The focus is on independent study but Workbook activities can equally be exploited in class.

Cambridge Learner Corpus informed exercises, in each unit of the Workbook, help your students avoid common pitfalls.

Finally, in units 1, 4, 7 and 10, you'll find extra practice of lexical chunks taught in the **WordWise** and **Phrases for Fluency** sections of the corresponding unit of the Student's Book.

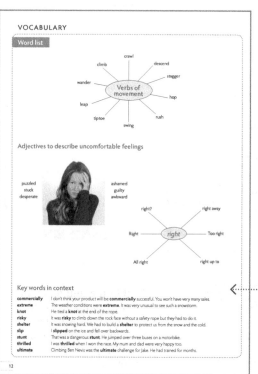

In addition to grammar and vocabulary practice activities, you'll also find a **word list** in each unit of the Workbook with examples of target lexis in context. This serves as a useful written record for your students.

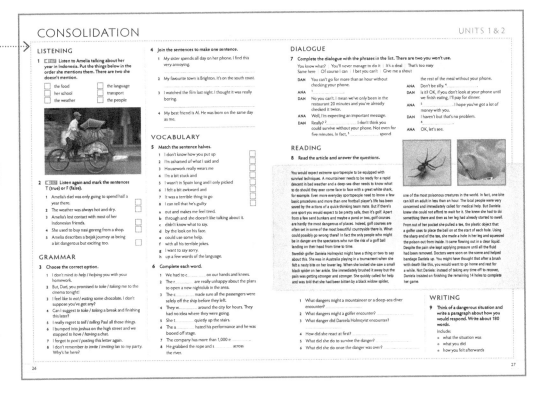

10 SPREADING THE NEWS

DEVELOPING WRITING

An article for the school magazine

1 Read Kate's article 'Around the World with Twitter' and find the answers to these questions.

1 Who?
2 When?
3 Where?
4 What?
5 How?

Around the world with Twitter

[1]
This is the amazing story of how one man travelled the world using Twitter.

[2]
In March 2009, Paul Smith, a British blogger, writer and former radio executive from Gateshead in the Northeast of England travelled around the world using the social media network Twitter. His journey started with an overnight ferry from Newcastle to Amsterdam and ended in New Zealand on the other side of the world.

[3]
Paul had the idea whilst he was in a supermarket. Two days later, he wrote his first Tweet and 'Twitchhiker' was born. Paul's aim was to travel as far from his home as possible in thirty days without spending any money on accommodation or travel. The only money he could spend was on food and drink and things that he could fit in his suitcase. The other rules were that he could only make travel plans three days in advance. If he was stuck anywhere for more than 48 hours, he had to go home.

[4]
After thirty days and with the aid of over 11,000 Twitter followers, Paul Smith had travelled as far as Stewart Island in New Zealand, and he had also raised over £5,000 for charity. Twitter had made it possible for one man to travel round the world, relying only on the kindness of strangers. What other great adventures can Twitter make possible? So far no one else has attempted the challenge. Maybe you or I could be next. Or maybe we'll look for a new challenge.

2 Read these tips for planning your article and number them in the correct order. Then label Kate's article.

☐ **Closing paragraph and a quotation**
Find something that sums the article up in a few words. You can also end your story with a link to more information on the Internet.

☐ **Lead sentence**
Grab your reader's attention.

☐ **Main body**
In this paragraph, answer 'How' and 'Where' and go into more detail. What happens? What are the events of the story?

☐ **Introduction**
Tell your readers 'Who?' 'What?' and 'When?'

3 You are going to write an article. Choose one of the topics below. Use the Internet to help you research your article.

1 an interesting way to travel round the world
2 an interesting train journey
3 a recent news story that caught your attention

Complete the plan below for your article.

Lead sentence

Introduction

Main body

Closing paragraph

4 Now write your article. Write between 200–250 words.

Write your own checklist.

CHECKLIST ✓

95

Each unit includes a full page devoted to developing your students' **writing** skills via a guided approach based on a model text. This staging focuses students on **why** they're writing and **who** the target reader is, thereby encouraging them to plan their writing appropriately. Students are also presented with a checklist to encourage them to edit their writing once they've finished.

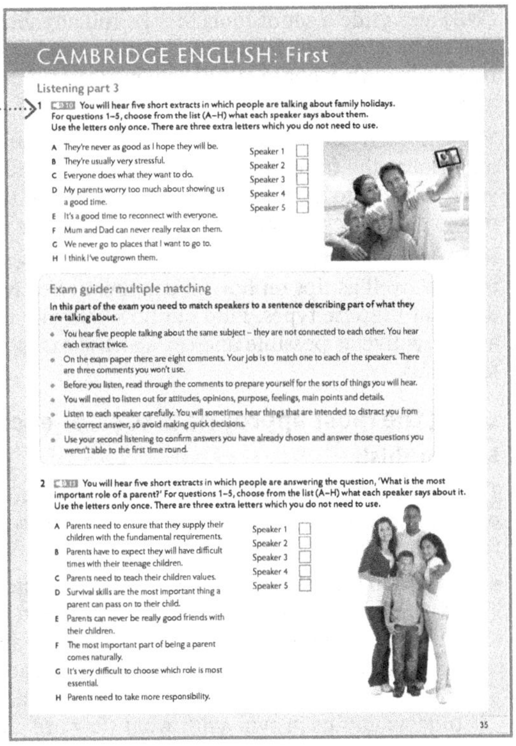

CAMBRIDGE ENGLISH: First

Listening part 3

1 You will hear five short extracts in which people are talking about family holidays. For questions 1–5, choose from the list (A–H) what each speaker says about them. Use the letters only once. There are three extra letters which you do not need to use.

A They're never as good as I hope they will be.
B They're usually very stressful.
C Everyone does what they want to do.
D My parents worry too much about showing us a good time.
E It's a good time to reconnect with everyone.
F Mum and Dad can never really relax on them.
G We never go to places that I want to go to.
H I think I've outgrown them.

Speaker 1 ☐
Speaker 2 ☐
Speaker 3 ☐
Speaker 4 ☐
Speaker 5 ☐

Exam guide: multiple matching

In this part of the exam you need to match speakers to a sentence describing part of what they are talking about.

• You hear five people talking about the same subject – they are not connected to each other. You hear each extract twice.
• On the exam paper there are eight comments. Your job is to match one to each of the speakers. There are three comments you won't use.
• Before you listen, read through the comments to prepare yourself for the sorts of things you will hear.
• You will need to listen out for attitudes, opinions, purpose, feelings, main points and details.
• Listen to each speaker carefully. You will sometimes hear things that are intended to distract you from the correct answer, so avoid making quick decisions.
• Use your second listening to confirm answers you have already chosen and answer those questions you weren't able to the first time round.

2 You will hear five short extracts in which people are answering the question, 'What is the most important role of a parent?' For questions 1–5, choose from the list (A–H) what each speaker says about it. Use the letters only once. There are three extra letters which you do not need to use.

A Parents need to ensure that they supply their children with the fundamental requirements.
B Parents have to expect they will have difficult times with their teenage children.
C Parents need to teach their children values.
D Survival skills are the most important thing a parent can pass on to their child.
E Parents can never be really good friends with their children.
F The most important part of being a parent comes naturally.
G It's very difficult to choose which role is most essential.
H Parents need to take more responsibility.

Speaker 1 ☐
Speaker 2 ☐
Speaker 3 ☐
Speaker 4 ☐
Speaker 5 ☐

35

The **Cambridge exam practice** page is designed to enable your students to further develop their exam skills. It covers all the different task types included in Cambridge English: First tests, together with a step-by-step guide outlining how to tackle each one effectively.

Every two units, a double-page consolidation spread provides skills and language practice based on what students have covered in the preceding two units.

CONSOLIDATION

UNITS 1 & 2

LISTENING

1 Listen to Amelia talking about her year in Indonesia. Put the things below in the order she mentions them. There are two she doesn't mention.

☐ the food   ☐ the language
☐ her school   ☐ transport
☐ the weather   ☐ the people

2 Listen again and mark the sentences T (true) or F (false).

1 Amelia's dad was only going to spend half a year there.
2 The weather was always hot and dry.
3 Amelia's lost contact with most of her Indonesian friends.
4 She used to buy nasi goreng from a shop.
5 Amelia describes a bejak journey as being a bit dangerous but exciting too.

GRAMMAR

3 Choose the correct option.

1 I don't mind to help / helping you with your homework.
2 But, Dad, you promised to take / taking me to the cinema tonight!
3 I feel like to eat / eating some chocolate. I don't suppose you've got any?
4 Can I suggest to take / taking a break and finishing this later?
5 I really regret to tell / telling Paul all those things.
6 I bumped into Joshua on the high street and we stopped to have / having a chat.
7 I forgot to post / posting this letter again.
8 I don't remember to invite / inviting Ian to my party. Why's he here?

4 Join the sentences to make one sentence.

1 My sister spends all day on her phone. I find this very annoying.

2 My favourite town is Brighton. It's on the south coast.

3 I watched the film last night. I thought it was really boring.

4 My best friend is Al. He was born on the same day as me.

VOCABULARY

5 Match the sentence halves.

1 I don't know how you put up
2 I'm ashamed of what I said and
3 Housework really wears me
4 I'm a bit stuck and
5 I wasn't in Spain long and I only picked
6 I felt a bit awkward and
7 It was a terrible thing to go
8 I can tell that he's guilty

a out and makes me feel tired.
b through and she doesn't like talking about it.
c didn't know what to say.
d by the look on his face.
e could use some help.
f with all his terrible jokes.
g I want to say sorry.
h up a few words of the language.

6 Complete each word.

1 We had to c_____ on our hands and knees.
2 The r_____ are really unhappy about the plans to open a new nightclub in the area.
3 The c_____ made sure all the passengers were safely off the ship before they left.
4 They w_____ around the city for hours. They had no idea where they were going.
5 She t_____ quietly up the stairs.
6 The a_____ hated his performance and he was booed off stage.
7 The company has more than 1,000 e_____.
8 He grabbed the rope and s_____ across the river.

DIALOGUE

7 Complete the dialogue with the phrases in the list. There are two you won't use.

You know what? | You'll never manage to do it | It's a deal | That's too easy
Same here | Of course I can | I bet you can't | Give me a shout

DAN   You can't go for more than an hour without checking your phone.
ANA   1_____
DAN   No you can't. I mean we've only been in the restaurant 20 minutes and you've already checked it twice.
ANA   Well, I'm expecting an important message.
DAN   Really? 2_____ I don't think you could possibly go wrong there! In fact the only people who might be in danger are the spectators who run the risk of a golf ball the rest of the meal without your phone.
ANA   Don't be silly. 4_____
DAN   Is it? OK, if you don't look at your phone until we finish eating, I'll pay for dinner.
ANA   5_____ I hope you've got a lot of money with you.
DAN   I haven't but that's no problem.
ANA   OK, let's see.

READING

8 Read the article and answer the questions.

You would expect extreme sportspeople to be equipped with survival techniques. A mountaineer needs to be ready for a rapid descent in bad weather and a deep-sea diver needs to know what to do should they ever come face to face with a great white shark, for example. Even more everyday sportspeople need to know a few basic procedures and more than one football player's life has been saved by the actions of a quick-thinking team mate. But if there's one sport you would expect to be pretty safe, then it's golf. Apart from a few sand bunkers and maybe a pond or two, golf courses are hardly the most dangerous of places. Indeed, golf courses are often set in some of the most beautiful countryside there is. What could possibly go wrong there? In fact the only people who might be in danger are the spectators who run the risk of a golf ball landing on their head from time to time.

Swedish golfer Daniela Holmqvist might have a thing or two to say about this. She was in Australia playing in a tournament when she felt a nasty bite on her lower leg. When she looked she saw a small black spider on her ankle. She immediately brushed it away but the pain was getting stronger and stronger. She quickly called for help and was told she had been bitten by a black widow spider,

one of the most poisonous creatures in the world. In fact, one bite can kill an adult in less than an hour. The local people were very concerned and immediately called for medical help. But Daniela knew she could not afford to wait for it. She knew she had to do something there and then as her leg had already started to swell. From out of her pocket she pulled a tee, the plastic object that a golfer uses to place the ball on at the start of each hole. Using the sharp end of the tee, she made a hole in her leg and squeezed the poison out from inside. It came flowing out in a clear liquid. Despite the pain she kept applying pressure until all the fluid had been removed. Doctors were soon on the scene and helped bandage Daniela up. You might have thought that after a brush with death like this, you would want to go home and rest for a while. Not Daniela: instead of taking any time off to recover, Daniela insisted on finishing the remaining 14 holes to complete her game.

1 What dangers might a mountaineer or a deep-sea diver encounter?
2 What dangers might a golfer encounter?
3 What danger did Daniela Holmqvist encounter?

4 How did she react at first?
5 What did she do to survive the danger?
6 What did she do once the danger was over?

WRITING

9 Think of a dangerous situation and write a paragraph about how you would respond. Write about 180 words.

include:
• what the situation was
• what you did
• how you felt afterwards

26   27

Think offers exciting digital components to aid the learning process for both teachers and students. Knowing how to make the most of these components will save you time and add variety and impact to your lessons and to the homework you set for your students.

HEADS-UP LEARNING!

The **presentation software** includes a digital version of both the Student's Book (SB) and the Workbook (WB) alongside a set of tools to take full advantage of this material in the classroom. It can be used with an Interactive Whiteboard (IWB) and projector, but also with a projector on its own.

You can easily facilitate class participation by using the material at the front of the class, and successfully getting your students to interact with it, with you and with each other. The presentation software can make this possible.

Read on for an explanation of the various presentation tools, as well as tips on how to use them effectively with different exercise types. Find out how to make your lessons as interactive as possible and see specific examples of how to do this.

Using the most appropriate tool for each activity
Look at this!

The **zoom** tool allows you to enlarge part of the page in order to draw students' attention to a specific section of, for example, a text, a photo or an exercise.

- **Making predictions based on titles and pictures:** ask students to work with their books closed and focus their attention on unit or reading text titles and pictures. Asking students to make predictions is an excellent way to activate prior or background knowledge and get the students' brains in sync with what they are going to read, see or listen to.

- With the title of a reading text you can ask students what they expect to read about, or if they know anything about the topic.

- **Describing pictures:** zoom in on a picture and students describe it to reactivate or pre-teach vocabulary.

- **Making connections:** use the zoom tool to display the pictures one by one and then ask students to find the link between them and describe what they see.

- **Guessing game:** focus on a small part of a picture to ask students to guess what it is, then zoom out to reveal the bigger picture.

Showing what's important

The **highlight** tool allows you to use one or more colours to select specific words, phrases, sentences or paragraphs. Different colours can be used to show different categories or to identify different students' suggestions.

- **Answers:** As an alternative to displaying all of the answers in one go, in multiple-choice exercises you can highlight the correct answers as you check the exercise. In reading comprehension exercises, during feedback highlight the parts of the text which contain the answers to the questions.

- **Lexical sets:** highlight the set of target vocabulary e.g. for places in a town: *market, football stadium, hotel, café.*

- **Chunks of language:** in reading texts ask students to highlight examples of the target language, for example, different ways of comparing: *different from, much lower than, ten centimetres taller than, even taller,* etc.

- **Pronunciation issues:** ask students to highlight the three different past *-ed* pronunciations in a text using different colours.

Life and how to live it

Life! It's a lot of fun but it can also be challenging. Things don't always go our way. Life can let us down and can sometimes fail to deliver what we were hoping for. That's just the way it is. But sometimes the problems that trouble us are the ones that we create in our own minds so maybe it's time to stop blaming other people, bad luck, the weather, our football team or whatever, and look to ourselves. Here are a few simple tips we can use to instantly change the way we live for the better.

1   'My life's a mess. I just wish I could disappear'; 'Why do these things always happen to me?'; 'If only someone understood me'. Thoughts like these help no one. Overdramatising a situation only makes it worse. Try and put things into perspective a little, take a step back, sleep on it, ask a friend for help. Things are rarely as bad as they seem.

2   So your teacher didn't give you the part in the school play that you really wanted and that you tried your hardest for at the audition. Well, that's a shame – things don't always work out the way we'd like them to, but it doesn't mean your teacher doesn't like you. Maybe there were other students who were more suited to the role. Similarly, when your football team loses, they don't lose just to upset you. Maybe they didn't play very well. Things go wrong for a million and one different reasons. It's not all about you.

3   Not all teachers are the enemy. Not all adults are out of touch. Not all younger brothers and sisters are annoying. Try not to look at people so simplistically. Everyone is an individual. Open your mind to other possibilities. Get to know people as individuals, they might surprise you.

4   Do you sometimes snap at your parents just because they've asked you to tidy your room or to do your homework? Just because you feel angry, it doesn't mean they're being unreasonable. Maybe you're tired or hungry. Maybe other problems with school or friends are getting in the way of you thinking clearly. Maybe you're overreacting. It's good to feel but it's important to take a step back before you act on those feelings.

5   No one gets it right all of the time, and that includes you! So don't expect life to always work out the way you think it should. If others let you down, be kind to them. If you're not living up to your own expectations, be kind to yourself. If you're always looking for perfection in others, you're sure to be disappointed.

6   Don't dwell on the past. There's no point thinking 'If only I'd studied harder for that test' or 'I wish I hadn't said those things to my parents'. You didn't study and you failed. You said those things and you got into trouble. There's nothing you can do to change any of that. Learn from it, and make sure you don't make the same mistakes again.

So there you go. Keep these tips in mind and next time life doesn't go exactly the way you want it to, try and use one or two. It's time to take control of your life.

Hide and elicit

The **mask** tool allows you to cover a part of the page so that students can't see it.

- **Matching words to pictures:** in these exercises mask the vocabulary, show the pictures and elicit the vocabulary from the students to find out what they already know.

- **The photostory:** cover the photostory dialogues and ask students to predict what the characters are talking about.
- **Listening comprehensions with photos:** hide the exercise below the pictures and ask students to predict the topic of the listening to help them engage fully with it before they listen so that they'll be better able to comprehend while they listen.
- **Manipulating dialogues (disappearing sentences):** Students practise a dialogue in pairs. Cover a small section of the dialogue, beginning from the right-hand side of the screen. Students repeat the dialogues trying to remember the whole thing, including the parts they can no longer see. Cover more and more of the dialogue, with students practising at each stage, until eventually nothing is left on the board. This activity involving lots of repetition is a fun way for students to memorise useful chunks.

Gap fill as a class

The **pen** tool allows you to write in different colours. With the **eraser** tool you can delete what you have written.

- **Eliciting grammar rules:** when presenting grammar rules you can ask students to go to the front of the class and write the answers directly onto the IWB or board.

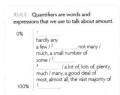

- **Annotating texts:** you can use any text in the book to focus students on specific language. For example, students can write definitions of new words or synonyms in the margin of a text.
- **Labelling pictures:** you can use any picture in the book to focus students on specific vocabulary by asking them to label items.

Remember!

The **sticky notes** tool allows you to write notes on the pages of the book.

- **Reminders to yourself:** add ideas or notes that you think of when preparing your lessons.
- **Task extension ideas for students:** the Teacher's Book offers Fast finishers options on a regular basis. Write these activities on sticky notes and display them for students who are ready to move on to an additional exercise.
- **Prompts for students:** adding extra words for students to work with or reminders related to the target language, for example, 'Don't forget to use the third person *s*.'

Engage and interact

The IWB software offers multiple opportunities for student interaction. What used to be heads-down activities can now be turned into heads-up ones! Students can close their books and focus on the IWB during lead-in activities and speaking tasks, therefore creating a more open, inclusive and dynamic classroom atmosphere. Also, asking students to come to the front to perform tasks on the IWB will vary the class dynamics and offer students the chance to be active participants in the lesson. At the same time, you will be able to ensure that everyone is engaged!

Heads-up teaching and interaction can be carried out in pairs, small groups or as a whole class with any of these activity types.

- **Multiple-choice, match, complete and drag and drop activities:** These can be solved by asking one student to come up to the board and prompting the other students to call out the answers from their seats. The student at the board can complete the activity based on instructions from the rest of the class. In the case of drop down menu tasks, ask students to guess the right answer before showing the options.
- **Gap-fill activities:** These can become more dynamic if they are set up as team competitions. One member of each team at a time, calls out and spells the word for another member of the same team, who is at the board, to solve the task.

Remember that answers are provided for all activities. These can be displayed on the board, making it a good way to reduce the time spent checking answers. Many activities also have the script or related rules, which can be used to extend the learning opportunities.

HEADS-DOWN LEARNING!

The **Online components in the LMS** complement the presentation software by providing 'heads-down' teaching resources. They can be used in the classroom or set for homework. They offer multiple advantages for teachers and students.

Motivated students …

- Students enjoy more interactivity in the exercises.
- Students receive immediate feedback on their performance by being shown the right and wrong answers, which in turn increases motivation.
- Students have the opportunity to choose what they want to do and when, where appropriate.

… Satisfied teachers!

- Teachers can see which exercises each student has done.
- Teachers can see average marks for each exercise and see whether a student has done better or worse than the average.
- Teachers can see if there is a particular exercise that a number of students have had difficulties with and then focus on that exercise or language area or skill in class.
- Teachers can then use class time more effectively for revision or speaking skills development, for example.
- Teachers can save classroom time by showing the answers in class after the students have done the exercises at home, without having to go through them one by one.
- Teachers will save time spent marking thanks to the automatic gradebook.

The LMS also offers extra resources for teachers, which are printable. These resources are course-specific, carefully graded and aligned to the syllabus and can save valuable time for teachers.

- Tests
- Readings
- Grammar worksheets and presentations
- Video worksheets
- Bilingual word lists

WELCOME

A WHAT A STORY!

A lucky pilot

1 🔊 1.02 Books closed. As a warm-up, divide the class into pairs and ask students: *Have you ever flown in an aeroplane? Where did you fly to? Which of you has flown the furthest?* Give students a couple of minutes to discuss in pairs, and then listen to some of their answers in open class. For further speaking practice, ask students to work in pairs and make a list of reasons why people are afraid of flying.

Books open. If there is an interactive whiteboard (IWB) available in the classroom, this activity would best be done as a heads-up activity with the whole class. Display the picture on the IWB. Ask: *Have you ever flown in a plane like this? How is this plane different from the planes you have flown in?* Tell students they are going to read about a flight in a small aeroplane. Ask students to read the instructions and the list of verbs and check understanding. Check/clarify: *engine*; *fuel tanks*; *parachute*; *life raft*. Ask students to read the text quickly, ignoring the gaps, to answer the question: *Why was the pilot lucky?* (He survived when his plane crashed into the sea.) Students work individually to complete the gaps. When the majority of students have completed the exercise, divide the class into pairs or small groups for students to compare their answers. Play the audio for them to check their answers.

> **Answers**
>
> 1 set   2 added   3 carry   4 dive   5 hit   6 destroyed
> 7 managed   8 pulled   9 end   10 find   11 screamed

2 Give students a minute to read through the questions. Check/clarify: *safely*; *rescued*. Students work with a partner to decide which key information they need to look out for in the conversation. Students read the conversation and complete the exercise. As they read, encourage them to underline the parts of the article that support their answers. During whole-class feedback, ask students to refer to the text and to explain why they chose their answers.

> **Answers**
>
> 1 From California to New Orleans.
> 2 Because it's usually too far for a small plane.
> 3 He tried to use a parachute.
> 4 People from a fishing boat rescued him.

Descriptive verbs

1 Students work with a partner to complete the exercise. During whole-class feedback, say the verbs for students to repeat and check pronunciation. Ask: *Which three of the verbs have an irregular past tense?* (flee–fled; strike–struck; dive has two past forms, dived and dove).

> **Answers**
>
> 1 d   2 c   3 b   4 f   5 h   6 e   7 a   8 g

> **Fast finishers**
>
> Students can write sentences including some of the verbs to describe any recent news events they've heard.

2 If you're short on time, set this exercise for homework. Give students time to read through the sentences and check understanding. Students work individually to complete the exercise. Allow them to compare answers with a partner before whole-class feedback.

> **Mixed-ability**
>
> Stronger students may like to cover the rest of the page and try to complete the sentences before looking back at Exercise 1 to check their answers.

> **Answers**
>
> 1 had fled   2 demolished   3 Grab   4 had been raging
> 5 had smashed   6 screamed   7 dived

> **Optional extension**
>
> Divide the class into pairs. Ask students to think of a story (a news story? a film? a TV programme?) in which:
>
> 1 there was a raging fire
> 2 something demolished something else
> 3 someone screamed
> 4 someone grabbed something
> 5 someone fled a place
> 6 something was smashed
>
> Monitor and help with any questions about vocabulary or to give students ideas for storylines. Make sure all students are taking notes to help them remember their stories. Put students with different partners to tell each other their stories. As feedback, ask some volunteers to tell their stories in open class.

Phrasal verbs

1 Students complete the sentences, then look back at the conversation to check their answers.

Answers

1 set off   2 end up   3 find out

2 Students work individually to complete the exercise before comparing answers with a partner. Monitor and help with any questions about vocabulary. Check answers in open class. Point out the use of the *-ing* form after the prepositions in sentences 1, 4 and 8. During feedback, elicit/explain the meanings of each of the options in the sentences.

Answers

1 gave up   2 take up   3 sort it out   4 carry on
5 looking forward to   6 stands out   7 broke down
8 ended up

Fast finishers

Students think of three examples of things that break down and three things that people find hard to give up.

Childhood memories

1 SPEAKING Books closed. To introduce the topic of cinemas, divide the class into pairs or small groups and ask students to take turns to describe films they have seen recently to their partners/groups, who must guess the film. During whole-class feedback, ask students which films they described. You could also initiate a class discussion around this question: *Which is better, watching films at home or at the cinema? Why?*

Books open. Ask students to discuss the questions in pairs. Nominate individuals to describe what they remember in open class and write some of their memories on the board.

2 Tell students they are going to read about a man's memories of cinemas in his childhood. Set a three-minute time limit and encourage students not to worry about unknown vocabulary, but to focus on answering the question. Allow students to compare answers with a partner before a whole-class check. During feedback, compare the memories in the passage to the ones written on the board.

3 Ask students to read the questions and check understanding. Give students a minute to try to answer the questions without looking back at the text. Before students re-read, check/clarify: *front row*; *boo*; *cheer*; *villain*. Students re-read the text and answer the questions. Allow them to compare answers with a partner before whole class-feedback.

Answers

1 Adults couldn't go.
2 He went with his older brother.
3 They went early so they could get seats near the front.
4 They cheered when they saw the opening pictures and when the hero won.
5 They booed when they saw the villain.

Elements of a story

1 Books closed. Choose a film or story that the majority of your students will know and write the title on the board. Ask individuals to describe what happens in the film/story and try to elicit the words from the list.

Books open. Ask students to work with a partner to complete the exercise. During whole-class feedback, say the words for students to repeat and check understanding. When checking pronunciation, write the words on the board and mark the stress for clarification.

Answers

1 set   2 hero   3 characters   4 villain   5 plot
6 ending   7 dialogue

2 SPEAKING Before asking students to work together, you may like to elicit some examples in open class to give them some ideas. Divide the class into small groups and give students five minutes to think of as many examples of each of the four things as they can. Monitor and encourage competition. After five minutes, establish which group came up with the most ideas. For feedback, regroup students and ask them to take it in turns to describe one of their ideas for the rest of their group to guess who/what is being described.

Talking about past routines

Before asking students to complete the exercise, you may like to review the difference between *would* and *used to*. Write the following sentences on the board.

I used to live in France.

When my brother was young, he loved chocolate and would eat three chocolate bars a day.

Elicit/explain that we use *used to* to describe a repeated past action or past state that no longer occurs. *Would* is also used to describe repeated past actions but not states.

Students work individually to complete the four sentences. Allow them to compare answers with a partner before checking in open class. During feedback, clarify that *used to* would be acceptable in all four sentences, but *would* only in sentences 1 and 3, which mention a time frame.

Answers

1 used to (*would* is not possible as the sentence is describing a state)   2 used to (*would* is possible)
3 would (*used to* is also possible)   4 used to (*would* is also possible)

Optional extension

Write the following questions on the board and ask students to write five sentences about themselves using *used to* and *would*.

Think about yourself when you were in primary school.

What routines did you have?

What things did you regularly do?

Divide the class into pairs or small groups for students to compare their answers.

B AN UNCERTAIN FUTURE

Future plans

1 🔊 1.03 Write the following questions on the board, or dictate them, and ask students to discuss them in pairs or small groups: *Do you want to go to university when you finish school? Why (not)? If so, what do you want to study? If not, what do you want to do?* Listen to some of their ideas in open class.

Ask students to read the conversation quickly in order to answer the question: *Has Greg decided what to do in the future?* (no). Ask students to work individually to complete the exercise before comparing answers with a partner. Play the audio for students to check their answers.

> **Answers**
>
> 1 get a good degree   2 then retire   3 when you leave school   4 and then travel the world   5 before I think about settling down   6 to start a family

2 Ask students to read the sentences and try to complete the exercise based on their first reading. Students re-read the conversation to decide if the sentences are true or false or if the information is not mentioned in the text (DS). Ask them to underline key text that supports their answers. Allow students to compare answers with a partner before feedback in open class. During feedback, ask students to correct the false sentences.

> **Answers**
>
> 1 T   2 DS   3 F   4 T   5 T

Life plans

1 To introduce the topic, you might like to tell students what your life plans are (or what they were when you were younger). Try to include some of the words from the list in your plans. Ask students to work with a partner to complete the sentences. Check answers in open class. During feedback, it is good practice to check students' understanding of vocabulary by asking concept check questions e.g. *Do you intend to travel the world when you are older? How would you feel if you got promoted? Why?* etc.

> **Answers**
>
> 1 travel   2 leave   3 degree   4 promoted   5 retired   6 career   7 settled   8 start

> **Fast finishers**
>
> Ask students to write down a list of things that they want to do before they're 30. Listen to some of their ideas in open class after feedback on Exercise 1.

2 SPEAKING Divide the class into small groups and ask them to discuss the questions. For better results, you may like to give students a few minutes to think about their ideas before they start their discussions. Monitor and answer any questions about vocabulary, but as this is a fluency practice activity, do not interrupt the conversations unless inaccuracy hinders comprehension. Listen to some of their ideas in open class as feedback.

Future continuous

1 To remind students of the future continuous, write the following sentence on the board:

At 7 o'clock tonight I _____ _____ eat___ dinner.

Elicit words to complete the gaps (*will be eating*). Give them the answer if they are unable to guess. Tell them we call this tense the future continuous. Remind students that we use continuous tenses to refer to an activity <u>in progress</u> at a particular point in time.

To check understanding at this point, ask a few students to give you an example of their own for each verb in the list.

Ask students to work individually to complete the exercise. Check answers in open class. During feedback, point out the double *l* in *travelling*.

> **Answers**
>
> 1 be travelling   2 be living   3 be studying   4 be working   5 be listening   6 be wondering

> **Fast finishers**
>
> Students write sentences imagining what they will be doing five, ten years from now.

2 SPEAKING Divide the class into pairs or small groups. Students discuss which statements are true for them. Monitor to prompt them to use the future continuous in their answers and to check they are using it correctly. Listen to some of their ideas in open class as feedback.

> **Optional extension**
>
> Ask students to work in pairs to ask each other questions with the future continuous.
>
> For example: *What will you be doing tomorrow at 3 pm?*
>
> You could extend this and ask students to speculate about their futures.
>
> For example: *What do you think you will be doing in 2027?*

Future perfect

To remind students of the future perfect, write the following sentence on the board:

By 2050 we will have used up our planet's resources.

Ask students if the action will take place before, in or after 2050 (*before*). Ask them if we know exactly when (*no, we don't – we only know it will be sometime before 2050*). Emphasise that the future perfect action is something that will be completed before a given time in the future. Compare this with the future continuous, where the action will still be in progress at a particular point in the future.

Students read the text. Do the first sentence in open class if necessary, making sure students understand why *will have left* is the correct answer. Working individually, students complete the exercise. Check answers with the whole class.

Answers

1 will have left   2 will have saved   3 will have travelled
4 will have decided   5 will have settled   6 will have
started

> **Optional extension**
>
> Divide the class into small groups. Ask them to work
> individually and write sentences making predictions about
> their partners. Students can then share and discuss their
> predictions.

Being emphatic: *so* and *such*

1 Ask students to try to complete the sentences from
memory before looking back at the conversation
on page 6 to check. Check answers in open class.
Elicit rules for the use of *so* and *such*. (We use them
to make statements more emphatic. We use *so* +
adjective and *such* + *a/an* + *adjective* + *noun*.)

Answers

1 so   2 such

2 Working in pairs, students complete the sentences.
Check answers in open class. During feedback, say
the statements for students to repeat, and check
pronunciation. Make sure students are putting the
main stress on the words *so* or *such*.

Answers

1 The thought of working in the same job for 40 years is
  so terrifying.
2 Travelling gives you such important experience.
3 It's such an awful waste of time to go travelling.
4 Deciding to settle down is such a huge decision.
5 It's such amazing news that you want to start a family.

3 Students work with a partner to discuss who might
have said statements 1–5. Check answers in open
class.

Answers

1 G   2 G   3 M   4 G   5 M

4 SPEAKING In open class, say: *Going to university is
such a fantastic idea. Do you agree?* Listen to some of
their ideas and encourage discussion.

Ask students to work with a partner and discuss
which of the five statements in Exercise 2 they agree
or disagree with. Encourage them to give reasons for
their answers. Monitor and help with vocabulary, but
do not interrupt unless errors impede conversation.
Listen to some of their ideas in open class.

Extreme adjectives

1 Ask students to try to remember words to complete
the exercise before looking back at the statements in
Exercise 2 to check. Remind students that we do not
use *very* with extreme adjectives so we can say *very
scary* but we can't say *very terrifying*.

Answers

1 terrifying   2 fantastic/amazing   3 awful   4 huge

2 Books closed. If there is an IWB available in the
classroom, introduce this language point with a
heads-up activity in open class. Before the lesson,
use the text icon to prepare a screen with the twelve
words, each in a separate text box. Ask students
to categorise the words into gradable or extreme
adjectives. After two minutes, ask individuals to
come to the board to drag and drop one of the words
into the correct column. Ask other students to agree
or disagree.

Books open. Ask students to put the adjectives into
the correct place. Allow them to compare answers
with a partner before feedback in open class.

Answers

1 terrible   2 brilliant   3 interesting   4 scared
5 funny   6 delighted   7 miserable   8 exciting
9 huge   10 tiny   11 freezing   12 hot

3 If you're short on time, set this exercise for
homework. Go through the example in open class.
Students work individually to complete the exercise.
Remind them to look back at the lists in Exercise 2
before they make their choice. Allow them to check
answers with a partner before feedback in open class.

Answers

1 delighted   2 hilarious   3 tiny/minute
4 fantastic/wonderful/brilliant/amazing
5 terrified   6 awful/terrible

4 WRITING Ask students to read the instructions,
and then work with a partner to write dialogues.
Monitor and give suggestions for how students could
use extreme adjectives. Give students time to practise
their dialogues several times before listening to some
examples in open class.

Student's Book pages 8–9

C   HOW PEOPLE BEHAVE

Conversations

1 ◄))1.04 Books open. If there is an IWB available in
the classroom, this activity would best be done as a
heads-up activity with the whole class. Display the
pictures on the IWB. Ask students: *What's happening
in the pictures?* Listen to some of their ideas in open
class but do not comment at this stage. Play the
audio while students listen and match the pictures to
the conversations. Students compare answers with a
partner before a whole-class check.

Answers

1 C   2 A   3 B

2 ◄))1.04 Give students two minutes to read the
conversations and try to complete the gaps from
memory. Play the audio again for students to
listen and check their predictions. When students
have compared answers with a partner, check in
open class.

Answers

Conversation 1 kind, rude, shouldn't
Conversation 2 have, allowed, unfriendly
Conversation 3 mind, hang, have, let

Optional extension

Disappearing sentences: You'll need to write out the dialogues on the board or IWB for this one. Make AB pairs so that half of the class are A and half are B. Students practise the conversations from Exercise 2 in their pairs. Cover a small section of the dialogue, beginning from the right-hand side of the screen or board. Students repeat the dialogues in their same AB pairings trying to remember the whole thing, including the parts they can no longer see. Cover more and more of the dialogue, with students practising at each stage, until eventually nothing is left on the board and students have memorised the entire conversation. Ask for volunteers to perform for the class or have all As and all Bs perform in unison. This activity involving lots of repetition is a fun way for students to memorise useful chunks.

3 SPEAKING Read the instructions in open class. Point out the use of *would have* + past participle to refer to a possible past situation. Students work with a partner to complete the exercise. Listen to some of their ideas in open class as feedback.

Mixed-ability

Stronger students could create new conversations based on the pictures.

Personality

SPEAKING Books closed. As a lead-in, give students three minutes to work in small groups and make a list of personality adjectives. Elicit examples and create a mindmap on the board, grouping similar adjectives where possible. Encourage students to copy the mindmap into their notebooks for future reference.

Books open. Ask the class: *Which, if any, are on your mindmaps?* Read through the list of adjectives and check understanding. Students work in pairs or small groups to complete the activity. Listen to some examples in open class as feedback.

Mixed-ability

Give weaker students time to prepare their answers before saying them to their partner.

Using *should*

SPEAKING Ask students to read the instructions and the example. Ask: *Why do they say 'shouldn't have' in the example?* (to express regret or give advice about a past action). Elicit further possible responses to the example to check students understand how to use *should(n't) have*. Students work with a partner to complete the exercise. Listen to some of their ideas in open class as feedback, checking their use of *should* and correcting, as necessary.

Mixed-ability

Give weaker students time to think about whether their answers refer to the past, present or future before deciding whether to use *should have* + past participle or *should* + base infinitive.

Career paths

1 Books open. Look at the pictures with students and nominate individuals to name the jobs. Write the names on the board. If there is an IWB available in the classroom, the picture description would best be done as a heads-up activity with the whole class.

Answers

A engineer B nurse C bus driver D street cleaner
E child minder

2 Tell students they are going to read an article about choosing a career. Set a time limit of two minutes to encourage students to practise reading quickly to search for specific words. Tell them not to worry about unknown words, but to just focus on checking which of the jobs are mentioned. Check answers, referring back to the jobs listed on the board.

Answers

engineer, childminder

3 SPEAKING Students re-read the article to complete the exercise. Encourage them not to use dictionaries, but to try to understand difficult vocabulary from its context. Get them to underline the parts of the article that helped them decide on their answers. Students compare answers in pairs before a whole-class check. During feedback ask students to refer to the parts of the article they underlined to justify their answers. You could hold a class vote to find out which of the tips students found most useful.

Decisions

1 The article contains a variety of expressions connected to decisions. Give students two minutes to try to complete the questions from memory before looking back at the article to check. Confirm answers in open class. During feedback, elicit some possible answers to the questions in preparation for the following exercise.

Answers

1 make 2 mind 3 make up 4 come to 5 long, hard

2 SPEAKING Working individually, students make notes on their answers to the questions in Exercise 1. Monitor and help with ideas or deal with questions about vocabulary. Divide the class into pairs or small groups for students to compare and discuss their answers. Listen to some of their ideas in open class as feedback and encourage further discussion.

Permission

1 To quickly review this area of grammar, nominate individuals to describe school rules. Elicit sentences such as:

Our teachers (don't) let us bring our phones into the classroom.
We are (not) allowed to ride bicycles in the playground.
My teacher makes (doesn't make) us do homework every week/evening.

Point out the absence of *to* with *let* and *make* and the use of *be* with *allowed*. Also draw students' attention to the negative forms.

Ask students to work individually to complete the sentences. Encourage them to look carefully at the context of each one before deciding which verb to use. Allow students to compare answers with a partner before feedback in open class.

Answers

1 let   2 make   3 are allowed to   4 makes
5 was allowed to   6 lets

Optional extension

Ask students to describe rules at home. Elicit sentences such as:

My parents (don't) let me stay up until midnight at the weekend.

I am (not) allowed to play on my Xbox every day.

My dad makes/doesn't make me tidy my bedroom every week.

---

2 WRITING If you're short on time, set this exercise for homework. Ask students to work individually and write sentences about their perfect job or career. Monitor carefully to ensure students are using the structures correctly and to make a note of any common errors. Divide the class into pairs for students to read each other's work. During feedback, listen to some examples in open class and elicit corrections to any repeated errors.

Student's Book pages 10–11

D   NEW THINGS

A change of lifestyle?

1 1.05 Books closed. As a lead-in, write these questions on the board, or dictate them, and ask students to discuss their answers with a partner: *Do you like doing sports? What sports do you do? What sorts of clothes do you like wearing for sports?* Give pairs a few minutes to discuss and then listen to some of their answers in open class.

Tell students they are going to hear a conversation about going to the gym.

Play the audio while students listen, read and answer the questions. Tell them to focus on answering the questions and not to worry if they do not understand every word. Allow them to compare answers with a partner before a whole-class check.

Mixed-ability

Stronger students could be asked to close their books and answer the questions based solely on listening to the conversation.

Answers

1 They are at the sports/leisure centre.
2 Tom doesn't want to be there because he feels uncomfortable wearing sports gear.

2 1.05 Give students time to read the dialogue and clarify any difficult vocabulary. Play the audio again while students complete the dialogue. Ask them to compare answers with a partner before checking in open class.

Answers

1 impatient   2 agreed   3 unhealthy   4 persuaded
5 encouraged   6 uncomfortable   7 should   8 hadn't

3 Divide the class into pairs or small groups for students to complete the exercise. Check answers in open class.

Answers

1 Because he's fed up with his unhealthy lifestyle.
2 Because he's got thin legs.
3 Because they're too busy doing exercise.
4 Because Tom keeps complaining.

Reporting verbs

1 This activity could be done via a *Test-Teach-Test* approach. Read the instructions with students and ask them to work individually to complete the exercise (*Test*). Allow students to compare answers with a partner. During open-class feedback, focus on the different structures that follow each verb (*Teach*). If students have had difficulty with particular verbs, give them further examples (*Teach*) and ask them to think of examples of their own (*Test*). Approaching the exercise in this way allows you to see which areas students are already aware of and which they need further practice in.

Answers

1 He recommended I watch that film.
2 He refused to help Molly.
3 She explained that she was late because there hadn't been any buses.
4 He agreed to lend Tony his jacket.
5 Alice persuaded me to go to the cinema with her.
6 I encouraged Sue to ask him.

2 SPEAKING Give students two minutes to read the sentences and think about their answers. Divide the class into pairs or small groups for them to discuss. Monitor to check students are using language correctly and to make a note of any repeated errors. Write these up on the board, ensuring anonymity and ask students to correct them during whole-class feedback. During feedback, ask students to share any interesting information they discovered about their partner.

Negative adjectives

1 Books closed. Write *happy* on the board and elicit the negative form (*unhappy*). In open class, brainstorm a list of other prefixes used to make adjectives negative and write them on the board.

Books open. Ask students to work with a partner to complete the exercise. Write answers on the board, and elicit and mark the stress during feedback. Say the adjectives for students to repeat and check pronunciation.

Answers

1 unhappy   2 impatient   3 impossible   4 unconcerned
5 irregular   6 illegal

2 Ask students to read the instructions and example. Check/clarify: *logical; responsible*. Students work with a partner to complete the exercise. During feedback, pay attention to pronunciation of the adjectives, and correct as necessary.

Answers

1 informal   2 unimportant   3 illogical   4 impolite
5 irresponsible

Another country

1 If there is an IWB available in the classroom, this activity would best be done as a heads-up activity with the whole class. Focus on the pictures on the left of the page, or ask students to cover the text on the right of the page in their books. Nominate individuals to describe the things in the photograph and write their answers on the board. Students then read the blog and complete the exercise. Tell them not to worry if they don't understand every word; they should just focus on answering the question. Ask students to check their answer with a partner before feedback in open class.

Answer

the temple

2 Check/clarify *get used to* by giving an example situation, for example: *driving abroad on the other side of the road felt very strange at first, but after a few weeks, I got used to it and it seemed normal.* Students read the text again to complete the exercise. Tell them to underline information in the text that helped them answer each question. Students check answers with a partner before whole-class feedback. During feedback, students can justify their answers by quoting the text they have underlined.

Answers

the traffic, the time it takes to get to school, the language

3 **SPEAKING** Working individually, students think of two more things Hayley has to *get used to*. Divide the class into pairs for students to compare their ideas. Listen to some of their answers in open class as feedback.

Suggested answers

the noise   a different currency   the climate

Changes

Ask students to work with a partner and complete sentences 1–7. During whole-class feedback, say the words for students to repeat and check pronunciation.

Answers

1 taking up   2 struggle   3 doing well   4 form
5 give up   6 ways   7 break

Regrets: *I wish … / If only …*

1 Ask students to try to complete the sentences from memory before looking back at the text to check their answers.

Answers

1 had told   2 I'd listened

2 Get students to read the instructions and the list of verbs. Elicit the past participle of each verb to remind students to use them in their answers. Students complete the exercise individually before comparing answers with a partner. Check answers in open class.

Answers

1 I'd brought   2 I'd worn   3 I'd known   4 had found

Optional extension

Write the following question on the board:

What things would you change about the last year if you could?

Ask students to write three sentences beginning *I wish …* or *If only …*

Divide the class into pairs. Ask students to take turns to read one of their sentences to their partner. Their partner asks them questions about it. Listen to some examples in open class as feedback.

Alternatively, you could ask students to think of celebrities who have done things they wish they hadn't. Students could find pictures of celebrities and write their thoughts in a speech bubble, for example a footballer might think: *If only I'd scored that goal!*

---

1 SURVIVAL

Objectives

FUNCTIONS	making and accepting a challenge
GRAMMAR	verbs followed by infinitive or gerund; verbs which take gerund and infinitive with different meanings: *remember, try, stop, regret, forget*
VOCABULARY	verbs of movement; adjectives to describe uncomfortable feelings

Student's Book pages 12–13

READING

1 Books closed. As a lead-in, ask students: *Have you ever been up a mountain? What was it like? What did you see there?* Listen to some of their answers in open class.

Books open. If there is an interactive whiteboard (IWB) available in the classroom, this activity would best be done as a heads-up activity with the whole class. Display the photos on the IWB. Say *a summit*, and nominate a student to point to the photo on the board. The rest of the class agree or disagree with the answers. Alternatively, students do the matching activity in pairs before checking answers with the whole class. Say each of the four words for students to repeat and check pronunciation.

2 Divide the class into pairs or small groups for students to discuss the questions and make a list of dangers. Listen to some of their ideas in open class and write a list on the board.

3 🔊1.06 Tell students they are going to read and listen to an article about two mountain climbers. Play the audio while students read the text to find the answer to the question. Tell them it is not important to understand every word. Students compare their answer with a partner before checking in open class.

4 This exercise is closely modelled on Reading and
✳ Use of English Part 6 of the Cambridge English: First exam. Read through the sentences with students and check/clarify: *failed, survive, crawl, stove, fuel, exhausted.* Encourage students to underline the key information in the sentences that will help them place the sentences in the text (e.g. *Then* in sentence A; *him* in sentence B). Students read the text in more detail to complete the exercise. Suggest that they underline the parts of the text that helped them find their answers. Students check their answers with a partner before whole-class feedback. During feedback, ask individuals to refer to the parts of the text they underlined.

Answers

1 C 2 F 3 A 4 H 5 B 6 E 7 G
D is the extra sentence

5 SPEAKING Give students two minutes to read the instructions and the questions. Check/clarify *paradoxical, owe*. Divide the class into pairs or small groups for students to discuss the questions. Monitor and help with any questions about vocabulary but, as this is a fluency activity, do not interrupt conversations unless errors impede communication. Listen to some of their ideas in open class for feedback and encourage further discussion.

Mixed-ability

Make similar-ability pairings. Allow weaker students some time to think about their answers before discussing them. Monitor, helping with vocabulary as required. Listen to some of their answers in open class.

Optional extension

A reading race: Ask students to find as many different infinitives and gerund forms in the text and the A–H sentences as they can in three minutes (not including *to be/ to have*). Get them to work in pairs. When the time is up, students count how many verbs they have found. Ask the pair with most verbs to read them out and make a list on the board. Ask other pairs to add to the list where they can.

There are thirteen infinitives and seven *-ing* forms:

to climb, reaching, to go, to melt, to descend, lowering, hanging, dying, to leave, to understand, giving, to cut, to descend, crawling, hopping, to cross, to leave, to save, to survive, to crawl

▌▌▌ TRAIN TO THiNK ▌▌▌

Thinking rationally

1 Read the introduction in open class.

To encourage students to think about relevant and irrelevant ideas, say: *I am looking for a present for my sister and I need to decide what to buy, which of the following is relevant to my decision?*

Read out the following sentences and ask students to say *relevant* or *irrelevant* in response to each one.

I have got a dog. (irrelevant)
I have got £20. (relevant)
My sister's name is Sally. (irrelevant)
Sally loves chocolate. (relevant)

Ask students to work with a partner and decide which of the facts were relevant. Check answers in open class.

2 SPEAKING Students work with a partner to discuss the question. Encourage students to think of several different feelings that Simon may have had. Listen to some of their ideas in open class.

3 SPEAKING Ask students to work individually to note down their answers to questions 1–3. Remind them that they should write what they *should do* and what they *might do* in each situation. Divide the class into pairs or small groups for students to discuss the questions. Monitor and help with vocabulary as necessary. Avoid error correction unless errors really hinder comprehension. The focus of this task is on fluency, not on practice of structures or lexis. Listen to some of their ideas in open class as feedback and encourage whole-class discussion.

> **Optional extension**
>
> Organise a simple balloon debate. Elicit the names of four famous people, historical or living, real or fictional. This activity works best if the four characters have different backgrounds or professions e.g. a politician, a sportsman, an actor and a cartoon character.
>
> Tell students that the four characters are in a hot air balloon which is falling from the sky due to the number of people on board. Students have to throw the characters out of the balloon, one at a time, in order for the remaining character to survive. Divide the class into groups of four and ask students to discuss the order in which the characters should be thrown from the balloon. During whole-class feedback, ask students to share their orders and also get them to give one relevant and one irrelevant reason for throwing each character from the balloon. Their classmates should say which is the relevant and which is the irrelevant reason.

PRONUNCIATION

For practice of alternative spellings of dipthongs go to Student's Book page 120.

Student's Book pages 14–15

GRAMMAR

Verbs followed by infinitive or gerund

1 Remind students that there are a variety of verb patterns in English. Look at the sentences from the article. Ask students to look back at the article and check which is the correct form. Students work with a partner to complete the rule before all answers are checked in open class.

> **Mixed-ability**
>
> Stronger students can complete the exercise before looking back at the article to check their answers. Allow weaker students to look directly at the article.

> **Answers**
>
> 1 to climb 2 to lower/lowering 3 dying 4 giving
> 5 to cut 6 to descend/descending

> **Rule**
>
> 1 a gerund 2 an infinitive 3 a gerund/an infinitive
> 4 an infinitive/a gerund

> **LANGUAGE NOTE**
>
> Point out that there are no specific rules to decide which verb is followed by what form and that verb patterns need to be learnt individually.

2 If you're short on time, set this exercise for homework. Students work individually to complete sentences 1–8. Allow them to compare answers with a partner before feedback in open class.

> **Mixed-ability**
>
> Stronger students can complete the exercise before looking back at the rule to check their answers. Encourage weaker students to look at the rule to help them with their answers.

> **Answers**
>
> 1 climbing 2 going 3 to show 4 reading 5 walking
> 6 to buy, to get/to get, to buy 7 helping 8 being

> **Fast finishers**
>
> Students can write sentences including some of the verb patterns from the rule which are not used in Exercise 2.

> **Optional extension**
>
> Ask students to work in threes to practise using the different verb patterns. Students take it in turns to say a verb for their partners to race to respond with a full sentence. For example:
> A: suggest
> B or C: My brother suggested going to the cinema.
> The first student to offer a correct sentence scores one point.

Workbook page 10 and page 122

 Be aware of common errors related to verb patterns. Go to Get it right! on Student's Book page 122.

VOCABULARY

Verbs of movement

1 Ask students to complete the sentences and then look back at the article to check their answers. During feedback, ask concept-check questions, for example: *Do you hop on two feet or one?* (one); *When you crawl, where are your hands?* (on the floor); *When you descend, are you going up or down?* (down).

> **Answers**
>
> 1 climb 2 descend 3 crawling, hopping

2 Divide the class into pairs and ask students to discuss the meaning of the verbs. Listen to some of their ideas in open class, but do not comment at this stage. Ask students to match the verbs to the definitions. Allow them to use English–English dictionaries if necessary. Check answers, giving further examples or demonstrating to clarify meaning, as required.

Answers

a 3   b 4   c 8   d 6   e 10   f 1   g 9   h 7   i 2   j 5

Fast finishers

Students think of more verbs to add to the list of verbs of movement. Allow them to use a dictionary. Listen to some of their examples in open class after feedback.

3 If you're short on time, you can set this exercise for homework.

Give students time to read sentences 1–10 and to ask about any difficult vocabulary. Check/clarify: *harbour, steep, ankle*. Students work individually to complete the gaps, being careful to put the verbs into the correct tense. Ask them to check with a partner before whole-class feedback.

Mixed-ability

Stronger students can cover the verbs in Exercise 2 and complete the sentences before looking back at the pictures to check their answers.

Answers

1 descending/to descend   2 wandering   3 swinging
4 climbed   5 tiptoed   6 to stagger   7 hop   8 rushed
9 crawl   10 leaped

Optional extension

Divide the class into pairs. Ask students to make a list of situations when they might have to or want to: 1 climb, 2 crawl, 3 hop, 4 tiptoe, 5 leap, 6 rush.

Listen to some of their ideas in open class as feedback.

Workbook page 12

LISTENING

1 ◖◗1.09 As a lead-in, write the following questions on the board:

What radio shows or podcasts do you listen to?
Do your parents/grandparents listen to different radio shows or podcasts to you?

Divide the class into pairs for students to discuss the questions. Monitor and help with vocabulary and prompt students to describe programmes in detail. Listen to some of their answers in open class.

Tell students they are going to listen to part of a radio show called *Desperate Measures*. Nominate students to guess what the show might be about in open class, encouraging as much speculation as possible. Play the recording while students listen and answer the question, checking their predictions. Students can check answers with a partner before whole-class feedback.

Answer

Contestants are given 30 seconds to give an original and humorous answer to a question.

Audio Script Track 1.09

Radio Host Good morning. This is *Desperate Measures*, our programme *for* young people, *with* young people. We have three of them on the show. We gave each of them today's question three minutes ago, so they've had time to think a bit. The person with the most original and humorous answer is the *Desperate Measures* Champion of the Week. And today's question is: 'Imagine you are in an awkward situation, how do you get out of it?' And here we go. Our first guest is Dawn.

Dawn Hi.

Radio Host Hi, Dawn. Give us your answer. You've got 30 seconds.

Dawn If you have food in your mouth, no one can expect you to speak. It would even be rude to talk with your mouth full, wouldn't it? So remember to take a snack with you wherever you go. Just imagine you are in class, and your teacher has asked you a question but you're stuck and can't answer it … that can be awful, right? But you don't need to feel ashamed. Just stuff your face with things to eat, chips, fruit, chewing gum … whatever you have. And if you want to be absolutely safe, put toffees in your mouth. At least seven and …

Radio Host Lovely answer. I remember eating a sandwich during a Maths class once because I was so hungry. I regret doing it as the teacher saw me and told me off. And now we have Philip. Hello.

Philip Hi!

Radio Host Philip. Give us your answer. You've got 30 seconds.

Philip When was the last time you were in an awkward situation? Wasn't it awful? I'm sure it was. But did you have a choice? Yes, you did. It's your own fault! Want to know why? Because the only way of getting out of an awkward situation is not to get into it. So here's my point. Never leave your room again. Just stay inside forever. If you stay in your room forever, you'll never get into any embarrassing situations in your whole life any more. Nothing to regret …

Radio Host Sorry, Philip, but I regret to tell you that you've run out of time. And now our third guest on the show, Amanda. Give us your answer. You've got 30 seconds.

Amanda Imagine you're in a shopping centre, hanging out with some friends, and suddenly you can see someone you want to avoid. You can try pretending that you don't feel awkward but it won't work. But don't worry. Playing Dead is a simple trick. Try to find a place where you can sit down, and pretend you're asleep. It's always worked for me … as long as you have your eyes closed, you and the other person can't see each other … and there's one more point. This strategy gives you a chance to relax, and gain energy for the rest of the day.

Radio Host Perfect, thanks so much, Amanda, and thanks too to Philip and Dawn. And now it's time to …

---

2 ◖◗1.09 This exercise is closely modelled on
✳ Listening Part 2 of the Cambridge English: First exam. Give students some time to discuss what they remember from the first listening and to read sentences 1–8. Check/clarify: *rude, awkward, scenario, tactic*. Play the audio again while students listen and complete the sentences. Allow them to compare answers with a partner before a whole-class check.

If necessary, play the audio again, pausing to clarify answers, during feedback.

> **Answers**
>
> 1 young people   2 original, humorous   3 food   4 fault
> 5 stay in   6 shopping centre   7 asleep   8 eyes

GRAMMAR

Verbs which take gerund and infinitive with different meanings: *remember, try, stop, regret, forget*

1 Books closed. As an introduction write *to go* and *going* on the board. In open class, read out verbs from the rule on page 14 and nominate individuals to say whether they are followed by *to go* or *going* or both. This could be turned into a game with the class divided into two groups, answering questions in turn and scoring a point for each correct answer.

Books open. Remind students that certain verbs are followed by *to* + infinitive or the gerund form with no difference in meaning (give examples of *begin*, *start* and *continue* from page 14). Explain/elicit that other verbs can be followed by *to* + infinitive or the gerund form but with a change in meaning.

Ask students to work with a partner and complete the exercise. Check answers in open class. During feedback, check understanding with concept-check questions (e.g. *Which sentence is giving advice? Which sentence refers to the past?*).

> **Answers**
>
> 1 to take, eating   2 doing, to tell   3 pretending, to find

2 Books closed. If there is an IWB available in the classroom, this activity would best be done as a heads-up activity with the whole class. Display the pictures on the IWB. Nominate individuals to describe each one. Read out sentences 1–4 in turn and ask a student to match a sentence to one of the pictures A–D, giving reasons for their choice. The rest of the class agree or disagree with the answers. If they disagree, ask them to say why. Alternatively, students do the matching activity in pairs before completing the rule. Check answers in open class.

> **Answers**
>
> 1 B   2 C   3 D   4 A

> **Rule**
>
> 1 gerund   2 infinitive   3 gerund   4 infinitive
> 5 gerund   6 infinitive   7 infinitive   8 gerund
> 9 gerund   10 infinitive

3 If you're short on time, set this exercise for homework. Students work individually to complete sentences 1–8. Allow students to compare answers with a partner before feedback in open class.

> **Answers**
>
> 1 to buy   2 telling   3 to get   4 to buy   5 playing
> 6 to find   7 putting   8 loving

> **Fast finishers**
>
> Students write sentences about themselves or people they know, and include some of the verb patterns. You could ask them to write two true and two false sentences. They could then read them out to another fast finisher, who should guess which are the false sentences.

> **Optional extension**
>
> Write the following on the board:
> *Think of:*
> * something you remember doing as a child
> * something you often forget
> * something you regret doing
> * something you have tried to do but failed
> * something you have stopped doing
>
> Monitor to help with vocabulary and ideas. Divide the class into pairs to discuss their answers.

Workbook page 11 and page 122

Be aware of common errors related to verb patterns. Go to Get it right! on Student's Book page 122.

Student's Book pages 16–17

VOCABULARY

Adjectives to describe uncomfortable feelings

1 In pairs, students choose an adjective for sentences 1–6. Do not let them refer to dictionaries at this stage. Check answers.

> **Answers**
>
> 1 awkward   2 ashamed   3 guilty   4 desperate
> 5 puzzled   6 stuck

2 Students match the adjectives to the definitions. Ask concept-check questions to check understanding and give further explanation if necessary to clarify meaning.

> **Answers**
>
> 1 ashamed   2 puzzled   3 stuck   4 awkward
> 5 guilty   6 desperate

> **Optional extension**
>
> Students write three sentences beginning: *I felt awkward/ guilty/ashamed when* … Tell them they can write about real or invented situations. When students have come up with some ideas, divide the class into pairs for students to discuss their answers. Listen to some of their examples in open class.

Workbook page 12

SPEAKING

1 Ask students to work individually to complete the exercise and then compare answers with a partner. Listen to some of their ideas in open class.

2 **WRITING** Look at the examples in the book and give further examples of your own to get students started. While students write their sentences, monitor to help with vocabulary and to encourage them to use adjectives from the Vocabulary exercise to describe uncomfortable feelings.

3 Refer back to the problems in Exercise 2 and ask students to read the example advice. Point out the use of imperatives and verb patterns with *stop*; *remember*; *start*; *try*. Divide the class into pairs to listen to each other's problems and give each other advice. Monitor to make a note of any examples of good usage. Praise students who make attempts to expand on their answers. Nominate individuals to feed back problems and advice in open class.

READING

1 A recording of this text is available with your digital resources. Books closed. As a lead-in, write the following situation on the board: *Your plane has crashed in a remote forest. Everybody has survived. What skills will you need to survive in the forest?*

In pairs, students discuss the question. Listen to some of their answers in open class.

Books open. Look at the photos and the headline of the article with students. Check/clarify: *GPS, shelter, survive, tie knots.* Divide the class into pairs for students to complete the exercise. Focusing on the topic in this way encourages prediction, a useful technique for improving reading speed.

> **BACKGROUND INFORMATION**
>
> **Edward 'Bear' Grylls** (born 7 June 1974) is a British television presenter, famous around the world for his television series such as *Born Survivor*, *Man vs Wild* and *Running Wild with Bear Grylls*. As well as teaching survival techniques, the shows involve stunts such as parachuting, ice climbing, fighting wild animals and so on. Among his other death-defying feats, he has climbed Mount Everest, spent 30 days circumnavigating the British Isles on jet skis and crossed the North Atlantic in an inflatable boat.

2 Give students a three-minute time limit (or longer with weaker classes) to read the text and check their predictions. Tell them not to worry about understanding every word and to just focus on checking their predictions. Allow students to compare with a partner before whole-class feedback.

> **Answers**
>
> how to build a fire ✓
> how to build a shelter in the wild ✓
> how to survive outdoors in bad weather ✓
> how to tie knots ✓

3 Divide the class into pairs or small groups for students to discuss the questions. Encourage them to underline the parts of the text that support their answers. Listen to some of their ideas in open class as feedback.

> **Optional extension**
>
> Ask students to work in pairs and make a list of films, books or television dramas which deal with people surviving in the wild. Regroup students into different groups for them to compare their lists, discuss what happens in each one, and make recommendations.

THiNK SELF-ESTEEM

How adventurous are you?

1 SPEAKING Ask students to work individually to make a list of four or five adventurous activities. If students have difficulty coming up with ideas, brainstorm activities in open class and create a group list on the board. Ask students to work with a partner to discuss which activities they have tried or would like to try. Encourage them to go into detail and give reasons for their answers. Listen to some examples in open class as feedback.

2 SPEAKING In pairs or small groups, students complete the exercise. Encourage them to use the language in the list of points when describing the activities. When students have discussed several activities, ask: *Following your discussion, would you like to try any different activities? Why?* Listen to some of their ideas in open class.

> **Optional extension**
>
> Ask students to work in pairs or small groups. Tell them that they have a friend coming to stay and they need to plan a week of adventurous activities which should include as many of the points in Exercise 2 as possible. Make sure all students note down their ideas. Re-group students for them to explain their plans to other groups.

WRITING

An email about an experience

This exercise can be done for homework or in class. Ask students to read the instructions and work in pairs or small groups to discuss the topic and note down their answers. Monitor and help students with any questions. Students work individually to expand their notes into an email. In the next lesson, put students back into the same groups to read each other's emails. Encourage them to work together to correct each other's mistakes and to say what they like about each other's emails.

Student's Book pages 18–19

PHOTOSTORY: episode 1

The challenge

1 To introduce the concept of challenges, say *I bet you can't say the alphabet in 15 seconds.* Tell students that you are issuing a challenge. You could ask for volunteers to accept the challenge and say the alphabet quickly in open class, to change the pace and add an element of fun to the lesson.

Tell students they are going to read and listen to a story about a group of students. If you are using an IWB, project the images on to the board and ask students to close their books. Students look at the title and photos and read the questions. Ask them to guess answers to the questions. Write some of their ideas on the board.

> **Answer**
>
> 2 To not use their phones at all during the whole weekend.

2 ◀ 1.10 Play the audio for students to read, listen and check their answer to Exercise 1. During whole-class feedback, refer to students' ideas on the board. Ask: *Who guessed correctly?*

DEVELOPING SPEAKING

3 Ask students what they think happens next. Get them to brainstorm possible endings to the story, in groups, with one student in each group acting as secretary and taking notes. During whole-class feedback, write students' ideas on the board to refer back to once they have watched the video. Don't give away answers at this stage.

4 ◀ EP1 Play the video for students to watch and check their answers. During whole-class feedback, refer to students' ideas on the board. Ask: *Who guessed correctly?*

5 Divide the class into pairs and ask students to complete the exercise. Monitor and help with any difficulties. Play the video again, pausing as required for clarification. Check answers with the whole class.

Answers

1 He thinks she doesn't want him to overhear what she's saying.
2 She watched YouTube videos on her phone.
3 He didn't last one night without using his phone.
4 Three hours.
5 She spoke to her friend Julia on the phone.

PHRASES FOR FLUENCY

1 Ask students to locate expressions 1–6 in the story on page 18 and underline them. To encourage speed-reading, you could do this as a race and ask students to find the expressions as quickly as possible. Ask students to compare their answers with a partner before whole-class feedback.

Answers

Nicole says phrases 1–5. They all say phrase 6.

2 Working in pairs, students complete the dialogues. Check answers. Drill the dialogues in open class (for students to repeat together), paying attention to the intonation of sentences and questions. Give students time to practise saying the dialogues with a partner.

Answers

1 something or other, Same here   2 give me a shout, It's a deal   3 You know what   4 where were we

WordWise

Expressions with *right*

1 Books closed. To introduce this activity, write the word *right* in the middle of the board. In open class, ask students to think of different meanings for *right* and any words that could go before or after *right*. Write any correct answers on the board.

Books open. Ask students to work with a partner and complete the exercise. Check answers in open class. Give further examples to outline meaning of the phrases if necessary.

Answers

1 right away   2 Too right   3 right up to   4 right?
5 Right   6 All right!

2 Students work individually to complete the sentences using phrases from Exercise 1. During whole-class feedback, say the phrases for students to repeat and check pronunciation.

Answers

1 right   2 right up to   3 right away   4 Right
5 Too right   6 All right

> **Optional extension**
>
> Divide the class into AB pairs. B closes his/her book. A says each sentence (in random order) replacing the *right* expression with *beep* for A to guess it. Repeat the activity with B asking A.

Workbook page 12 ▶

FUNCTIONS

Issuing and accepting a challenge

1 Look at the eight phrases. Students work with a partner to decide which are used to issue a challenge and which to accept or turn one down. Check answers. Say the phrases for students to repeat and check pronunciation.

Answers

1 issue a challenge
2 accept a challenge
3 issue a challenge
4 accept / turn down a challenge
5 issue a challenge
6 accept a challenge
7 issue a challenge
8 accept a challenge

2 WRITING Check/clarify: *doughnut, licking your lips.* Students work with a partner to write short dialogues, then practise acting them out. Encourage them to sound enthusiastic when issuing or accepting challenges. Listen to some examples in open class as feedback. Ask: *Why would these challenges be difficult?* Students discuss in pairs.

> **Mixed-ability**
>
> Weaker students can write their dialogues and practise them before trying to act out their dialogue without looking at their notes. Stronger students can perform dialogues spontaneously.

> **Optional extension**
>
> Ask students to work in pairs and issue each other challenges that could be taken up in the classroom.

2 GOING PLACES

Objectives

FUNCTIONS	expressing surprise
GRAMMAR	relative clauses (review); *which* to refer to a whole clause; omitting relative pronouns; reduced relative clauses
VOCABULARY	groups of people; phrasal verbs (1)

Student's Book pages 20–21

READING

1 Books closed. As a lead-in, write the names of three countries on the board including the country in which you are teaching. Ask students: *What are the differences between these countries?* Students discuss the question in pairs. Listen to some of their answers in open class and write some of their ideas on the board.

Books open. Draw students' attention to the photos and nominate one or two students to describe them. If there is an interactive whiteboard (IWB) available in the classroom, the picture description would best be done as a heads-up activity with the whole class. Focus attention on the exercise. Ask students to work individually to choose two more things and rank the items 1–6. Monitor and help with any difficulties.

2 SPEAKING Divide the class into pairs or small groups for students to compare their answers. Listen to some of their findings in open class and hold a class vote to find out which things students think would be most difficult to get used to.

3 SPEAKING Check/clarify: *shortage, workshops, refugees, renovation*. Students work with a partner to predict the topic of the article. Listen to some of their ideas in open class and write them on the board, but do not comment on them at this stage.

4 ◁)) 1.11 Students read and listen to the article to check their ideas. To encourage students to skim-read in order to get an overall understanding of the text, set a two-minute time limit for this exercise. Allow students to compare answers with a partner before doing feedback in open class.

5 Before students read the text again, ask them to work with a partner and choose and underline the key information in the sentences that they will need to look for in the article. Students read the article and complete the exercise. Encourage them to underline parts of the text that support their answers and to correct any false information. Allow them to check answers with a partner before whole-class feedback.

Answers

1 Many people in the 1990s left Riace because of a shortage of jobs.
2 The refugees had to work to get food and accommodation.
3 The refugees had to learn Italian.
4 The refugees lived in empty houses.
5 Between two and three hundred immigrants live in Riace now.
6 More local people are staying in Riace.
7 Many politicians have tried to use Lucano's ideas.
8 Lucano came third in the 2010 'World Mayor' award.

6 SPEAKING Students work in pairs or small groups to discuss the questions. Nominate students to share their ideas during whole-class feedback. Ask: *Do you think this would be successful in your town? Why (not)?*

▰ TRAIN TO THiNK ▰

Distinguishing fact from opinion

1 Books closed. As an introduction to this topic, write the following on the board:

A: *Drinking water is good for you.*
B: *Children eat too many sweets.*

Ask: *Are these sentences fact or opinion?* (A is fact, B is opinion). Elicit answers in open class prompting students to explain their answers and to react to each other's ideas.

Books open. Ask students to read the introduction and statements. Point out the use of *Does that mean that …?* and *What evidence is there that …?* to start the questions. Elicit answers in open class.

Answer

The purpose of question B is to check if statement A is true.

2 Ask students to read the statements and check understanding. Get students to work with a partner and think of questions to separate opinions from facts. Monitor and help if students are having difficulties thinking of questions. Listen to some of their ideas in open class and write good answers on the board.

Mixed-ability

Stronger students can write questions for all five statements. Weaker students can focus on just the first three statements.

Student's Book pages 22–23

GRAMMAR

Relative clauses (review)

1 At this level, students will have seen relative clauses before, but may still make mistakes when using them, particularly with the use of commas in non-defining clauses.

Ask students to read through the sentences and then work with a partner to complete the rule. Check answers. Read the sentences without the relative clause to show that B and C define the noun and A and D add extra information.

Rule

1 B   2 C   3 A   4 D

LANGUAGE NOTE

Remind students that we do not use *that* as a relative pronoun in non-defining relative clauses.

2 SPEAKING Students work with a partner to complete the sentences. Check answers in open class. Ask students to work in small groups to discuss whether or not they agree with the statements. Monitor to help with any difficulties and to prompt students to give reasons for their answers. Listen to some of their opinions during whole-class feedback.

Answers

1 who/that   2 who/that   3 who/that   4 which/that
They are all defining relative clauses.

3 If you're short on time, set this exercise for homework but perhaps do number 1 in open class to make sure students are clear on what they have to do. Students work individually to complete sentences 1–4. Allow them to compare answers with a partner before feedback in open class.

Answers

1 The locals, who were very kind, gave them food.
2 Rome, which is my favourite city, is an exciting place.
3 I've been reading a book by William Boyd, who is one of my favourite writers.
4 My neighbour Rubens, who is from Guatemala, has been living here for ten years.

which to refer to a whole clause

4 Look back at sentences A and B in Exercise 1 and ask students what *which* refers to (A: Calabria; B: buildings). Explain that *which* can be used to refer to specific things or to whole clauses. Ask students to read sentences 1 and 2 and decide what *which* refers to. Check answers.

Answers

1 Calabria   2 Città Futura has 13 local employees

5 This exercise gives more examples of *which* being used to refer to whole clauses. Read the example in open class and point out that *which* is used to join the two sentences and makes the language sound more fluent and interesting. Students work in pairs to complete the exercise. Check answers in open class.

Answers

1 Some people go and live in another country, which is not always easy.
2 You have to learn new customs, which can be challenging.
3 Some people are nervous about strangers, which makes life difficult for new arrivals.
4 Sometimes there are differences in culture, which often results in misunderstandings.

Workbook page 18 and page 122

 Be aware of common errors related to relative clauses. Go to Get it right! on Student's Book page 122.

VOCABULARY

Groups of people

Books closed. To introduce this topic, write *groups of people* in the centre of the board and brainstorm names of different groups. Give one or two examples to get them started (*footballers, students, men*, etc). Alternatively, if you have access to an IWB, do an internet search for photos of different groups and display them on the board for students to name.

Books open. Ask students to read the list and check understanding. In pairs, students complete the gaps in sentences 1–11. Check answers in open class.

Answers

1 pedestrians 2 the staff 3 motorists 4 the crew
5 Inhabitants 6 employees 7 politicians 8 Refugees
9 Employers 10 residents 11 Immigrants

Fast finishers

Ask students to add further examples of groups of people to the list.

Workbook page 20

LISTENING

Migration in nature

1 SPEAKING Books closed. As a lead-in, ask students: *Do wild animals always stay in the same place? Which animals migrate from one place to another?* Give students two minutes to discuss their answers, and make a list in pairs. Listen to some of their answers in open class and write any correct answers on the board.

Books open. If there is an IWB available in the classroom, this activity would best be done as a heads-up activity with the whole class. Display the pictures on the IWB. Say *wildebeest*, and nominate a student to choose the correct migration route 1–3. The rest of the class agrees or disagrees. Alternatively, students do the matching activity in pairs before a quick show of hands in open class and tally their answers on the board. Do not give answers at this stage.

2 ◁)) 1.12 Tell students they are going to listen to a radio interview about animal migration. Play

the recording while students check their answers to Exercise 1. Tell them not to worry if they don't understand every word, but to just focus on checking they've matched the right route with the right animal. Confirm answers in open class.

Answers

A 3 B 1 C 2

Audio Script Track 1.12

Man Now, I've been reading a new book called *On the Move* by wildlife expert Sally Harker, and she's with us in the studio today to tell us a bit about it. Hi, Sally.

Sally Hello.

Man So, tell the audience what your book is about.

Sally Well, it's about the movement of animals and birds. All over the world, the natural world, there are examples of how birds and animals don't stay in one place, but move around, either all the time, like whales, or at certain times, like a lot of migrating birds. And there are some really extraordinary cases, amazing stories of the journeys that animals or birds make.

Man Why do you say 'extraordinary'?

Sally Well because sometimes the journeys are incredibly long, in others they're very, very risky, dangerous for the animals, and in some cases we just don't understand how the animals do it at all!

Man So can you give us some examples? Let's start with really long journeys.

Sally OK, for really long journeys it's hard to beat the grey whale. In the winter, grey whales can be found near California or Mexico; the whales have their babies there. And then in the summer, the grey whales like to be near Alaska, where the sea is full of food for them. So, every year, they swim from one place to the other and back again – it's a trip of about 18,000 kilometres altogether.

Man That's quite a distance!

Sally It certainly is! Now, in terms of dangerous trips, it's hard to beat the wildebeest of central Africa. Every year, more than a million wildebeest travel from Tanzania to Kenya, where there's more food. It's a trip of over 2,000 kilometres. The real danger is near the end of the journey, when they're already tired, hungry and thirsty, they have to cross the Mara River. The river flows very fast, and it's full of hungry crocodiles. And the wildebeest are very scared of water. But they jump in and struggle to swim across. Thousands of them don't get to the other side. We think that every year, about 250,000 wildebeest die on this journey.

Man Unbelievable! Good heavens.

Sally Yes, it's amazing isn't it? And here's a third example. Birds, this time – the Arctic tern. This bird, you know, every year, it flies a distance of about 70,000 kilometres from the north of Canada down to Antarctica, and back.

Man Wow. That's phenomenal.

Sally And so in its lifetime, a single bird could fly about 2 million kilometres – that's like going to the moon and back five or six times! And, the big question for us is, how do the birds manage to find exactly the same places every year?

Man No GPS.

Sally That's right. They fly thousands of kilometres and arrive, every year, in exactly the same place.

Man That's incredible. Do we really have no idea how they do it?

Sally Not really, although of course research is being done all the time …

---

3 ◄))1.12 Ask students to work with a partner to try to remember what the numbers referred to. Play the audio again for students to check their answers. During feedback, encourage students to answer in full sentences by prompting them and praising those who do.

> **Answers**
>
> 1 The distance in kilometres swum by grey whales every year.
> 2 The number of wildebeest that travel from Tanzania to Kenya every year.
> 3 The distance in kilometres travelled by the wildebeest.
> 4 The number of wildebeest that die on the journey every year.
> 5 The distance in kilometres flown by Arctic terns every year.
> 6 The distance in kilometres flown by an Arctic tern during its lifetime.

4 ◄))1.12 Give students time to read the sentences and check understanding. Clarify that all the sentences contain incorrect information. Students work together to correct the information. If necessary, play the recording a third time for students to check their answers.

> **Answers**
>
> 1 Grey whales swim to Alaska to find food.
> 2 Grey whales can be found near California or Mexico in the winter.
> 3 The Mara River is near the end of the wildebeests' journey.
> 4 The Mara River is full of crocodiles.
> 5 Arctic terns do their journey every year.
> 6 People don't know how the terns always arrive at the same place.

5 SPEAKING Divide the class into pairs or small groups for students to discuss the questions. If students have access to the Internet in the classroom, ask them to do a search to find further examples of migratory animals or birds to share with the class. Monitor and help with any questions about vocabulary. For feedback, nominate students to share their group's ideas with the class and encourage reaction and further discussion.

FUNCTIONS

Expressing surprise

1 ◄))1.12 Books closed. Elicit/explain that there were many phrases used to express surprise in the recording. Ask students if they can recall any of them, and if they can think of any other phrases used to express surprise. Write all correct expressions on the board.

Books open. Look at the gapped sentences 1–5 with students. Play the recording again for students to listen and complete the gaps. Pause after each phrase and ask students to repeat the phrase using suitable intonation. Encourage students to sound enthusiastic! Repeat the phrases several times chorally and individually.

> **Answers**
>
> 1 That's quite a distance.   2 Unbelievable! Good heavens.
> 3 It's amazing, isn't it?   4 Wow. That's phenomenal.
> 5 That's incredible.

2 Divide the class into AB pairs to create dialogues. Give some examples of your own to get them started. For example:
A: My brother can run 100m in 10.3 seconds.
B: Wow. That's phenomenal! Is he going to be at the next Olympics?
Or *A: I have been to 37 different countries.*
B: That's incredible. Which was your favourite?

Monitor to make sure students are asking follow-up questions and encourage them to continue the conversation where possible. If space allows, this activity also works well as a mingle with students swapping partners after each exchange. Listen to some examples in open class as feedback.

Student's Book pages 24–25

READING

1 A recording of this text is available with your digital resources. Books closed. As a lead-in, ask: *If you could live in a foreign country, where would you live? Why?* Give students one minute to think of their answers and make notes. Divide the class into small groups for students to compare answers. During feedback, hold a class vote to find out which country would be the most popular destination and why.

Books open. Ask students to work individually and make notes on the questions.

> **Answers**
>
> 1 She's in France.   2 She's from the UK / England.
> 3 It's about living abroad.

2 Ask students to read the blog and check their ideas. Tell them not to worry if they do not understand every word, but to focus on finding the answers to the questions. Allow students to compare answers with a partner before feedback in open class.

3 Give students time to read the questions and check understanding. Check/clarify: *deal with, homesickness*. Students re-read the blog and answer the questions, then compare with a partner before feedback in open class.

> **Answers**
>
> 1 She's studying.
> 2 Because some films give that impression of living abroad. / Because she has to do lots of things you wouldn't do on holiday.
> 3 Because she has to speak French all day.
> 4 Some were unhappy and wanted to leave.
> 5 Keep going because it won't last forever.
> 6 She tries to ignore them and concentrate on nice people she meets.

VOCABULARY

Phrasal verbs (1)

1 Divide the class into pairs. Ask students to cover the blog and try to complete sentences 1–8. When the majority of the class have completed the sentences, students can look back at the text to check answers. Ask students to discuss the meaning of the phrasal verbs and to try to deduce their meanings from context. During whole-class feedback, elicit/clarify the meaning of each phrasal verb with further examples as necessary.

> ### Mixed-ability
>
> Divide students roughly according to level. Ask stronger students to cover both the blog and the list of phrasal verbs and try to complete the sentences before looking at the list of phrasal verbs to check.
>
> Weaker students can complete the exercise with any verbs (phrasal or otherwise) that fit the context. They then try to match with phrasal verbs from the list before checking in the blog. This approach will help them more quickly grasp the meaning of the target phrasal verbs.

> ### Answers
>
> 1 pick up   2 go through   3 put up with
> 4 hang out with   5 wears, out   6 turning out
> 7 ran into   8 bring about

> ### Fast finishers
>
> Ask students to close their books and write down as many of the eight phrasal verbs as they can remember. Students then open their books to check.

PRONUNCIATION

For practice of phrasal verb stress go to Student's Book page 120.

2 Students work with a partner to match the phrasal verbs to their meanings. Check answers in open class. During whole-class feedback, clarify the meaning of the phrasal verbs by giving/eliciting further examples, as necessary.

> ### Answers
>
> 1 run into   2 pick up   3 put up with   4 go through
> 5 turn out   6 hang with   7 bring about

> ### Optional extension
>
> This activity could be done as a game of pelmanism, allowing for extra focus on the meanings of the verbs. Write each of the phrasal verbs and definitions on separate cards. Give one set of cards to each group of three or four students. Ask students to put all the cards face down on the table and take turns to turn over two cards until they find a matching pair (phrasal verb/definition). The winner is the player with most matching pairs at the end of the game.

3 Ask students to read questions 1–6 and check understanding. Students discuss the questions in pairs or small groups. Monitor to encourage students to use the phrasal verbs in their answers and to check they are being used correctly. Make a note

of any particularly good usage and nominate these individuals to repeat their answers during whole-class feedback.

Workbook page 20

GRAMMAR

Omitting relative pronouns

1 If you're not using an IWB, write the two example sentences on the board for clarity when explaining the answers. Give students a minute to work with a partner and answer the questions. In open class, elicit answers and the position of *that*, adding it to the sentences on the board with an arrow pointing to the object in each case. Then ask students to complete the rule in pairs before a whole-class check.

> ### Answers
>
> 1 It's a phase that you have to go through. (*phase* is the object)
> 2 I concentrate on the nice people that I meet. (*people* is the object)
> *That* refers to the object.

> ### Rule
>
> 1 object   2 subject

2 Remind students/elicit that we can remove the relative pronoun when it refers to an object, but we need to keep it if it refers to a subject. Students work with a partner to complete the exercise. During whole-class feedback, ask individuals to say what the relative pronoun refers to in each sentence.

> ### Answers
>
> 1 ✓   2 ✗   3 ✓   4 ✗   5 ✓   6 ✗

Reduced relative clauses

3 If you're not using an IWB, write the sentences on the board. Give students a minute to work with a partner and answer the questions. In open class, elicit answers and add *that is/who is* to the sentences on the board. Point out that we use reduced relative clauses in written English to make sentences flow more easily and improve 'readability'. They are also a good way to show examiners that you are a high level, and so should be encouraged in written work.

Next, ask students to complete the rule with a partner. Check answers.

> ### Answers
>
> 1 I'm a student who is living and studying in France.
> 2 The experience that is gained by living abroad is invaluable.

> ### Rule
>
> B

4 Ask students to work individually to complete the exercise. Clarify that there is a mixture of reduced relative clauses and omitted relative pronouns in the

paragraph. Allow students to compare answers with a partner before feedback in open class.

Answers

2 ~~who are~~ 3 ~~who were~~ 4 ~~that~~ 5 ~~that~~ 7 ~~that~~

Fast finishers

Ask students to look back at the article on page 21 to find further examples of relative pronouns and any sentences where relative pronouns have been omitted.

> Workbook page 19 and page 122 ➤

 Be aware of common errors related to omitting relative pronouns. Go to Get it right! on Student's Book page 123.

▌▌ THiNK VALUES ▌▌

Learning from other cultures

1 Refer back to the blog on page 24. Give students two minutes to rank the five things, individually.

2 Give students a minute to read sentences 1–5 and check understanding. Working individually, students complete the exercise.

3 SPEAKING Divide the class into small groups for students to compare their answers. During feedback, hold a class vote and create a class ranking on the board. To develop discussion further, this exercise can be done as a mingle with students comparing their answers with different students until they find a student with the same, or very similar answers to themselves.

Optional extension

Divide the class into pairs or small groups. Ask students to make a list of the things that immigrants to their own country would find difficult to get used to. Write some general topics on the board to guide students if necessary e.g. *food*; *weather*; *working hours*; *daily timetable*; *transport*; *noise*, etc. During feedback, elicit and write up a list of things students have come up with on the board and ask students to work in pairs to rank them in order of difficulty to adapt to.

Student's Book pages 26–27

CULTURE

1 If there is an IWB available in the classroom, this activity would best be done as a heads-up activity with the whole class. If your IWB allows zooming, zoom in on the photos and nominate individuals to say what they have in common. Alternatively, students can look at photos in their books and answer the question.

Answer

They all have a nomadic way of life.

2 ◁) 1.15 Play the audio while students read and listen to the article. Tell students not to worry if

they don't understand every word; they should just focus on answering the question. Ask students to check their answer with a partner before feedback in open class.

3 Give students a minute or two to read the sentences and circle the key information that they need to look for. Students read the text again to complete the exercise. Tell them to underline information in the text that helped them answer each question. Students check answers with a partner before whole-class feedback. During feedback, ask students to justify their answers by quoting the text they have underlined.

Answers

1 The Shahsavan 2 Aborigines 3 Aborigines, the Tuareg
4 Aborigines 5 The Tuareg 6 The Tuareg, the Shahsavan

4 VOCABULARY Ask students to cover the definitions. Give them two minutes to find the highlighted words in the article and to try to deduce meaning from context. Get them to discuss what they think each word means with a partner. Students uncover the definitions to check their ideas and complete the exercise. Check answers in open class, giving further explanations to clarify meaning as necessary.

Answers

1 national borders 2 destination 3 diet 4 droughts
5 principally 6 possessions 7 annual 8 remain

SPEAKING

In pairs or small groups, students discuss the questions. Monitor and make a note of any nice expressions in English that students use during the activity. At the end write them on the board for the whole class to copy, and praise the student who used them. For feedback, ask for volunteers to report back to the class on their discussion.

WRITING

An informal email

BACKGROUND INFORMATION

The Inuit are a group of indigenous people in Greenland, Alaska, Canada and Denmark. There are roughly 135,000 Inuit people in the four countries. Traditionally, Inuit people were nomadic and live on hunted fish, seals, polar bears and whales. They lived in igloos or tents made from animal skins. While hunting is still a part of Inuit life, nearly all Inuit have migrated south to urban areas or live in Inuit communities with access to satellite television and the Internet.

---

1 Tell students they are going to read an informal email from a girl who is staying with the Inuit people. Check/clarify *Inuit*. Students read the article to answer the questions. Set a two-minute time limit to encourage them to read quickly for gist and focus on the questions. Allow them to compare answers with a partner before checking in open class.

Answers

1 10 days   2 A couple of days ago.   3 She's learning about patience, because Inuit hunting involves a lot of waiting in the cold.

2 Divide the class into pairs for students to complete the exercise. Monitor and help with any difficulties. Check answers in open class.

Answers

1 loads   2 Well, here I am at last   3 said I could go along with them   4 I'm over the moon   5 how I'm getting on with things   6 a couple of days ago

3 Give students a minute to discuss the question in pairs before checking in open class.

Answer

They are too formal for an email to a friend.

4 Working individually, students make notes in preparation for writing an email. Monitor to help with any questions. Encourage them to use some of the vocabulary and expressions from the article, adapting larger chunks of language as necessary.

5 If you're short on time, set this exercise for homework.

Students can either write the email individually or in pairs, as an exercise in collaborative writing in class. On completion, ask students to exchange their emails with another pair. If students have access to the Internet in the classroom, this could be done electronically for added authenticity. Ask them to read and evaluate on the basis of **content** (were all points included? how interesting were the ideas?); **organisation** (did each paragraph include a clear and distinct idea like the model answer?); **communicative purpose** (were you convinced by it?); and language.

If you mark the writing yourself, focus on how well students have communicated, how clear and easy their writing is to follow and whether they wrote about relevant details. Avoid focusing too much on accuracy, as a heavily marked piece of writing is more likely to de-motivate learners than to make them try harder next time.

Students book pages 28–29

CAMBRIDGE ENGLISH: First

▬ THiNK EXAMS ▬

READING AND USE OF ENGLISH

Part 4: Key word transformations

1

Answers

1 worn/tired me   2 regret going   3 which really annoyed   4 put up with   5 forgot to post   6 can't stand getting

Workbook page 17 ➤

TEST YOURSELF UNITS 1 & 2

VOCABULARY

1

Answers

1 wandering   2 ran into   3 refugees   4 go through   5 guilty   6 staff   7 residents   8 crawl   9 puzzled   10 turned out

GRAMMAR

2

Answers

1 to go   2 falling   3 to do   4 to live   5 doing   6 living

3

Answers

1 I really like that guy which **who** plays Sam on TV.
2 My brother Julian, that **who** lives in New York, is coming to stay with me.
3 It isn't a film **which/that** makes everyone laugh.
4 The man what **who** plays the drums in the band is on the left in the photo.
5 My brother broke my phone, what **which** means he has to buy me a new one.
6 She's the runner **who** won the gold medal.

FUNCTIONAL LANGUAGE

4

Answers

1 quite a, amazing   2 phenomenal, incredible   3 bet, can't   4 will, dare

THE NEXT GENERATION

Objectives

FUNCTIONS	emphasising
GRAMMAR	quantifiers; *so* and *such* (review); *do* and *did* for emphasis
VOCABULARY	costumes and uniforms; bringing up children

Student's Book pages 30–31

READING

1 As a lead-in, show some photographs of people wearing fancy dress. Ask students: *Have you ever worn fancy dress to a party? What sorts of thing have you dressed as? What was your favourite costume when you were little?* Students discuss the questions in small groups. Listen to some of their answers in open class as feedback. You could also brainstorm a list of typical fancy dress costumes to gauge how familiar your students are with the vocabulary explored later on in this unit.

If there is an interactive whiteboard (IWB) available in the classroom, this activity would best be done as a heads-up activity with the whole class. Read through the four captions, and nominate a student to choose a caption for each picture A–D. The rest of the class should confirm or reject answers. Alternatively, students do the matching activity in pairs before checking answers with the whole class.

> **Answers**
>
> A – Kiss the chef; B – Go Chargers!; C – King for a day;
> D – Batman and Boy Wonder

2 **SPEAKING** Ask students to work with a partner to predict what the blog is about. Elicit students' predictions during open-class feedback, prompting students to expand as much as possible on their ideas, and noting them on the board to refer to after Exercise 3.

3 **1.16** Play the audio while students listen and read to check their ideas from Exercise 2. Tell them not to worry about unknown words, but to focus on checking their ideas. The focus here is on gist understanding. Check answers, referring back to the ideas on the board. Ask: *Did anyone guess correctly?*

4 Ask students to read questions 1–8 and underline any difficult words or phrases. Clarify these in open class before students read the blog in more detail and answer the questions. Tell them not to use dictionaries, but to try to understand difficult vocabulary from its context. Encourage them to underline the parts of the article that helped them

find the answers. Students compare answers in pairs before a whole-class check. During this stage ask students to refer to the parts of the article they underlined to justify their answers.

> **Answers**
>
> 1 They waved from the doorstep.   2 180 days.
> 3 Rain's brother and his mum.   4 American football player; pirate.   5 $50
> 6 He used the family fancy-dress collection, and friends and neighbours helped.
> 7 He was embarrassed at the beginning, but thought he was pretty cool in the end.
> 8 He's going to get more sleep each morning.

5 **SPEAKING** In pairs, students discuss the questions. Monitor and help with any difficulties, but as this is a fluency activity, do not interrupt to correct errors unless they impede communication. Listen to some of their ideas in open class as feedback, encouraging students to react to and debate with each other.

TRAIN TO THiNK

Changing your opinions

1 Ask students to read the introduction and sentences 1–3. Ask them to work with a partner to complete the exercise. Check answers.

> **Answers**
>
> 1 Rain   2 Rain's friends   3 Rochelle

2 **SPEAKING** Point out the use of *Initially* and *with time*. Ask students to work in small groups to discuss how the opinions of the other people changed. Encourage them to find evidence in the article to justify their answers. Listen to some of their thoughts in open class as feedback.

3 **SPEAKING** Give students a few minutes to prepare their answers. Monitor, help with ideas if necessary and prompt students to make notes. Divide the class into small groups. Students discuss their answers. Monitor, encouraging all students to participate in the discussion, but avoid error correction unless errors really hinder comprehension. Ask each group to nominate a secretary to note down their answers (this could be one of the quieter students, as a way to encourage them to participate). When students have some ideas, regroup them into new groups and encourage them to share information. Listen to some of the best ideas in open class during the feedback stage.

Student's Book pages 32–33

GRAMMAR

Quantifiers

1 Students should have seen most of the quantifiers in these exercises before, but it is still an area in which students make a lot of errors, so certainly worth reviewing.

Ask students to try to complete sentences 1–6 before looking back at the article to check their answers. This encourages students to notice language and helps activate their curiosity around the target language. Check answers in open class.

Then ask students to work with a partner to complete the rule before checking answers. Use the sentences in Exercise 1 and further examples of your own to clarify.

Answers

1 many   2 all   3 loads   4 several   5 Some, most
6 little

Rule

1 none   2 a little   3 several   4 loads   5 all

2 Students work with a partner to complete the exercise. Refer them to the rule to help them decide on and check their answers. Check answers in open class.

Answers

1 loads   2 a lot of   3 most   4 Most   5 Most
6 hardly any

3 **SPEAKING** In pairs or small groups, students discuss the sentences. Monitor and encourage them to answer in full sentences. Make a note of any nice expressions in English that students use during the activity. At the end write them on the board for the whole class to copy, and praise the student(s) who used them. Also ask for volunteers to report back to the class on their discussion during feedback.

Workbook page 28 and page 123

 Be aware of common errors related to quantifiers. Go to Get it right! on Student's Book page 123.

VOCABULARY

Costumes and uniforms

1 Ask students to look at the photos on pages 30–31 and work with a partner to find the items. If there is an IWB available in the classroom, this activity would best be done as a heads-up activity with the whole class. Say each item individually and nominate a student to say in which picture the object appears. Say the words for students to repeat and check pronunciation.

Answers

sword and shield – 5   leather jacket – no picture
wig – no picture   belt – 6   sunglasses – 4   helmet – 2
cape – 7   mask – 8   apron – 1   football top – 3

2 Students work with a partner to answer the questions. Check answers. Give students two minutes to discuss the difference between *a costume, a uniform* and *a kit* (a costume is worn to create the appearance of a particular period or character e.g. a cowboy costume; a kit is worn for a specific sport e.g. football kit; a uniform is worn by members of an organisation for doing a specific job e.g. an army uniform). You could ask students to work in small groups and brainstorm further examples of each one to extend their vocabulary further. Write some of their ideas on the board.

Answers

A kit   B costume   C uniform

3 SPEAKING Give students time to read the questions and check understanding. Ask them to work individually for a few minutes to note down their answers. Monitor and make a note of any lexical errors to correct during feedback. Divide the class into pairs or small groups to discuss the questions. Listen to some of their answers in open class.

Workbook page 30

LISTENING

1 🔊 1.17 Books closed. As a lead-in, write the following questions on the board:

How often do you see your extended family (family members other than your parents and brothers/sisters)?

Do you have a fixed bedtime?

In pairs, students discuss the questions. Nominate students to report back on their discussions in open class.

Books open. Ask students to work in pairs to describe what they can see and to try to explain what the captions refer to. Listen to some of their ideas in open class. Play the audio while students listen and match the countries to the pictures. Students check answers with a partner before whole-class feedback.

Answers

No time for bedtime – Argentina
Let them solve their own problems – Japan
Introduce them early – France
Keep it in the family – Poland
Early to bed – Britain
Young chefs – Mexico

Audio Script Track 1.17

Hello and welcome to Family Matters.

What is the best way to bring up children? Now there's a question. Many parents are caught between what they think they should do and what they end up doing and feeling guilty about. Well a new book by sociologist Miriam Keating might just help make those parents feel a little bit better. In her new book *Bringing up Babies*, Miriam questions some of the ideas we have on parenting and looks to other cultures to show how they do things differently. In each chapter she takes a different problematic area and shows us how parents from other countries do things differently.

For example, in the first chapter, Miriam looks at the British obsession with bedtimes and making sure we get our children to bed before a certain hour. To look at this from a different perspective, Miriam takes us to Argentina where parents often let their children stay up late and where it's not uncommon to see children eating out late in restaurants with their parents. But it doesn't seem to do them any harm. What is important is that children get enough sleep. So if they go to bed late, they get up late. And that's exactly what they do. Furthermore, by going out in the evenings with their parents, Argentinian children also learn how to socialise well from a very early age.

Another familiar problem that Miriam looks at is food and most parents' fight to get their children to eat healthily. For a solution to this one she takes an example from France where children are introduced to all sorts of food from a very early age. French children are allowed to not like an item of food but they are not

allowed to not try it. And, if the child seems not to like a particular item of food, that's no reason to never try it again. Just wait a while and reintroduce it a little later. Unsurprisingly, Miriam found that French children were a lot less fussy than kids in the UK.

In Japan Miriam discovered an interesting idea on how to deal with children fighting. While watching children in one Japanese primary school she was surprised to see that when two five-year-olds started to argue about whose turn it was to use the computer, the teacher did nothing even though the children were getting quite loud. The teacher only did something if the children started to get physical. But she was even more surprised at how often the children were able to sort out their problem themselves. Instead of having an adult feeling they had to control the child's world, the children were learning the important life skill of negotiating from an early age.

Other chapters look at Poland, where the family is always kept very close together and Mexico where mothers teach their children how to cook from a very early age. Adults are bringing up children all over the world. The clear message from *Bringing up Babies* is that there is no single right way to do it and that it might be a good idea to take note of how parents in other cultures are doing it.

2 🔊 1.17 This exercise is closely modelled on
❋ Listening Part 4 of the Cambridge English: First exam. Check/clarify: *guilty, bring up, attention, strict, argue*. Play the audio again while students complete the exercise. Allow them to compare answers with a partner, encouraging them to explain their choices as they do this, before checking in open class. If necessary, play the audio again, pausing to clarify answers.

Mixed-ability

To increase the challenge for stronger students, give them the questions without the multiple choice options.

Give weaker students just two options for each question by identifying one incorrect option in each.

Answers

1 C   2 C   3 A   4 B   5 C

▰▰ THiNK SELF-ESTEEM ▰▰

Developing independence

1 Give students time to read the statements. Check/clarify: *set their own bedtimes, earn pocket money*. To check understanding, ask: *Who sets children's bedtimes?* (parents); *Who receives pocket money, children or adults?* (children); *What might you do to earn pocket money?* (clean cars, do gardening). Working individually, students complete the exercise. Monitor and help with any difficulties.

2 SPEAKING Divide the class into small groups. Nominate a secretary (or get students to do this) to make notes on the group's decisions. Students compare their answers. Monitor to encourage students to give reasons for their answers. During whole-class feedback, find out which questions the majority of the class agree/disagree on.

Student's Book pages 34–35

READING

1 A recording of this text is available with your digital resources. If there is an IWB available in the classroom, this activity would best be done as a heads-up activity with the whole class. Zoom in on the book cover and ask: *What kind of book do you think this is?* Elicit ideas in open class, but do not comment at this stage. Ask students to read the introduction. Tell them not to worry if they do not understand every word, but to focus on getting a general understanding of what the book is about. Check/clarify: *the Chinese Way.* Allow them to discuss their ideas with a partner before checking answers in open class. Ask: *Would you like to read the book?*

Answer

A story about bringing up children the 'Chinese way'.

2 Tell students they are going to read two different opinions on the book. Students read the two opinions and answer the questions. Ask them to underline any phrases that support their answers. Students compare answers with a partner before whole-class feedback. Encourage students to refer to the texts when giving their answers.

Answers

Stephanie's opinion is 'against'. She believes that children should be able to enjoy their childhoods and watch TV and play computer games.

Tim's opinion is 'for'. He thinks parents are too soft on their children and let them do what they want. They also don't have enough time for their children.

3 This exercise requires a deeper understanding of the texts. Give students time to read the sentences and check understanding. Clarify who Amy, Stephanie and Tim are. Working individually, students re-read the texts to complete the exercise. Divide the class into pairs for students to compare their answers and then check answers in open class.

Answers

1 Tim   2 Amy   3 Stephanie   4 Tim   5 Amy
6 Stephanie

SPEAKING

In pairs or small groups, students discuss the questions and make notes on their answers. Monitor and answer any questions about vocabulary, but as this is a fluency practice activity, do not interrupt the conversations to correct students unless inaccuracy hinders comprehension. Listen to some of their ideas in open class.

GRAMMAR

so and *such* (review)

1 Ask students to complete sentences 1–2 before finding the sentences in the text to check their answers. Ask students to work with a partner to complete the rule. Check answers in open class. Refer to the examples in Exercise 1 to clarify and add further examples if necessary.

Answers

1 so   2 such

Rule

1 such   2 so

2 If you're short on time, you can set this exercise for homework.

Students fill the gaps and complete the sentences with their own ideas. Divide the class into pairs for students to compare answers. Listen to some examples in open class as feedback.

Answers

1 so 2 such 3 so 4 such

do and did for emphasis

3 To promote noticing, ask students to fill the gaps, and then find the sentences in the text to check their answers. Before they look at the rule, you could ask them to consider the effect of *do* and *did* in the example sentences.

Answers

1 do 2 did

Look!

Read through the information with students. Check that they are clear on the different usage of *so/such* and *too/ not enough* by writing the following gapped examples on the board. Elicit the answers in open class:

It was ___ cold that we didn't go to the beach. (so)

It was ___ cold to go to the beach. (too)

It was ___ a cold day that we didn't go to the beach. (such)

4 This exercise is closely modelled on Reading & Use of
✷ English Part 4 of the Cambridge English: First exam. If you're short on time, you can set this exercise for homework.

Students work individually to complete the exercise, then check their answers with a partner before whole-class feedback. During feedback refer to the rules and Look! box for clarification.

Answers

1 weren't enough chairs 2 doesn't save enough
3 too boring to 4 did like 5 do think we shouldn't

Workbook page 28 and page 123

PRONUNCIATION

For practice of adding emphasis go to Student's Book page 120.

VOCABULARY

Bringing up children

1 Before filling the gaps, ask students to read the text to answer the question: *Does the text suggest that parenting is easy or difficult?* (The aim of this is to encourage students to read a text first for gist understanding and then only on a second read, to complete the task assigned.) Divide the class into pairs for students to complete the exercise. Check answers. Draw attention to the expressions: *do their best; get ahead in life; bring up; grow up; do well* and give further examples to clarify meaning as necessary.

Answers

1 do 2 get 3 bring 4 childhood 5 grow 6 do
7 strict 8 soft

2 Ask students to read the definitions and check that they understand the language used. Students work with a partner to match the expressions in the text with their meanings.

Answers

a to get ahead in life b bring up c grow up d do well
e soft f do your best g strict h childhood

Fast finishers

Ask students to circle the words to look for other interesting lexical chunks in the text. One approach would be for them to circle all of the words to the right of the space.

Optional extension

This exercise can be made into a matching activity. Before the lesson, write each expression and each meaning on cards. Create enough sets of cards to allow for one set per four students. Mix up all the expressions and meanings and distribute one set to each group of students. Either ask students to match the expressions and meanings or ask them to turn all the pieces of paper face down and play a game of pelmanism, taking it in turns to try to find a matching pair.

Workbook page 30

Student's Book pages 36–37

LITERATURE

BACKGROUND INFORMATION

Nick Hornby (born April 17, 1957) is an English novelist and screenwriter. His novels include *Fever Pitch* (1992), *High Fidelity* (1995), *About a Boy* (1998) and *A Long Way Down* (2005), all of which have been made into films. His novels mainly focus on music, sport and the difficulties of human relationships.

About a Boy was made into a film in 2002, starring Hugh Grant as a rich lazy man who lives off the royalties from his father's music. Nicholas Hoult plays a young boy who is bullied at school and brought up by his single mother (Toni Collette). The film focuses on the difficulties of growing up, both for the young boy and the older man. It is an excellent film to show to teenagers in the classroom and can lead to a lot of discussion about relationships, bullying, parenthood, life as a teenager and so on.

---

1 Books closed. As a lead-in, brainstorm a list of films about teenagers and write the titles on the board. Divide the class into pairs for students to take turns to describe the plot of the films listed for their partners to guess the title. Listen to some examples in open class and write any repeated themes on the board.

Books open. If there is an IWB available in the classroom, this activity would best be done as a heads-up activity with the whole class. Ask students to look at the photos and read the introduction. Check/clarify: *depressed, bullied.* Ask students to quickly discuss the question with a partner. Listen to some of their ideas in open class and write them on the board to facilitate feedback on Exercise 2.

2 ◄))1.20 Play the audio for students to listen and read to check their answer to Exercise 1. Tell them to concentrate on answering the question and not to worry about understanding every word. Allow

students to compare with a partner before feedback in open class. Nominate students to give reasons for their answer.

3 Check/clarify *think highly of*. Ask students to underline the key information they will need to read for. You could encourage students to try to answer the questions before reading again. Students then read the text again in order to check. Let students compare answers with a partner before feedback in open class. During feedback, ask students to refer to the parts of the text that support their answers.

Answers

1 when you were only twelve?
2 Marcus looked out of the bus window
3 neither of them was doing all right
4 But his mum seemed to be saying that there was more to it than that. / He hadn't even known until today
5 (there were loads of kids at school, he reckoned, kids who stole and swore too much and bullied other kids, whose mums and dads had a lot to answer for).
6 Marcus thought he was lucky to have found him.

4 **VOCABULARY** Students work individually to complete the exercise, then check their answers with a partner before feedback in open class.

Mixed-ability

Stronger students can refer solely to the context provided by the extract in order to deduce meaning before referring to the definitions to check.

Answers

1 trendy   2 mess it up   3 doesn't know the first thing
4 straightforward   5 for nothing   6 swore
7 off her head   8 whichever way

5 **SPEAKING** In pairs or small groups, students discuss the questions. Monitor and encourage students to answer in full sentences. Make a note of any nice expressions or lexical errors to refer to during feedback. At the end write both questions on the board to discuss and ask students to identify and correct the errors. Also ask for volunteers to report back to the class on their discussion.

FUNCTIONS

Emphasising

1 Books closed. As a lead-in, ask students: Which words can we use to make sentences more emphatic? Elicit answers in open class and write *so/such/do/did* on the board. If students have difficulty, write the following on the board and point out where the words should go in each sentence.

He is (such) a nice man.
I am (so) tired.
I (do) like swimming in the sea.
I (did) do my homework.

Books open. Students work with a partner to complete the exercise. During whole-class feedback, say the sentences for students to repeat and check pronunciation. Encourage them to be emphatic!

Answers

1 He's <u>such</u> a good father.
2 She gets on <u>so</u> well with children./She <u>does</u> get on well with children.
3 She's <u>so</u> patient.
4 My dad <u>did try</u> his best.
5 My parents <u>did make</u> some mistakes.
6 She's <u>so</u> soft on her children.
7 He's <u>such</u> a strict father.
8 Parents <u>do</u> get it wrong sometimes.

2 Students discuss the question in pairs. Monitor to answer any questions and to help with ideas. Listen to some of their answers in open class.

3 **WRITING** Students work in pairs and develop one of the sentences into a dialogue. Students then practise their dialogues. Monitor during both stages. Do not correct errors unless they hinder comprehension. You could note down any repeated errors to discuss later as a class. Ask a few pairs to perform for the rest of the class.

Mixed-ability

If your class has a mix of levels, make similar-ability pairings where you can.

Encourage stronger students to speak spontaneously and to perform their dialogues without looking at their notes.

Encourage weaker students to write their dialogues in full before practising them.

4 Give an example of your own to get students started. Use emphasis when describing the person's personality and anecdotes to show how the person is good with children. Ask students to work individually to complete the exercise.

5 In pairs or small groups, students talk about the person they've chosen. Monitor to encourage students to use emphatic structures where possible. During feedback, ask for volunteers to share their descriptions with the class.

Mixed-ability

With stronger groups, ask students to give a two-minute presentation on their chosen person.

WRITING

An essay

This could be done as a collaborative writing activity in class or planning for this exercise can be done in class with the writing set as homework.

Ask students to discuss which essay they'd like to choose. Before writing, students should write a plan for their essay. This involves thinking of ideas for and against the statement and imagining other people's opinions, not just their own. Their own opinion should be presented and argued in the final paragraph.

When students have completed their essay, ask them to exchange with a partner/another pair and read each other's essays. Ask them to add a comment to the article of the type you might make in response to an online article. You may like to display the essays around the class for students to circulate and read.

4 THINKING OUTSIDE THE BOX

Objectives

FUNCTIONS	expressing frustration
GRAMMAR	*be / get used to (doing)* vs. *used to (do)*; adverbs and adverbial phrases
VOCABULARY	personality adjectives; common adverbial phrases

Student's Book pages 38–39

READING

BACKGROUND INFORMATION

The **Masai** are a nomadic tribe in Kenya and Tanzania, numbering roughly 1.6 million people. Despite modern influence, they largely maintain their traditional lifestyle of desert farming. They are famous as warriors and herders of cattle. They measure wealth by the number of cattle owned and the number of children in a family. If you have access to the Internet in the classroom, students may like to see examples of Masai people who have particular clothes, body modifications and dances.

1 Books closed. As a lead-in, divide the class into teams and give them two minutes to make a list of countries in Africa. Who can write the most? After two minutes, find out which team listed the most and ask them to read their list to the class while others cross off countries which also appear on their lists. Ask students: *What do you know about Africa? How do people live? What problems do they have? What places or things would you like to visit there?*

Students discuss the questions in pairs. Listen to some of their ideas in open class.

Books open. If there is an interactive whiteboard (IWB) available in the classroom, this activity would best be done as a heads-up activity with the whole class. Say *lions* and nominate a student to point to the correct picture on the board. Alternatively, students do the matching activity in pairs before checking answers with the whole class.

Answers

lions – C   cattle – D   a scarecrow – A   a light bulb – E
a battery – B   a solar panel – B

2 SPEAKING Divide the class into pairs for students to complete the exercise. Give some examples of your own to get them started if necessary (e.g. they could put a scarecrow on the back of some of the cattle to scare the lions). During feedback, listen to some of their ideas in open class and praise the most creative ideas.

3 Tell students they are going to read an article about lions in Africa. Students read the article to find the answer to the question. Tell them it is not important to understand every word, but to focus on matching the summaries to the sections. To encourage students to read quickly, set a two-minute time limit. Students compare their answers with a partner before checking in open class.

Answers

A 4   B 3   C (extra summary)   D 1   E 5   F 2

4 This exercise is closely modelled on Reading and ✳ Use of English Part 6 of the Cambridge English: First exam. Check/clarify *cowsheds, posed, kept well away, conflict.* Tell students that the best approach for this type of exercise is to first underline the key information in the sentences that will help them place the sentences in the text (e.g. *that* in sentence A; *this motionless thing* in sentence B). Next, they should read the words around the gap in the text and look for connections between the text and the sentence in the gap. Do the first one as an example in open class and clarify how the sentence in the gap is connected to the text. Students complete the rest of the exercise individually. Suggest that they underline the parts of the text that helped them find the answers. Students check their answers with a partner. Do not confirm answers at this stage.

Answers

1 G   2 A   3 B   4 E   5 D   6 H   7 C

5 ◀》1.21 Play the audio for students to check their answers to Exercise 4. Confirm answers in open class, asking students to refer to the parts of the text to explain the answers.

6 SPEAKING Divide the class into pairs or small groups to answer the questions. Monitor to help with vocabulary and to prompt students to give reasons for their answers. Asking students to come to an agreement as a group focuses their speaking towards the achievement of a tangible goal, which in turn motivates them to speak more. Listen to some of their answers during open-class feedback. Have a quick show of hands to find out how impressive they think the invention was and nominate students to give reasons for their opinions.

<table>
<tr><td>

Optional extension

Make groups of three. One student in each group is Richard the inventor and the other two are members of the audience. The audience members can ask their questions for Richard to respond.

</td></tr>
</table>

■■■ TRAIN TO THiNK ■■■

Lateral thinking

1 Books closed. Refer students to the title of the unit *Thinking Outside the Box*. Ask students to work with a partner and discuss the meaning of the phrase. Elicit ideas and explain the correct meaning with examples. Ask: *Is this a useful skill? Why?* Listen to some of their ideas in open class.

Books open. Ask students to read the text in the yellow box and try to think of answers before they read the text that follows to see if any of the ideas they came up with are mentioned.

2 SPEAKING Give students time to read situations 1–3. Check/clarify: *operating theatre*. Divide the class into pairs or small groups for students to discuss possible answers. Remind students that there may be more than one possible solution and encourage them to come up with as many ideas as they can. Monitor and praise students who make the effort to explain their ideas in English rather than reverting to their first language. Nominate two or three students to share their ideas in open class and have a class discussion as to which are the most likely answers.

> **Possible answers**
>
> 1 The doctor is the boy's mother.
> 2 The woman is in a hotel room and the person in the next room is snoring loudly. She calls the number to wake them up and to stop the snoring.
> 3 The man is not tall enough to reach the button for the twelfth floor.

<table>
<tr><td>

Optional extension

Here are two more lateral thinking problems:

A cowboy rode into town on Friday, spent one night there, then left on Friday. How is that possible? (His horse is called Friday)

A women had two sons, Billy and Bobby, who were born at the same hour on the same day of the same year, but they were not twins. How is this possible? (They were two of a set of triplets)

Alternatively, do an internet search for lateral thinking problems and choose two which would be suitable for your group.

Divide the class into AB pairs and give each student a different problem with the solution. Give students time to read and understand their problem and solution. Ask students to exchange problems, but not solutions. Students ask each other questions to find the solution to each problem. Tell them they can only ask *yes/no* questions (Not *Who, What, Why*, etc.) as this makes the exercise more difficult and maximises language practice.

</td></tr>
</table>

Student's Book pages 40–41

GRAMMAR

be / get used to (doing) vs. *used to (do)*

1 Ask students to read sentences 1–4. Ask: *Which two words are in all of the sentences?* (used to). Ask students to work with a partner to complete the exercise. During feedback, point out that in sentence 2, *used to* is preceded by *are* and in sentence 3 by *got*. Students work with a partner to complete the rule. Encourage them to refer to the example sentences to help them. Check answers.

> **Answers**
>
> 1 exist   2 attacking   3 seeing   4 play

> **Rule**
>
> 1 used to do   2 be used to doing   3 get used to

<table>
<tr><td>

LANGUAGE NOTE

Students often make the following mistake due to L1 interference:

I am used to get up early.

Point out that we use the gerund form here to talk about something familiar, not to describe something as a regular or habitual event.

I am used to getting up early. = Getting up early is normal for me, it's not particularly difficult.

</td></tr>
</table>

2 Ask students to work individually to choose the correct form in each sentence and encourage them to refer to the rule to check their answers. Allow them to compare answers with a partner before feedback in open class.

> **Answers**
>
> 1 to look after   2 to hearing   3 to seeing   4 to watch
> 5 to imagine   6 to speaking

<table>
<tr><td>

Fast finishers

Ask students to write sentences about famous people with *used to* and *be/get used to + -ing*. For example: *Lionel Messi used to live in Argentina. Now he lives in Spain. When he arrived in Spain, he found the language quite different, but now he's used to Castilian Spanish.*

</td></tr>
</table>

3 If you're short on time, set this exercise for homework.

Ask students to work in pairs and complete the exercise. Remind them to check if the sentence requires a positive or negative form. Check answers with the whole class, checking students' pronunciation of *used to*. Draw attention to the elision of the /d/ and /t/. If necessary, refer back to the rule to clarify understanding.

> **Answers**
>
> 1 am/'m   2 get   3 got   4 get   5 Are   6 weren't

4 SPEAKING Divide the class into pairs for students to discuss their answers. Encourage them to go into detail and to ask each other questions. Monitor as they are doing this and make a note of common errors with *used to* and *be/get used to* + *-ing*. Write these up on the board, ensuring anonymity, and ask students to correct them as part of whole-class feedback.

► Workbook page 36 and page 123

 Be aware of common errors related to *used to*. Go to Get it right! on Student's Book page 124.

VOCABULARY

Personality adjectives

1 Books closed. As a lead-in, brainstorm personality adjectives in open class and write them on the board.

Books open. Ask students to work with a partner to discuss meaning of the adjectives. During whole-class feedback, ask questions to check understanding. For example: *Does a decisive person take a long time to make a choice?* (no); *If you are confident, do you get shy when you meet new people?* (no). When checking pronunciation, you may like to write the words on the board and elicit and mark the stress.

> **Answers**
>
> bright, responsible

> **Optional extension**
>
> As a further check on understanding, ask students to work in pairs to group the adjectives into positive and negative. Check answers.
>
> Positive: bright, responsible, decisive, imaginative, organised, practical, confident, cautious
>
> Negative: bad-tempered, impatient, arrogant, dull

2a Ask students to work individually and read the sentences to complete the exercise. Allow them to check their answers with a partner before feedback in open class.

> **Answers**
>
> 1 ✓ 2 ? 3 ✓ 4 ✗ 5 ✓ 6 ? 7 ✓ 8 ✓

b Students work with a partner to choose a word from Exercise 1 for each sentence. Check answers in open class. During feedback, ask concept-check questions to check understanding, for example: *Which adjective would describe a boring film?* (dull); *Do impatient people like waiting?* (no). Also make sure students are pronouncing the words correctly, paying particular attention to word stress.

> **Answers**
>
> 1 bright 2 cautious 3 decisive 4 dull 5 imaginative
> 6 impatient 7 organised 8 responsible

> **Fast finishers**
>
> Ask students to think of things that someone who is each adjective does. For example, an imaginative person has a lot of ideas, makes up stories, dreams a lot, etc.

> **Optional extension**
>
> Higher level students may like to work with a partner to rank the adjectives from best to worst. This can lead to some interesting discussions – Is it better to be decisive or responsible? Dull or arrogant?

► Workbook page 38

SPEAKING

1 Ask students to read the instructions and the example. Students can do the exercise together but make sure that they all write the sentences. Monitor and help with any questions about vocabulary. Be alert to students describing other class members negatively. Encourage stronger students to write about adjectives that are new to them.

> **Mixed-ability**
>
> Weaker students can write sentences about three different people.

2 Regroup students and ask them to read their sentences to their partner, who should then guess which adjective is being described. Encourage students to sit facing each other and to hold their books up to force students to speak and listen, rather than just read each other's sentences. During feedback, listen to some examples in open class.

3 Students ask each other extra questions about the adjectives. Monitor and help with vocabulary as necessary. Avoid error correction unless errors really hinder comprehension. Make a note of any nice expressions in English that students use during the activity, emphasising lexical range over accuracy. At the end, write them on the board for the whole class to copy, and praise the student who used them. Giving positive feedback like this will encourage students to be more adventurous in similar communication tasks.

> **Mixed-ability**
>
> Give weaker students time to work with a partner and think of further questions before completing the exercise.

LISTENING

Being imaginative

1 Books closed. As an introduction to this activity, take a piece of realia (a frying pan or coat hanger are good examples) into the classroom and show it to students without saying anything. In open class, brainstorm possible uses for the object, encouraging students to be as inventive as possible by praising those who come up with the most imaginative ideas.

Books open. Read through the task with students and ask them to work individually to complete the exercise. Divide the class into pairs for students to compare their ideas with a partner. Listen to some of their ideas in open class as feedback.

2 ◀)) 1.22 Ask students to read the instructions. Play the audio for them to listen and answer the questions. Ask students to check answers with a partner before whole-class feedback.

Answers

1 paperweight, doorstop, laptop stand, something to stand on, hammer, car wheel chuck
2 two faces, tree, broccoli, human brain

Audio Script Track 1.22

Boy So, did you do the one with the brick?

Girl Yes.

Boy OK. So. How many things did you think of?

Girl Well I only came up with six things.

Boy Only? I think six is a lot! What are they, then, your six?

Girl Well, first of all, a paperweight – you know, put it on top of a pile of papers to stop them blowing away when you open the window.

Boy Right. Of course! Why didn't I think of that?

Girl Then, a doorstop, to stop a door banging in the wind. Then, er, something to put your laptop on, make it higher so you don't have to look down at the screen. Erm then you can use the brick to stand on …

Boy What?

Girl You know, when you're at a concert or something, and you can't see, you stand on the brick. That's four. And the other two are … a hammer, to knock nails into a wall, and lastly you can put the brick behind the wheel of a car to stop it moving.

Boy You're not serious, are you?

Girl About what?

Boy About using a brick as a hammer. I mean, it's too soft, the brick would break.

Girl Oh please. It's only a game. Don't take it so seriously.

Boy Yeah, OK. What about the picture one?

Girl I haven't done that one yet. Have you?

Boy Yes, and I got four things.

Girl Come on then. What are they?

Boy Well, I can see … two people's faces looking at each other if you focus on the trunk … and I can see a tree …

Girl Yes, yes. That's obvious. What else? Come on!

Boy OK, OK, don't be so impatient! A piece of broccoli …

Girl OK … hmm, yes, OK, although any tree could be said to look like a piece of broccoli. And …?

Boy … and then lastly, a human brain …

Girl What? How do you see a human brain in this picture?

Boy Can't you see it? Look – there! The top bit … if you ignore the trunk.

Girl Oh come on! You can't just base it on one part of the picture and ignore the other … that's cheating!

Boy Now who's taking things too seriously?

Girl Yes, sorry. But honestly – who makes these things up? Do you think they really say anything about a person?

Boy Well they're supposed to show how imaginative you are. And I'm a bit hopeless, so I guess it means I'm not very imaginative!

Girl No, don't be so hard on yourself. What's so creative about thinking of things to do with a brick?

Boy You've got a point, I guess. Fun, though, isn't it?

---

3 SPEAKING Divide the class into pairs for students to compare their ideas with those of Briony and Mark.

4 ◀ 1.22 This exercise is closely modelled on
✳ Listening Part 2 of the Cambridge English: First exam. Ask students to read the sentences and check the meaning of any unfamiliar words or phrases. Get them to underline the key information they will need to listen for and to make predictions as to possible answers or the types of word needed to complete the sentences, before listening. Play the audio while students check their answers. Let students compare with a partner before feedback in open class.

Answers

1 comes up with 2 pile of papers 3 nails 4 cheating
5 how imaginative 6 hard

▰▰ THiNK VALUES ▰▰

Appreciating creative solutions

1 Ask students to work individually to choose the best ending for the sentence. Tell students that there isn't only one correct answer. Students compare ideas with a partner. During feedback, have a quick vote to find out which sentence students chose. Nominate one or two students to give reasons for their choice.

2 Working individually, students rank the five items in order of importance. Remind them to think about what is important for themselves, not for people in general. Encourage them to reflect on the reasons for their choices and to note these down.

3 SPEAKING Ask students to compare their answers in pairs or small groups. Listen to some of their ideas in open class during feedback and also decide on the best order to rank the five items, as a class.

Optional extension

Write the following questions on the board:

1 In which school subjects do you have to be imaginative? Do you like those subjects? Why (not)?

2 Do scientists need to be imaginative? Why (not)?

3 What would a society full of very imaginative people be like? What about a society where nobody had any imagination?

Ask students to discuss the questions in pairs or small groups, then listen to some of their ideas in open class and encourage further debate and discussion.

Student's Book pages 42–43

READING

1 A recording of this text is available with your digital resources.

Books closed. As a lead-in to this exercise, ask students: *Do you know what you want to do when you finish school? Go to university/start work? Is there anything that worries you about going to university or starting work?* Ask students to work with a partner and discuss the questions. During feedback, make a note of the most common worries and elicit ideas on the best way to overcome them.

Books open. Tell students they are going to read a post from a student who is worried about university. Working individually, students quickly read the text and answer the question. Set a two-minute time limit to encourage them to read quickly, for gist, rather than getting bogged down in trying to understand every word. Check answers with the whole class.

Answer

He's worried about the course he's planning to do at university because he doesn't think he's creative enough to be able to succeed at it.

2 **SPEAKING** Working in pairs, students discuss the best way to reply to Paul's post. Listen to some of their answers in open class and make a note on the board for future reference, but do not comment at this stage.

3 Tell students they are going to read a reply from Sarah. Check/clarify: *relate, denying, brought up, assumption, enthusiasm*. Ask students to read the reply and underline the sections that refer to specific advice for Paul. Allow them to compare answers with a partner. During whole-class feedback, refer back to the ideas on the board. Ask: *Did anyone suggest the same advice?*

4 Do the first one with students to clarify the task. Before reading the text again, ask students to underline the key words in the statements that will help them decide if the sentence is true or false. Students read the letters again and complete the activity. Check answers with the whole class. Ask students to correct false statements.

Answers

1 F (He wants to work in TV.)
2 T
3 T
4 F (She says she can completely relate to his post.)
5 T
6 T
7 F (She thinks we shouldn't see things as 'right' or 'wrong'.)
8 T

5 **SPEAKING** Divide the class into pairs or small groups for students to discuss the questions. Monitor and help with vocabulary as necessary. Try the 'silent tick' – writing a tick on a student's notebook if they speak well. Students can be quite motivated by this! Ask some of the students to share their opinions with the whole class and encourage open-class discussion.

PRONUNCIATION

For practice of pronouncing words with *gh* go to Student's Book page 120.

GRAMMAR

Adverbs and adverbial phrases

1 Books closed. Divide the class into two teams and have a game of 'vocabulary tennis'. Teams take it in turns to say an adverb. Elicit one or two in whole class to check students are clear on what an adverb is. If a team makes a mistake or takes more than five seconds to think of an adverb, the other team scores a point. To avoid stronger students dominating the game, nominate a different student for each answer. As well as acting as an introduction to this language point, this game will give you an idea of the extent of students' current knowledge of adverbs.

Books open. Ask students to read the instructions. Check/clarify *time, manner, place* and *certainty* with adverbs that do not appear in the exercise (e.g. *finally, happily, outside* and *certainly* or *clearly*). Ask students to work with a partner and complete the exercise. Check answers in open class.

Answers

1 T   2 C   3 C   4 P   5 M   6 P   7 C   8 T   9 M

2 Check understanding of *qualify*. Do number 1 in class to make sure students understand the activity. Students look back at the text on page 42 to complete the exercise. Allow them to check answers with a partner before whole-class feedback.

Answers

1 relate   2 start, believe   3 think   4 thinking   5 work

3 Explain to students that an adverbial phrase is a group of words that act in the same way as an adverb i.e. they qualify a verb. Look at the examples in lists A and B with students. Ask students to work with a partner and complete the exercise. Check answers in open class.

Read through the rule in open class and elicit answers. Refer back to the sentences in Exercise 3 for examples of the two types of adverbial phrase. Put the adverbial phrases into sentences for further clarification. For example *He completed the exercise without difficulty*.

Answers

A	B
friendly	fear
interesting	surprise
strange	enthusiasm

Rule

1 adjective   2 noun

4 If you're short on time, set this exercise for homework. Ask students to work individually and complete the sentences with an adverbial phrase of their choice. Allow students to compare answers with a partner before feedback in open class.

Answers

1 a friendly / strange / horrible way
2 difficulty / interest / enthusiasm
3 a / an interesting / strange / different way
4 excitement / interest / enthusiasm
5 enthusiasm / excitement / interest

Fast finishers

Ask students to close their books and write down all of the adverbs and adverbial phrases from page 43 that they can remember. When they have completed their lists, students open their books to check.

Workbook page 37 and page 123 ▶

VOCABULARY

Common adverbial phrases

1 Look at the example in open class. Ask students to work with a partner and complete the exercise. Check answers in open class. During feedback, say the adverbial phrases for students to repeat. Pay particular attention to the pronunciation of *row* /rəʊ/ and *purpose* /ˈpɜːpəs/.

Answers

1 in public   2 in private   3 on purpose   4 by accident
5 in a panic   6 in a hurry   7 in a row

2 Give students time to read through the sentences. Check/clarify: *behaved, staring*. Working individually, students choose the correct option for each sentence. Students compare answers with a partner before feedback in open class.

Answers

1 in private   2 on purpose   3 in public   4 in a row
5 in a hurry   6 in a panic   7 by accident   8 in secret

Optional extension

Divide the class into AB pairs. Ask As to close their books and Bs to read sentences from Exercise 2 at random, replacing the adverbial phrases with 'beep' for A to guess them. After three minutes ask students to switch roles and repeat.

---

3 SPEAKING Ask students to read the questions and reflect on their answers. As these questions are difficult to answer spontaneously, give students some thinking time to make notes on their answers. You could also give some example answers of your own to get them started. Students discuss the questions in pairs or small groups. Monitor and answer any questions about vocabulary, but as this is a fluency practice activity, do not interrupt to correct mistakes unless inaccuracy hinders comprehension. Listen to some of their ideas in open class for feedback.

Workbook page 38 ▶

Student's Book pages 44–45

PHOTOSTORY: episode 2

Writer's block

1 Look at the title and elicit/explain the meaning. If you are using an IWB, project the photos on the board and ask students to close their books. Ask students to try to remember the names of the teenagers (Emma, Liam, Justin and Nicole) from episode 1. Students look at the photos and read the questions. Ask them to predict answers to the questions based solely on the photos. Write some of their ideas on the board.

2 ◀◗1.25 Play the audio for students to listen and check their answers from Exercise 1. During whole-class feedback, refer to students' ideas on the board. Ask: Who guessed correctly?

Answers

1 To write a story.   2 She's anxious about it.
3 No, he isn't being helpful.

DEVELOPING SPEAKING

3 Ask students: *What do you think happens next?* Get them to brainstorm possible endings. Students work in groups, with one student in each group acting as secretary and taking notes. During whole-class feedback, write students' ideas on the board to refer back to once they have watched the video. Don't give away answers at this stage.

4 ◀◖ EP2 Play the video for students to watch and check their answers. During whole-class feedback, refer to students' ideas on the board. *Who guessed correctly?*

5 Ask students to complete the exercise in pairs. Monitor and help with any difficulties. Play the video again, pausing as required for clarification.

Check answers with the whole class.

Answers

1 c   2 e   3 g   4 a   5 f   6 d   7 b

PHRASES FOR FLUENCY

1 Ask students to locate expressions 1–6 in the story on page 44 and underline them. To encourage speed-reading, you could do this as a race and ask students to find the expressions as quickly as possible. Ask students to compare their answers with a partner before whole-class feedback.

Answers

1 Emma   2 Justin   3 Nicole   4 Emma
5 Nicole   6 Liam

2 Working in pairs, students complete the dialogues. Check answers. If you'd like to do some pronunciation work with your students, focusing on intonation, drill the dialogues in open class (for students to repeat together).

Answers

1 again   2 can't be serious   3 Calm down
4 give it a rest, out of order   5 That's just it

Answers

1 It's all good   2 for good   3 not very good
4 It's a good thing   5 So far, so good   6 it's no good

Workbook page 38

Optional extension

Disappearing sentences: you'll need to write out the dialogues on the board or project them on the IWB for this one. Make AB pairs so that half of the class are A and half are B. Students practise the conversations from Exercise 2 in their pairs. Cover a small section of the dialogue, beginning from the right-hand side of the screen or board. Students repeat the dialogues in their same AB pairings trying to remember the whole thing, including the parts they can no longer see. Cover more and more of the dialogue, with students practising at each stage, until eventually nothing is left on the board. Ask for volunteers to perform for the class or have all As and all Bs perform in unison. This activity involving lots of repetition is a fun way for students to memorise useful lexical chunks.

WordWise

Expressions with *good*

1 Books closed. To introduce this activity, write *good* in the centre of the board. Divide the class into pairs and ask students to make a list of as many expressions with *good* as they can in three minutes. Elicit and write any correct answers on the board.

Books open. Ask students which of the expressions on the board appear. Next, ask them to work with a partner and complete the exercise. Check answers in open class.

Answers

1 not very good at   2 So far, so good.   3 It's all good.
4 It's no good   5 It's a good thing

2 Students work individually to match the phrases from Exercise 1 with the meanings. During whole-class feedback, say the phrases for students to repeat and check pronunciation. Give further examples to outline meaning of the phrases if necessary.

Answers

1 for good   2 It's no good.   3 It's all good.
4 So far, so good.   5 not very good at   6 It's a good thing

Optional extension

Ask students to work with a partner to complete sentences 1–6 with one of the phrases from Exercise 1. Check answers in open class.

1 _____ – the children are asleep. We can watch a film!

2 She's not going to Australia just for a holiday – she's going there _____ .

3 Oh no! This food is awful! Well, I guess I'm _____ at cooking.

4 A It's really cold today.
   B Yes. _____ we're wearing our coats.

5 A How are you getting on?
   B _____ . I think I'll finish in ten minutes.

6 I've apologised three times to her, but _____ – she's still angry with me.

FUNCTIONS

Expressing frustration

1 To introduce the concept of frustration, tell a story about something frustrating that happened to you. For example: running for a flight only to find that it has been delayed, or finding it impossible to memorise something. Include some of the phrases to express frustration in your anecdote. Ask students to work with a partner to think of examples of frustrating things that have happened to them. Listen to some of their ideas in open class.

Look at the seven phrases. Students work with a partner to answer the questions. Ask students to find the phrases in the photostory before checking answers in open class. Say the phrases for students to repeat and check pronunciation.

Answers

She doesn't say 2, 3, 5 or 6.
The sentences all express a negative opinion about personal ability or a situation.

2 In open class, elicit as much information as students can recall about the woman who loses her key in the photostory. Refer students to the first sentence in Exercise 1 (I can't (do that)) and ask students what the woman might have thought using this expression. Nominate one or two students to share their ideas and then ask students to work in pairs to think of and write down three thoughts using other sentences from Exercise 1. Monitor to check that students are using the sentence stems appropriately. During feedback, ask students to share their ideas with the class and review any common errors.

WRITING

A story

The planning for this exercise can be done in class and the writing can be set as homework.

Tell students they are going to write a story ending with the words *Thanks, you saved my life!* and that the story doesn't have to be true. You could tell them a story of your own to act as an example or elicit Emma's story.

Give students a short while to think of ideas for a story and to make notes. Divide the class into pairs for students to share their ideas with a partner. Encourage partners to ask questions to elicit further details about the story and to give suggestions as to how they might make their stories more interesting. In open class, brainstorm adverbs or adverbial phrases (from page 43) and personality adjectives (from page 40) that students could use in their stories. When students have told their stories, ask them to work individually to expand on the notes they have made in order to make the story as interesting as possible and to try to use four items of vocabulary from the unit. Finally, students should write their final version in class or at home.

Student's Book pages 46–47

LISTENING

1 🔊 **1.26**

Audio Script Track 1.26

You will hear five different people talking about an after-school art group. Choose from the list (A–H) what each speaker likes most about the group. Use the letters only once. There are three extra letters that you do not need to use.

Speaker 1

There's a massive emphasis at our school on sport and we're really encouraged to get involved. There are clubs for loads of different sports and most kids want to get into at least one team. It's definitely the thing to do if you want to be in. Being into art is most definitely not cool so if you're creative like me, you usually don't talk too much about it. When I heard Mr Bowden was starting an art club I got really excited. Not only is he a really inspiring teacher but it was my chance to find out if there were any other secret artists like myself at school. It turns out there are and I've made loads of new friends. I couldn't be happier.

Speaker 2

I've been into art as long as I can remember. When I was a little kid I was always colouring in and cutting out and making things. It's my favourite subject at school by a long way, and I know that when I leave school, I'm definitely going to art college. So this club was always going to be for me. It's been really interesting and a good chance to learn about different ways of doing things. I've never had lessons with Mr Bowden before. He's an absolutely amazing teacher and he really brings out the best in me. I've made a massive improvement and it's all been with his help. He's been the best part of this club, for sure.

Speaker 3

I'd always thought of myself as a bit of a maths geek. I mean I already know that I want to work in IT when I leave school. I never really thought of myself as having much imagination so I've been really surprised at the kind of work I can produce with a paint brush or a camera in my hand. I'm learning all sorts of things I never knew about myself. In truth, I only went to art club because I wanted to make new friends. I wasn't really all that interested in art. I have met some really nice people but what has surprised me most is how much I'm enjoying being creative.

Speaker 4

I consider myself to be a really creative person and I love painting and drawing so this was the perfect after-school club for me. The fact that it's run by Mr Bowden, my favourite teacher, and that my two best friends go to it too, are just bonuses. What's really great is that we don't just do painting and drawing. Mr Bowden introduces us to other types of art too and encourages us to have a go. We've done sculpture, photography – we've even made a short film too. I can't wait to see what we do next. I really enjoy the class; even the short lectures about famous artists aren't too bad.

Speaker 5

If I'm honest, I didn't really want to do extra art classes but my parents made me because they didn't want me in the house on my own after school. I'd rather have gone to a history club, but there isn't one. But it's not as bad as I thought it would be because the teacher gives us quite a bit of art history too. It's good to learn about which famous artists were doing what and when. I'm not really a very creative kind of person so I don't really enjoy the practical side of the lessons, although we do do different stuff, which makes it less boring.

Answers

Speaker 1 – G   Speaker 2 – F   Speaker 3 – H
Speaker 4 – A   Speaker 5 – E

Workbook page 35 ➤

TEST YOURSELF UNITS 3 & 4

VOCABULARY

1

Answers

1 strict   2 organised   3 helmets   4 bad-tempered
5 well   6 public   7 imaginative   8 panic
9 secret   10 grow

GRAMMAR

2

Answers

1 enthusiasm   2 None   3 live   4 few   5 living
6 little

3

Answers

1 The test was ~~such~~ **so** difficult that nobody got everything right.
2 Harry was used to be**ing** alone in the old house so he wasn't worried.
3 Sara was ~~much~~ **too** scared to stay there after dark.
4 Manu listened with ~~interesting~~ **interest** to the interview with the local politician.
5 There was hardly any ~~of~~ space on the shelf, so I couldn't put the books there.
6 My grandmother always preferred her laptop. She never **got** used to using a tablet.

FUNCTIONAL LANGUAGE

4

Answers

1 'll never, so   2 such, I can't   3 so, such   4 hopeless, so

---

5 | SCREEN TIME

Objectives

FUNCTIONS	advice and obligation
GRAMMAR	obligation, permission and prohibition (review); necessity: *didn't need to / needn't have*; ability in the past (*could, was / were able to, managed to, succeeded in*)
VOCABULARY	technology (nouns); technology (verbs)

Student's Book pages 48–49

READING

1 Books closed. As a lead-in, ask: *On an average day, how long do you spend looking at a screen (e.g. TV, PC, mobile phone)?* Ask students to write their answer on a piece of paper, then divide the class into small groups to compare answers and find out who spends the longest and who, the least amount of time looking at screens. Encourage students to detail how long they spend looking at different types of screen. Take feedback in open class.

Books open. If there is an interactive whiteboard (IWB) available in the classroom, this activity would best be done as a heads-up activity. Display the pictures on the IWB and nominate a student to describe one of the pictures. Give students two minutes to think of as many different types of screen as they can in pairs. During feedback, elicit and write a list of different types of screen on the board.

2 Students discuss in pairs or small groups. Make sure they are thinking about the advantages and disadvantages of so much screen time in general, rather than discussing individual screens, by eliciting one advantage and one disadvantage in open class. You could encourage groups to compete with each other to come up with the most advantages and disadvantages. During feedback, elicit and list advantages and disadvantages on the board, possibly by asking the group with the most items to read their list to the class.

3 ◀)) 1.27 Tell students they are going to read and listen to three texts about screens. Tell them to just focus on checking which of the advantages and disadvantages listed on the board are mentioned, and not to worry if they don't understand every word. After playing the audio, allow students to compare answers with a partner before whole-class feedback. Refer back to the lists on the board at this stage.

4 Ask students to try to match the titles to the paragraphs individually, before re-reading the texts to check. Allow them to compare answers with

a partner, giving reasons for their choices before conducting feedback in open class.

Answers

A 3 B (extra title) C 1 D 2

5 Check/clarify: *harm, implications*. Students read the article again to match the questions with the answers. Ask students to underline the parts of the text that helped them find the answer. Students can compare answers in pairs before whole-class feedback. During feedback, ask students to explain which parts of the text helped them decide on their answers.

> **Mixed-ability**
>
> Put students into mixed-level groups. Students discuss and agree on their answers as a group. One student acts as secretary, noting down the group's answers. This adds an extra layer of thinking about the texts, gives students practice in negotiating, and involves a valuable element of peer teaching with stronger students explaining answers to weaker students.

Answers

a 2 b 3 c 1 d 3 e 2 f 1

6 **SPEAKING** Give students time to reflect and make notes. Divide the class into pairs or small groups for students to discuss their answers. Monitor and help as necessary, encouraging students to express themselves at length, expanding on and justifying their opinions, in English. Ask pairs or groups to feed back to the class and discuss any interesting points further.

> **Optional extension**
>
> Ask students to draw a pie chart showing how their screen time is divided. Draw an example of your own and explain it to students (e.g. *I spend 40% of my screen time watching TV, 40% on my laptop and 20% on my mobile*). When students have drawn their charts, divide the class into pairs for students to ask each other questions and compare.

TRAIN TO THiNK

The PMI strategy

1 Refer students back to Exercise 2 on page 48 and emphasise the need to weigh up advantages and disadvantages before making decisions. Divide the class into pairs and ask students to add as many ideas to each column as they can. Listen to some of their ideas in open class and encourage further

discussion. To focus on the importance of asking questions before making decisions and considering the consequences of different decisions, stress the particular relevance of the third column.

Optional extension

Divide the class into two groups, one supporting the idea of banning books from schools and the other opposing it. Ask students to work in small groups and debate the pluses and minuses of their group's position. They should also discuss any questions in the 'interesting' category. Make new groups of four students with two in favour and two against, and get them to debate.

---

2 SPEAKING Divide the class into three groups and ask students to find a partner within their group. Assign one of the three situations to each group. Students use the PMI strategy to come to a decision on their situation, in pairs. When the majority of students have reached a decision, regroup students into the original three larger groups for them to discuss their ideas and agree on the best decision for their situation.

Fast finishers

Ask students to discuss one of the other situations.

Optional extension

Ask students to work in small groups and think of a situation of their own. Monitor while they do this. Ask them to write their situation at the top of a piece of paper and draw the three PMI columns underneath. Students then hand their situation to another group and give them two minutes to add an idea to one of the columns. Repeat this process until all the groups have seen each situation, at which stage the situation returns to the original group. Give students time to read all of the ideas and then nominate one student from each group to respond to the ideas in open class. Finally, encourage discussion around how useful students find the PMI strategy as a way to make decisions.

Student's Book pages 50–51

GRAMMAR

Obligation, permission and prohibition (review)

1 Books closed. As a simple introduction, write the letters *l, m, s, n t* and *n a t* on the board. Tell students that they are the initial letters of five modal and semi-modal forms (*let, must, should, need to* and *not allowed to*). Elicit the forms in open class and once they are written on the board, give students one minute to silently reflect on their knowledge of the form and meaning of each verb. This will focus students on the verbs and ready them for the exercise.

Ask students to work in pairs to read the three sentences and try to complete them before looking back at the article to check. During feedback, remind students that modal verbs are followed by an infinitive without *to*. This is of course not the case for semi-modal verbs. In pairs, students then complete the rule. Elicit answers in open class giving further examples to clarify the usage of each modal verb, as necessary.

Answers

1 should   2 must   3 let

Rule

1 must   2 should   3 need to   4 let   5 not allowed to

LANGUAGE NOTE

Students may be confused by the difference between *have to* and *must*. A simple distinction is that we use *must* when the obligation comes from the speaker [*their parents*], as in sentence 2 in Exercise 1 (*… their parents say they must switch their electronic devices off*).

If the speaker is describing a rule or obligation imposed by somebody else, they use *have to*, for example: *I have to switch my electronic devices off* [*because my parents tell me to*]. An added difficulty is that the negative form in each case is *mustn't*: *You must arrive by 9 a.m. = You mustn't arrive late; I have to arrive by 9 a.m. = I mustn't arrive late I don't have to arrive late.* Reinforce that *don't have to* expresses a lack of obligation in a similar way to *don't need to*.

Look!

Read through the information in the Look! box in open class. Write the following examples on the board:

1 *This suitcase is very old. We **had better** buy a new one before we go on holiday.*

Point out that *we had* contracts to *we'd* and should not be confused with *we would*.

2 *Drivers **are supposed to** drive slowly when they are near a school (but sometimes they don't).*

2 This exercise is closely modelled on Reading and
✳ Use of English part 4 of the Cambridge English: First exam. Ask students to work individually to complete the exercise. Allow them to compare answers with a partner before feedback in open class. During feedback, refer to the rule and the Look! box to clarify answers, as necessary.

Answers

1 isn't allowed to   2 're supposed to   3 don't let
4 'd better turn

Fast finishers

Ask students to write sentences describing five things they are supposed to do, but don't always do.

Optional extension

Ask students to imagine that they are allowed to introduce new rules in their house. Ask students to make a list of the rules that they and their parents will have to follow, in pairs. Tell them to use modals appropriately to express obligation, permission and prohibition. When students have completed their lists, regroup them into new pairs for students to role-play a conversation in which they describe the new rules to their parents, with one student playing the role of parent, and the other the child.

Workbook page 46 and page 124

Be aware of common errors related to modals.
Go to Get it right! on Student's Book page 124.

FUNCTIONS

Advice and obligation

1 Check/clarify: *exchange student*. Working individually, students write down three rules and three pieces of advice. To get students started, elicit one rule and one piece of advice in open class. Encourage students to use *supposed to* and *had better* where possible. Monitor to help with vocabulary and to check students are using the verbs correctly.

> **Mixed-ability**
>
> Allow weaker students to create their list in pairs before comparing with another pair in Exercise 2.

2 **SPEAKING** Divide the class into pairs for students to compare their sentences. For feedback, ask pairs to read out the most important rule and the best piece of advice they came up with.

VOCABULARY

Technology (nouns)

1 Ask students to cover the words and work with a partner to try to name the objects in the pictures. After two minutes, ask students to uncover the words, check their answers and match any remaining pictures with the correct words. Check answers in open class and take the opportunity to say the words for students to repeat and check pronunciation. Pay attention to the unstressed schwa sound in the final syllable of *adaptor, charger, power* and *router*.

> **Answers**
>
> A 3 B 1 C 6 D 2 E 9 F 10 G 4 H 5 I 7 J 8

> **Optional extension**
>
> Ask students to close their books and write down as many of the items as they can remember in one minute, then open their books to check. Alternatively, ask students to work in pairs and take it in turns to say the first letter of one of the words for their partner to recall the whole word without looking in their books.

2 Give students time to read the sentences. Check/clarify: *out of battery* (item 3). Ask students to work individually to complete the sentences then compare answers with a partner before feedback in open class.

> **Mixed-ability**
>
> Stronger students can cover the words in Exercise 1 and attempt to complete the sentences from memory.

> **Answers**
>
> 1 'at' symbol   2 adaptor   3 charger   4 wireless router
> 5 USB port   6 power lead   7 headset   8 plug

> **Fast finishers**
>
> Ask students to underline the verbs in the sentences and use them in sentences of their own.

> **Optional extension**
>
> If students are interested in this topic, brainstorm more nouns connected to technology and create a mindmap on the board for students to copy into their notebooks.
>
> Or
>
> Ask students to work in pairs or small groups to discuss the following questions relating to students' use of technology:
>
> 1 Which of the things have you used today?
> 2 Which of the things do you never use?
> 3 What other technology do you use?

Workbook page 48 ▶

LISTENING

1 **SPEAKING** Books closed. In open class, elicit ten popular TV programmes from the class. Ask students to rank them individually from best to worst before agreeing on a joint ranking in pairs. Listen to their choices in open class and have a quick show of hands to find out which are the most popular programmes.

Books open. Ask students to work individually to complete the exercise. Divide the class into small groups for students to compare their findings. Encourage students to justify their choices. In open class, compare findings by asking students to raise hands if they agree with a statement. Nominate individuals to give reasons for their choices.

2 🔊 1.28 Tell students they are going to listen to a conversation between a girl (Sheena) and a boy (Aaron) about television. Tell them to just concentrate on checking which of the statements in Exercise 1 the girl mentions and not to worry about understanding every word.

> **Audio Script Track 1.28**
>
> | | |
> |---|---|
> | Sheena | Hi, Aaron. Why weren't you at the stadium on Saturday? You missed a really good game. |
> | Aaron | Well, I didn't need to go because I was able to watch it live online. |
> | Sheena | What! |
> | Aaron | Yeah, we had wifi installed a couple of weeks ago, and I've just been watching films and TV on my tablet for the past two weeks. |
> | Sheena | What! |
> | Aaron | Yeah, it's great. I watch anything I want anytime. Anyway, what have you been doing? |
> | Sheena | Reading actually. In fact I've just read an article called 'Three reasons why you shouldn't watch too much TV' – something you might be interested in? |
> | Aaron | On no, here we go. |
> | Sheena | So the first reason – you know what a 'couch potato' is, don't you? |
> | Aaron | You're not saying I'm turning into one, are you? |
> | Sheena | Well, you'd better be careful. Medical studies have shown that when people watch films and other things on screens too much, their brains become slower, and they feel sleepy. |
> | Aaron | That probably explains why I'm half asleep most of the time. Mind you I can't remember the last time I went to bed before two in the morning. |
> | Sheena | Second reason. Not watching too much TV actually saves you money! |

Aaron	What? You mean watching TV costs me money? How come?
Sheena	OK, any regular one-hour segment on TV is made up of 40 minutes of actual content and 20 minutes of advertising. That's a third of all TV viewing time.
Aaron	But I don't spend that much time watching TV actually. I watch downloaded films mostly so I don't see the advertising.
Sheena	Right. But did you know that there's a lot of product placement in the films themselves, which is like being brainwashed? People buy what they see on TV and in films, and not what they need. This is why watching less TV or fewer films saves you money!
Aaron	I'd never thought of that.
Sheena	OK, and finally the third reason and this is the key, the key to changing your life NOW.
Aaron	Can't wait to hear it.
Sheena	It's so much more rewarding to spend time with real people than with the people you see on TV or in films.
Aaron	Eh?
Sheena	You know what I mean. Life's about friendships. It's about getting together with your friends, talking about the music you like, and sports, and other things. It's about caring for real people, as I've said, and not about worrying about the people on screen.
Aaron	Well, of course I know that! I'm not a fool. In fact I just wanted to ask you … erm.
Sheena	To watch a film with you?
Aaron	No! But there's a concert in the park on Sunday, and I bought two tickets.
Sheena	Hey, you needn't have done that!
Aaron	Why?
Sheena	Because I did the same thing.
Aaron	Oh no!

Answers

1, 4 and 5

3 🔊 1.28 Check/clarify *hidden advertising* by eliciting an example. Ask students to underline the key information they will need to listen for in each sentence. Students may like to work in pairs and try to answer the questions from memory and by making predictions before listening to the audio again to check their answers. Let students compare answers with a partner before conducting feedback in open class.

Answers

1 the game   2 watching films and TV   3 couch potato
4 two/2 am   5 product placement   6 concert (in the park)

GRAMMAR

Necessity: *didn't need to / needn't have*

1 Ask students to work with a partner to answer the questions. Check answers, and then draw students' attention to the words that follow *need to* and *needn't have*. Next, students complete the rule in pairs. Check answers in open class.

To check understanding at this point, elicit a few more examples from the class of things they didn't need to/needn't have done in the last week and check that their choice of *didn't need to* vs. *needn't have* is the correct one.

Answers

1 No   2 Yes

Rule

1 needn't have done   2 didn't need to do

LANGUAGE NOTE

Students may produce statements like *He needn't has bought a new bicycle.* Remind them that because *have* follows an auxiliary, it does not change in the third person.

---

2 Students work individually to complete the exercise. Let them compare answers with a partner before checking answers in open class. During feedback, insist on students explaining why they chose the answers they chose.

Answer

1 a   2 b   3 b   4 a   5 b   6 a

Optional extension

Tell students to imagine they are preparing for a party at their house. Write the following sentences on the board and ask students to work in pairs and think of how they would say them in a different way using the words in brackets.

1 I bought some cakes for the party, but my brother had already bought some. (needn't have)

2 My sister had already chosen some music. (didn't need)

3 Our neighbours are on holiday. (didn't need)

4 The party was very informal, but my friend John wore a suit. (needn't have)

Suggested answers

1 I needn't have bought any cakes.

2 I didn't need to choose any music.

3 I didn't need to tell the neighbours.

4 John needn't have worn a suit.

Workbook page 47 and page 124 ➤

VOCABULARY

Technology (verbs)

Books closed. If you are using an IWB, create two text boxes and copy and paste them nine times to make twenty boxes. Break up the verb phrases into smaller chunks and write one half in each of the boxes. Mix the boxes up on the board and ask students to work in pairs to match the boxes and create the ten phrases as quickly as possible. Ask the first pair to finish to come to the board and drag and drop the boxes to make correct phrases.

Books open. Go through the first item as an example in open class. Ask students to work with a partner to complete the exercise. During whole-class feedback, say the phrases for students to repeat and check pronunciation. Draw attention to the stress on the second syllable of _upgrade_, _extract_ and _connect_. Also point out that _upgrade_ and _extract_ are stressed on the first syllable if they are nouns (as is _update_).

Answers

1 streaming 2 connect to wifi 3 browsing the Internet
4 upgrading 5 sync devices 6 plugged in
7 posted an update 8 save

Fast finishers

Ask students to make a list of any other nouns that collocate with the verbs. Alternatively they could make a list of any other English verbs related to technology that are used in their language. Encourage students to share their lists with the class/a partner following feedback on Exercise 1.

Workbook page 48 ➤

SPEAKING

In pairs or small groups, students discuss the questions and make notes on their answers. Monitor and answer any questions about vocabulary, but as this is a fluency practice activity, do not interrupt the conversations unless inaccuracy hinders comprehension. During feedback, nominate one or two students, for each question, to share their ideas in open class.

PRONUNCIATION

For practice of the schwa sound, go to Student's Book page 120.

Student's Book pages 52–53

READING

1 A recording of this text is available with your digital resources.

Books closed. As a lead-in, ask students: _How much do your parents know about technology? What technology do they use? What about your grandparents?_ Divide the class into pairs for students to discuss these questions.

Books open. If there is an IWB available in the classroom, this activity would best be done as a heads-up activity with the photo projected on the board. Ask students to work with a partner and make predictions based on the photo.

Answers

1 probably grandson and grandmother 2 He's teaching her how to use a computer, how to use the Internet.

2 Students read the article quickly to check their predictions. Set a two-minute time limit for this to encourage students to read quickly and to focus on gist rather than specific information. During feedback, confirm answers to Exercise 1 in open class and ask if students' predictions were correct.

3 Students re-read the article and scan for examples. Allow them to compare answers in pairs before doing feedback in open class.

Answers

Skype, Facebook, email, making a YouTube cooking tutorial, making a rap video, reconnecting with people

4 Students answer the questions. Ask them to underline key text in the article that gives them their answers. Allow them to check answers with a partner, encouraging them to refer to the article to explain their answers, before whole-class feedback.

Answers

1 It's a documentary.
2 It shows the story of teenagers teaching elderly people to use the Internet.
3 Poppy and Amy Raynes
4 They were inspired after witnessing how the Internet had changed their grandparents' lives.
5 friends
6 in a local home for elderly people
7 using Facebook / getting ideas for travelling, learning how to play an instrument or cooking
8 making a YouTube cooking tutorial, making a rap video and reconnecting with people

5 SPEAKING Give students three minutes to read the questions and make notes to refer to in their discussions. In pairs or small groups, students ask and answer the questions. Encourage them to develop their answers as much as possible and monitor to praise students who are making attempts to speak at length.

GRAMMAR

Ability in the past: _could, was / were able to, managed to, succeeded in_

1 You might like to point out the use of _even_ in sentence 1. Elicit/explain that it is used to emphasise something surprising. Put students into pairs to complete the rule. Remind them to refer to the example sentences to help them to do this.

Rule

1 could 2 managed 3 succeeded 4 couldn't

LANGUAGE NOTE

You may like to tell students that _managed to_ and _succeeded in_ are usually used to describe the ability to do something difficult. For example: _On his fourth attempt, he finally managed to pass/ succeeded in passing his driving test._

---

2 Go through the first sentence as an example, if necessary, making sure students are clear on why that particular modal form is used, perhaps by eliciting an explanation from the class. Remind students to think about the context of each sentence and to refer to the rule if necessary. Check answers, asking students to explain their choice of answer each time.

Answers

1 B 2 A 3 B 4 B 5 B 6 C

Fast finishers

Ask students to write sentences of their own describing difficult things they managed to do or succeeded in doing in the past two years.

Optional extension

Write the following sentences on the board and ask students to work with a partner to find the error in each one. Then ask them to imagine a scenario in which they might say each sentence.

1 I finally managed pass my exam.
2 I succeeded at explaining the problem.
3 I could convince them after three hours of discussion.

Answers

1 I finally managed **to** pass my exam.
2 I succeeded **in** explaining the problem.
3 I **managed to** convince them after three hours of discussion.

> Workbook page 47 and page 124

▮▮ THiNK SELF-ESTEEM ▮▮

Learning from elderly people

1 Ask students to choose a person they admire. Perhaps allow them to discuss possible choices in pairs. It might be difficult for students to think of someone by themselves or without discussion. Once they've chosen someone, students can make notes individually. Encourage students to reflect on whether they admire the things the person does or their personality, or both. Monitor and help with ideas for people and qualities.

2 Ask students to read through their notes and work with a partner to discuss which of the qualities they would like to have themselves. Ask: *Why would that quality be useful to you?*

3 Students make notes of the ways in which they could develop these positive qualities. Encourage them to go into detail and think of examples. Get students to compare ideas in pairs and think of alternative/additional ways in which their partner might develop these qualities.

4 SPEAKING Make different pairs or put pairs together to form groups of four for students to discuss their answers to Exercises 1–3. Listen to some of their ideas in open class as feedback.

5 WRITING If you're short on time, set this exercise for homework. As a lead-in, ask the class to read the paragraph and answer the question: *What has the writer learnt from Mr Carter?*

Ask students to work individually and write their own paragraph summarising their notes from Exercises 1–3. When students have finished writing, make small groups and ask students to read each other's paragraphs. Ask students to give each other feedback on the content of the paragraph they read (without going into detail on grammatical or lexical accuracy) and encourage them to show interest by asking questions to get further information.

Optional extension

Divide the class into small groups. Ask students to decide on the three most important things that we can learn from elderly people. Nominate a student from each group to report their findings to the rest of the class and have a quick class vote to decide on the most important qualities.

Student's Book pages 54–55

CULTURE

1 SPEAKING Ask students to discuss the questions in pairs. Listen to some of their answers in open class. If you have access to the Internet, you could lead into the topic of cinema by showing a clip from a silent film of your choice. For example, films with the Keystone Cops or Buster Keaton. Ask: *Did you enjoy the clip? How were these films different from films today?*

2 Ask students to circle the key information in the questions that they need to look for in the article. Tell them that they need to scan for specific information and they do not need to read every word of the text to complete the exercise. Set a two-minute time limit to encourage students to scan quickly rather than attempt to read in detail.

3 ◄))1.31 Play the audio while students read and listen to the article to check their answers to Exercise 2. Allow them to compare answers with a partner before feedback in open class.

Answers

1 A magic lantern.
2 They invented a camera that took a picture every half a second.
3 The 1930s.

4 Divide the class into three groups (A, B and C). Ask Group A to re-read the first part of the text (*Early days: the magic lantern*), Group B to read the second part (*The invention of film*) and Group C to read the third part (*Hollywood*) and to prepare to give a summary of what they've read. Form new ABC groups for students to take it in turns to give their summaries and then to work together to answer the questions. Check answers in open class.

Answers

1 Hand-drawn pictures on a reflecting surface, a candle and a simple lens.
2 He projected images of witches, ghosts and other spooky creatures.
3 It could only be watched by one person at a time.
4 They filmed a train coming towards the camera.
5 It developed talkies, documentaries and Westerns, creating over 800 films a year.

5 VOCABULARY Ask students to complete the activity, looking back at the text to find the highlighted words or phrases that match the descriptions. Check answers and during feedback say the words for students to repeat and check pronunciation.

Answers

1 startled   2 reel   3 spooky   4 lens   5 forerunner
6 transparent   7 shutter   8 flourish

SPEAKING

Students should discuss the questions in pairs. Encourage them to develop their answers with examples where possible. Monitor and praise those expanding on their answers. Avoid error correction except in cases where errors really hinder comprehension. The focus of this task is on fluency, not on the practice of specific structures or lexis.

WRITING

Instructions

1 Books closed. As a lead-in, ask: *How often do you read instructions? If you need help with a computer, where do you get advice?* Ask students to read the instructions and answer the question. Allow them to compare answers in pairs before a whole-class check.

   Suggested answer

   It has been written for people who do not know how to save a file on a computer so that they do not lose files.

2 Ask students to complete the sentences in pairs. During feedback, point out that the words in the gaps are commonly used when giving instructions.

   Answers

   1 If, then   2 first thing   3 To do   4 To   5 This means
   6 Finally

3 Ask students to work with a partner to complete the sentences with the words or phrases from the list. Check answers.

   Answers

   1 first thing   2 If, then   3 this means   4 To   5 Finally

4 SPEAKING Ask students to make notes on why they think each of the tips is important. Put them into pairs or small groups to compare ideas. During feedback, nominate students to report back on their discussions and invite reactions and further comments from the class.

5 Students choose one of the processes and list all important stages, in preparation for writing their instructions. Monitor and help with any difficulties.

6 Students can do the preparation in class, and complete the writing at home. Or, this could be done as a collaborative writing task in class with students working in pairs to write their texts.

Students should organise their stages in the same way as the example. They should use words and phrases from Exercises 2 and 3. When they have finished, ask them to share their instructions with a (different) partner. Ask students: *How clear are your partner's instructions?*

6 BRINGING PEOPLE TOGETHER

Objectives

FUNCTIONS	using intensifying comparatives
GRAMMAR	comparatives; linkers of contrast
VOCABULARY	ways of speaking; love and relationships

Student's Book pages 56–57

READING

1 **SPEAKING** Books closed. As a lead-in, brainstorm different types of public transport and write them on the board. Divide the class into groups and assign one of the types of public transport to each group. Ask them to make a list of at least five advantages and five disadvantages of using that type of transport. Regroup students so that each type of public transport is represented within each group. Ask students to compare lists and come to an agreement on which is the best and worst way to travel.

Books open. Check/clarify: *stuffy* (lacking fresh air), *packed* (tightly filled). To check understanding, ask: *If you were at a very busy football match on a cold day, would you say it was packed or stuffy?* (packed); *If you are in a stuffy classroom, is it easy to breathe?* (no). Students work together in pairs to discuss the people in the photos. To encourage them to say as much as possible, you could ask students to take it in turns to say a sentence about a photo and to compete to continue adding details until their partner cannot think of anything else to say. You could also ask students to come to an agreement on where the people might be feeling most and least comfortable. Conduct feedback by nominating one or two students to share their ideas in open class.

2 **SPEAKING** Working individually students make notes about what they imagine to be the thoughts of one of the people in the photos. Get them to think about where the person they've chosen might have been, where they're going and why, etc. Students read out the person's thoughts (this is more fun if done in the first person) for their partner(s) to guess who it is. Listen to some examples in open class.

3 **1.32** Ask students to make predictions based on the title. Elicit some ideas in open class and write these on the board. Students read and listen to the blog to check which of the ideas on the board are mentioned.

4 Working individually, students re-read the blog and answer the questions. Encourage them to answer any from memory before they re-read and check, and to underline the sections of the blog that support their

answers. Allow them to compare answers with a partner before whole-class feedback.

Answers

1 20 minutes.
2 They complained about the trains.
3 Tourists' nationality and their holiday plans/experience, a businesswoman's mountain-climbing hobby, what an older fellow pupil from school thought about their teachers.
4 Offering each other food and drink, playing/singing music, medical assistance.
5 Because she helped a diabetic man.
6 Clapped, cheered and hugged.
7 The same as usual. People weren't as friendly as the day before.

5 **SPEAKING** Ask students to work with a partner and answer the questions. Monitor and help with vocabulary, but do not interrupt unless errors impede communication. Instead, note down any recurring mistakes, write them on the board, ensuring anonymity and ask students to correct them in open class.

Mixed-ability

Divide the class into pairs or small groups by level for this speaking exercise. Give weaker students a minute or two to think about their answers and make notes before they begin their discussions in pairs.

Stuck in a lift

ROLE PLAY Put students into groups of four and assign a letter (A, B, C and D) to each member. Give students time to read their role card. Put As, Bs, Cs and Ds together to check understanding of their roles and to brainstorm things they could say. Tell students that it is important to stay in character to make the activity interesting and fun. During the role playing stage, monitor to encourage quieter students to speak and to remind students that they need to reach agreement on what to do. During feedback, nominate a member of each group to report back to the class on what they decided to do.

TRAIN TO THiNK

Exaggeration

1 Books closed. To introduce the topic, tell students the same story twice. The first time you tell the story, use very ordinary adjectives (*good, nice, not bad,* etc.).

For example: I went on holiday last year. It was nice. The food was OK and the weather was good. I went on a trip to some mountains and I saw some trees and a lake. It was good. I took some pictures.

When you repeat the story, use language of exaggeration, as follows, stressing the adjectives:

I went on the best holiday of my life last year. It was absolutely fantastic. The food was delicious and the weather was incredible. I went on a trip to some really beautiful mountains and saw the tallest trees I've ever seen. They were touching the clouds. There was also a massive lake. It all felt like a dream. I took some amazing pictures!

Ask students: *What was the difference between the two stories?* Elicit that the second included more exaggeration and was possibly more interesting to listen to, as a result, though it might have not been any truer an account of my holiday than the first one.

Divide the class into pairs for students to discuss and answer the questions in Exercise 1. Check answers in open class.

Answers

1 five
2 journey was terrible; worst journey of my life; stopped for ages; middle of nowhere; so bored I thought I was going to go mad
3 journey was terrible = journey was annoying/ inconvenient
worst journey of my life = it wasn't a good journey
stopped for ages = stopped for quite a long time
middle of nowhere = not at a station/in the countryside
so bored I thought I was going to go mad = impatient with having to wait on a train

Optional extension

During feedback, read the example text (in the speech bubble) for students to repeat and check stress/intonation. Point out that we put a strong stress on words which we use to exaggerate meaning, e.g. *terrible – worst; two hours – ages.* Ask students to take it in turns telling the story to a partner using suitable stress and intonation.

2 SPEAKING Give pairs time to come up with an idea for a story, make notes and think about how they will exaggerate their story. Also, allow them time to take turns to practise telling it. Regroup students with different partners to tell each other their stories. Listen to some examples in open class as feedback.

PRONUNCIATION

For practice of linking words with /dʒ/ and /tʃ/, go to Student's Book page 120.

Student's Book pages 58–59

GRAMMAR

Comparatives

1 Working in pairs, students match the sentence halves before referring back to the text to check their answers. You could elicit the comparative forms in each sentence and ask students to underline them before they go on and complete the rule. To check understanding of these uses of comparatives during feedback, say some sentences and ask students to

decide if they are true or false. For example *Spain is not nearly as big as China.* (true); *The more you eat, the thinner you get.* (false) etc.

Answers

1 c 2 d 3 e 4 a 5 b

Rule

A 2 B 3,4 C 5 D 1

2 This exercise is closely modelled on Reading and ✳ Use of English Part 4 of the Cambridge English: First exam. You could do the first one in open class to clarify the task. Students work individually to complete the exercise before checking with a partner. Refer them to the rule to help them decide on their answers before doing feedback in open class.

Answers

1 nowhere near as difficult   2 practise, the better
3 more and more expensive   4 the less

Fast finishers

Ask students to write five sentences comparing themselves to a member of their family using some of the comparative structures in the rule box.

Optional extension

Write the following sentence openers/endings on the board. Ask students to work together to complete the sentences and fill the gaps.

1 *The older I get, …*

2 *… is far more exciting than …*

3 *… is getting better and better.*

4 *… are not nearly as expensive as …*

Nominate one or two students to share their answers with the class. For further practice, ask students to work in pairs to write sentences of their own using comparatives, then read them out to another pair without saying the adjectives for their partners to guess.

For example:

A *Barcelona is nowhere near as … as Madrid.*

B *Barcelona is nowhere near as big as Madrid.*

A *Correct!*

Workbook page 54 and page 124

 Be aware of common errors related to comparatives. Go to Get it right! on Student's Book page 124.

FUNCTIONS

Using intensifying comparatives

1 If there is an interactive whiteboard (IWB) available in the classroom, this activity would best be done as a heads-up activity with the whole class. Display the grid on the board, covering the second and third columns with the reveal tool. Alternatively, ask students to cover the second and third columns in their books. Read the information with students and elicit reasons for each statement. Encourage students to use comparative forms in their answers.

Reveal or ask students to uncover the second and third columns and work with a partner to match the three parts. During whole-class feedback, draw attention to the phrases in italics. Say the phrases for students to repeat. Point out that primary stress is often placed on the intensifying comparatives and that they are often used to exaggerate information in stories.

Answers

1 b ii   2 c i   3 a iii

2 Ask students to work individually and make a list of recommendations for visitors to their country. Divide the class into pairs for students to compare ideas. Encourage students to say whether they agree or disagree with each piece of advice and to agree on five 'top tips' as a pair. Monitor to make sure they are using intensifying comparatives. During feedback, nominate two or three students to each share their favourite piece of advice with the class and encourage reactions from the rest of the class.

VOCABULARY

Ways of speaking

1 Books closed. As a lead-in, read out the following sentences and elicit the communicative purpose of each one, in L1 if necessary, and using the first one as an example:

You should buy a new computer. (to recommend)
My neighbours make a lot of noise. (to complain)
The concert will begin in five minutes. (to announce)
Hello, I'm Brian. (to introduce)
I told him your secret. (to confess)
What time is it? (to enquire)

Write correct answers on the board.

Books open. With a partner, students answer the question. Do whole-class feedback prompting students to justify their answers.

Answer

6

2 In pairs, students match the verbs to the sentences in Exercise 1. During feedback, say the verbs for students to repeat and check pronunciation.

Answers

to recommend 2   to introduce 4   to announce 5
to confess 6   to enquire 1   to complain 3

LANGUAGE NOTE

While this exercise does not focus on reported speech, you might like to point out to stronger classes that some of these verbs can be used to report what has been said. You could elicit/give the following sentences and draw attention to the verb patterns in each:

He enquired about the train. (to enquire about + noun)
She recommended visiting Manchester. (to recommend + -ing)
He complained about the lack of free seats. (to complain about + noun)
She introduced herself and her friend. (to introduce yourself)
They announced a problem. (to announce a problem)
He confessed to eating the last piece of cake. (to confess to + -ing)

3 Look at the example with students and explain that we can form nouns from the verb roots using the suffixes in the list. Also point out that we can make verb phrases using *make* or *give* + noun, e.g. *make an enquiry*. Ask students to work with a partner and choose the correct suffix to make nouns. Check answers in open class.

Answers

2 confession   3 introduction   4 enquiry
5 announcement   6 complaint

Fast finishers

Ask students to make a list of more nouns that include the suffixes in the list.

4 Give students time to write three sentences. In pairs, students take turns to read out their sentences and identify the function.

Workbook page 56

LISTENING

1 Ask students to look at the pictures. Ask: *What do you think is the relationship between Sophie and Rob? What type of story do you think it is? Do you think it's a story with a happy or a sad ending? Why?* Working individually, students order the pictures to make a story. Divide the class into pairs for students to compare their ideas.

2 ◀))1.35 Tell students they're going to listen to Sophie and Rob's story. Tell them not to worry if they don't understand everything, but to just concentrate on checking the order they came up with in Exercise 1. Play the recording. Let students compare answers with a partner before whole-class feedback. *Did they guess the story correctly?*

Answers

A 4   B 3   C 2   D 1   E 8   F 7   G 6   H 5

Audio Script Track 1.35

And now it's that time in the morning to stop what you're doing, sit back and enjoy *Radio Romances*. Today's story comes from Sophie, who describes herself as a work-at-home mother.

Sophie used to work in a big law firm in London. She had friends, she had a job she liked, she was happy, but there was one thing missing in her life – she wanted to fall in love. She used to dream about meeting the perfect man. But at the same time, she used to believe that 'love at first sight' only happened in films. Until …

Sophie still remembers the first time she saw him on the platform. She was waiting for her usual train to work. She recognised lots of the regular passengers, but this time there was a new face. A tall, good-looking guy in his twenties. That was the beginning of Sophie's love story with the stranger she decided to call 'Train Man'.

In the mornings, on the train, she used to sit where she could see him. Soon all her friends at work knew about him and every day they would ask her: 'Did you see Train Man today?' And she'd smile back. There was only one problem: she had never spoken to him.

One day she came up with a plan. While he was walking past her, she dropped her ticket. Train Man picked it up and gave it to her. 'Thanks,' was all Sophie managed to whisper as he walked away.

Two months passed and nothing happened. Then Sophie decided she had to do something. One day she wrote him a note. It said: 'It's my birthday, and everyone should do something silly on their birthday. Would you like to go for a coffee sometime?' and included her email address. She walked by him as she was leaving the train, her hand shaking and gave him the note. Train Man looked confused. 'What's this?' he asked, but Sophie had already run away.

That evening Sophie got an email. It was from Rob. Train Man finally had a name. It was a lovely email but it mentioned that Rob had a girlfriend. The next day on the train, they smiled nervously at each other and that was all.

And so life went on, until a few months later when Sophie got the best email of her life. It was from Rob. He had split up with his girlfriend a few months before, and now that he'd got over her he had decided to write to Sophie. She couldn't believe it. He was asking her out! Three days later they went on their first date.

They started going out, and they fell in love. Some months later, on a train travelling across Australia on holiday, Rob asked Sophie to marry him. They got engaged and then they got married the following summer. A year later they decided to start a family. Today they have a daughter called Megan. And Sophie still calls Rob her 'Train Man'.

3 🔊1.35 This exercise is closely modelled on Listening Part 2 of the Cambridge English: First exam. Check/clarify: *proposed*. Ask students to predict the words or type of words that could go in each space before they listen a second time. Play the recording again while students complete the gaps. Check answers in open class. If necessary, play the recording a third time to clarify answers.

Answers

1 love/falling in love   2 platform
3 work friends/friends at work   4 note   5 email
6 girlfriend   7 few months   8 got engaged

VOCABULARY

Love and relationships

1 Books closed. As a lead-in, write the following phrases from the listening on the board in random order: *get engaged; split up; ask out; fall in love; first date; get married; start a family; meet someone*.

Ask students to work with a partner to order the phrases according to the typical chronology of a relationship. Listen to some of their ideas in open class. Remove the phrases from the board before asking students to open their books.

Books open. Students work with a partner to complete the phrases. During feedback, check understanding by eliciting meaning referring to the story of Sophie and Rob. You might also like to highlight dependent prepositions, e.g. *fall in love* **with** *someone*.

Answers

1 fall   2 split   3 get   4 get   5 ask   6 go   7 go
8 start   9 get

2 Students complete the exercise individually, then check answers in pairs before feedback in open class.

Answers

1 split up   2 got over   3 went on a date   4 going out
5 fell in love   6 got engaged   7 got married
8 start a family

Fast finishers

Ask students to close their books and write as many of the phrases from page 59 as they can remember. They can then open their books to check.

Optional extension

Make AB pairs. All Bs should close their books while As read phrases, at random, without the preposition for Bs to recall. For example:

A: *To fall in love beep someone*

B: *with*

3 SPEAKING In pairs, students tell the story of a famous couple. Get them to use as many phrasal verbs from Exercise 1 as they can. Once they've finished, nominate pairs or ask for volunteers to tell their story to the class. To give students a reason to listen, ask them to note down all of the phrasal verbs from Exercise 1 that they hear. The winning pair is the one who used the most phrasal verbs.

Workbook page 56

Student's Book pages 60–61

READING

1 A recording of this text is available with your digital resources.

If you have an IWB available in the classroom, this would best be done as a heads-up activity. Project the photos and ask students to discuss the two questions in pairs. Take some feedback in open class and write students' ideas on the board but don't give anything away at this stage.

Answers

1 They are throwing buckets of water over their heads.
2 They are probably doing it to raise money for charity.

2 Students quickly read the article to check their answers. The article contains some quite difficult language. Tell students not to worry if they don't understand every word but to just focus on checking their ideas. Refer them to the ideas on the board at this point. Allow them to compare answers with a partner before whole-class feedback.

Answers

'Cool' refers to both the popularity of the challenge and the icy water.

3 Give students time to read sentences 1–8 and underline key words. Check/clarify: *challenge, refused, donated*. Ask students to read the article again to

answer the questions. Encourage them to underline the parts of the text that give them their answers and correct any false statements. Students compare answers with a partner before whole-class feedback.

Answers

1 T   2 DS   3 F (You had to pay $10)   4 T   5 F (He refused to do the challenge. He gave $100 to charity)
6 F (They felt it put pressure on people)   7 F (only 10% of participants gave money to charity)   8 T

Optional extension

The article contains a variety of interesting vocabulary. Write the following phrases on the board.

1 weird; 2 swept across; 3 bright future; 4 cut short;
5 prove; 6 viewed; 7 put pressure on; 8 take part;
9 seen as being; 10 criticised

Ask students to find them in the article and work with a partner to work out their meaning from the context. Check answers in open class, giving further clarification where required.

SPEAKING

Put students into pairs or small groups to discuss the questions. Monitor and help as necessary, encouraging students to develop their answers. Make a note of any students with particularly interesting anecdotes and call on them to share them with the rest of the class during feedback.

GRAMMAR

Linkers of contrast

1 Draw attention to the words in bold and elicit/explain that they are used to join, or link, contrasting information. Divide the class into pairs for students to read the sentences and complete the rule. Monitor and help with any difficulties. During whole-class feedback, refer to sentences 1–6 and give further examples for clarification if required. Stress the importance of the position (beginning, middle or end of sentence) of the linker and the correct use of pronunciation.

Rule

1 in spite of   2 even though   3 nevertheless

LANGUAGE NOTE

In spite of and *despite* can be followed by a negative gerund, for example:
In spite of/Despite not having an umbrella, he walked home in the rain.

---

2 If you're short on time, do number 1 as an example in open class, then set the rest of the exercise for homework.

Students work individually to rewrite the sentences. Remind them to check the position of the linker and punctuation with the rule. Students check answers with a partner before whole-class feedback.

Answers

1 Despite studying hard for the test, I failed it.
2 He doesn't earn a lot of money. However, he gives a lot of it to charity.
3 Although I'd seen the film before, I still really enjoyed it.
4 In spite of starting to eat less, I didn't lose any weight. / I didn't lose any weight, in spite of starting to eat less.
5 It wasn't very warm. Nevertheless, we had a good time at the beach.
6 Even though I don't speak a word of Chinese, I understood what he said. / I understood what he said, even though I don't speak a word of Chinese.

Fast finishers

Ask students to rewrite the sentences using different linkers of contrast.

Optional extension

Divide the class into small groups. Write the following mixed-up sentences on the board one at a time. If you're using an IWB, write each word in a separate text box and drag and drop to order. Alternatively, you could dictate them. Ask students to race to be first to correctly order the words. Give a point for each correct answer.

1 a Despite managed the finish having she to finger race broken.
2 raining tennis at Even hard, we went though park it was to play the.
3 before met. had really Nevertheless on never, they They got well.
4 the was we Although meeting the late, arrived train at.
5 a friends doesn't big., he have family has He a lot However of.

Answers

1 Despite having a broken finger, she managed to finish the race.
2 Even though it was raining hard, we went to play tennis at the park.
3 They had never met before. Nevertheless, they got on really well.
4 Although the train was late, we arrived at the meeting.
5 He doesn't have a big family. However, he has a lot of friends.

---

3 Students work with a partner to do this.

Mixed-ability

Ask stronger students to complete the exercise without referring to the rule box. They can refer to Exercise 2 to remind them of the actual linkers.

Answers

Although I felt really tired, I stayed up till midnight to celebrate the new year. / I stayed up till midnight to celebrate the new year, although I felt really tired.
Even though I felt really tired, I stayed up till midnight to celebrate the new year. / I stayed up till midnight to celebrate the new year, even though I felt really tired.
I felt really tired. However, I stayed up till midnight to celebrate the new year.
Despite feeling really tired, I stayed up till midnight to celebrate the new year. / I stayed up till midnight to celebrate the new year, despite feeling really tired.
In spite of feeling really tired, I stayed up till midnight to celebrate the new year. / I stayed up till midnight to celebrate the new year, in spite of feeling really tired.
I felt really tired. Nevertheless, I stayed up till midnight to celebrate the new year.

Workbook page 55 and page 125

 Be aware of common errors related to linkers of contrast. Go to Get it right! on Student's Book page 124.

▓ THiNK VALUES ▓

Doing good

1 Divide the class into groups of four to complete this task. Monitor to help with vocabulary and ideas. As students are going to present their ideas to the class, you may like to ask them to consider using visual cues as part of their presentation. Depending on what's available in the classroom, you could ask them to produce a PowerPoint presentation.

2 **SPEAKING** Ask each group to decide who is going to present which part of their presentation and give them some time to practise. Groups take it in turns to present their ideas to the class. Ask students to think of one question to ask the group presenting. Allow time for questions after each presentation. Hold a class vote to decide on the best charity idea.

> **Optional extension**
>
> Before students vote on the best charity, ask them to work with their original group of four and discuss the other presentations. Ask them to discuss the positive and negative points of each charity idea and discuss ways they might have done things differently. When students vote, nominate individuals to give reasons for their choices.

Student's Book pages 62–63

LITERATURE

> **BACKGROUND INFORMATION**
>
> Stan Barstow (28 June 1928–1 August 2011) was an English novelist from Yorkshire in the North of England. His novels include *Ask Me Tomorrow* (1962) and *The Watchers on the Shore* (1966). **A Kind of Loving** (1960) was his most popular novel and was made into a film starring Alan Bates and June Ritchie. The story centres on a working-class man whose girlfriend has a baby. He is forced to marry her and change his lifestyle, learning the difference between the initial excitement of a relationship and the reality (and tedium) of everyday love.

1 Books closed. As a lead-in, task students with making a list of five romantic novels or films, in pairs or small groups. Encourage students to discuss the main plot points of each and to agree on a ranking of the five novels or films from best to worst. Nominate pairs to share their lists with the class during feedback.

Books open. If there is an IWB available in the classroom, this activity would best be done as a heads-up activity with the whole class. Check/ clarify: *attracted to, run into each other.* Draw students' attention to the photos and ask them to discuss the question with their partner. During feedback, note down students' ideas on the board.

2 🔊 1.36 Play the audio for students to listen and read to check their answer to Exercise 1. Tell them to concentrate on answering the question and not to worry about understanding every word. Allow students to check their answer with a partner before feedback in open class. Nominate individuals to give reasons for their answer. Check the answers on the IWB to see if anybody predicted correctly.

3 Ask students to read the questions and underline the key information they will need to read for. You could encourage students to try to answer the questions before reading again to check their answers. Let students compare answers with a partner before feedback in open class. During feedback, ask students to refer to the parts of the text that support their answers.

> **Answers**
>
> 1 She talks about the people who work at Whittaker's.
> 2 He's thinking about how to ask her out.
> 3 That he thinks the musical is good, and that he was thinking of seeing it that week.
> 4 Because he's excited that Ingrid has agreed to go to the musical with him.
> 5 Because he got there early.

4 **VOCABULARY** Students work individually to complete the exercise and then check their answers with a partner before feedback in open class.

> **Mixed-ability**
>
> Ask stronger students to look back at the extract and try and deduce meaning of the highlighted words using the context, without referring to the definitions in Exercise 4. Weaker students can match definitions and words directly.

> **Answers**
>
> 1 fib 2 That makes us quits 3 scandal 4 make it
> 5 draughtsman 6 whiff 7 tearing 8 chattering

5 **SPEAKING** In pairs or small groups, students discuss the questions. Monitor and encourage students to expand on their answers. Make a note of any nice expressions in English that students use during the activity and also of any repeated errors. At the end write your notes on the board praising students who produced nice expressions and eliciting corrections of any mistakes. Also during feedback, ask for volunteers to report back to the class on their discussion and encourage others in the class to react.

WRITING

An essay

1 To lead in to this activity, ask students: *When did you last write an essay? What was the topic?* Elicit answers in open class. Ask: *What do you need to do to write a very good essay?* Brainstorm ideas. You can then use students' answers to inform you as to their existing knowledge of essay writing and adapt your input accordingly. Students read the essay and answer the question. Let them compare their answers with a partner before checking in open class.

Answer

The author agrees.

2 Ask students to work with a partner to complete the exercise. Point out that in a well-structured piece of writing, each paragraph should have its own purpose, which is exactly why it is written as a separate paragraph. Check answers in open class.

Answers

1 D   2 B   3 C   4 A

3 Ask students to complete the sentences, and then check their answers in the essay. During feedback, elicit other linkers that could also fit into the sentences. If students find any of the linkers difficult, take the opportunity to go back to page 61 and review them.

Answers

1 However   2 As a consequence   3 Furthermore
4 As a result   5 Nevertheless   6 Therefore

4 If you're short on time, students can do the preparation in class and complete the writing at home. Alternatively, this could be done as a collaborative writing activity in class with pairs of students of a similar level working together.

Ask students to make a note of any vocabulary they could use in their essays and to include linkers of contrast. Remind them that they should leave their own opinion until the conclusion.

5 Students expand their notes into an essay.

On completion, you could ask students to swap their essays with a partner (or another pair where you opted for a collaborative writing approach) for them to read and give each other feedback on **content** (Is it interesting and engaging to read?) and **coherence** (Are linkers used? Are they used accurately? Have they followed the structure of the model answer?). Alternatively, you may prefer to collect their writing in for marking. When you mark their essays, check for the above points. The main focus should be on how successful you feel each piece is as an informative essay to read – not on particular grammar or lexical errors. Write short feedback for each student, saying first what you liked about each essay, and two or three things they may like to improve on in the future. Make a note of any persistent errors that occur in the class, then go over these points (and bring in extra practice for them) in a subsequent lesson.

Student's Book pages 64–65

■ THiNK EXAMS ■

READING AND USE OF ENGLISH

1 Part 7: Matching

Answers

1 C   2 B   3 D   4 A   5 B   6 A   7 C   8 D   9 C   10 A

Workbook page 61 ➤

TEST YOURSELF UNITS 5 & 6

VOCABULARY

1

Answers

1 split   2 going   3 confessed   4 introduced   5 zip
6 upgrade   7 back up   8 startled   9 complained
10 recommendation

GRAMMAR

2

Answers

1 even though   2 succeeded in   3 wasn't allowed to
4 nowhere near as   5 needn't have   6 been able

3

Answers

1 We ran as fast as we could, but we didn't manage **to** get there in time.
2 Despite ~~he earns~~ **earning** a good salary, Mario says he never has enough money.
3 Nicole's parents weren't as strict with her brother ~~than~~ **as** they were with her.
4 ~~Nevertheless~~ **Although/Even though** Barry's French isn't great, he understood a lot of the film.
5 It is very kind of you, but you don't need **to** pick me up at my house. I can walk to the restaurant.
6 James always does well in tests, ~~although never studying~~ **despite/in spite of never studying / although he never studies**.

FUNCTIONAL LANGUAGE

4

Answers

1 far and away, even   2 must, don't need to   3 let, have
4 easily, whole

7 ALWAYS LOOK ON THE BRIGHT SIDE

Objectives

FUNCTIONS	cheering someone up
GRAMMAR	ways of referring to the future (review); future continuous; future perfect
VOCABULARY	phrases to talk about the future: *about to, off to, on the point of*; feelings about future events

Student's Book pages 66–67

READING

1 Books closed. As a lead-in to the topic, ask students to work in pairs or small groups and make a list of blogs they have read, including the topic of each one. Elicit the names of a few blogs in open class and ask students: *Have you ever taken advice from a blog?*

If there is an interactive whiteboard (IWB) available in the classroom, this exercise would best be done as a heads-up activity. Focus attention on the pictures and ask students to discuss the questions in pairs. Monitor and encourage students to be as creative and open-minded as possible and to accept all of their classmates' ideas and interpretations equally. Nominate one or two pairs to share their ideas in open class. Have a quick show of hands to find out whether the majority thought that the pictures were mostly positive or negative, and invite comments.

2 **SPEAKING** Books open. Give students time to read the two statements before they begin their discussions in pairs. During feedback in open class, ask for volunteers to report on their discussions and to say who is more like them and why.

3 Check/clarify: *do for a living*. Ask students to read the blog and answer the questions. Set a three-minute time limit to encourage students to read quickly and not to focus on trying to understand every word. Allow students to compare answers with a partner before a whole-class check.

Answers

1 Jim 2 He owns a shop. 3 He's an optimist.

4 🔊 2.02 Check/clarify: *in a good mood, allergic, bullets*. Before reading, ask students to underline key words in the statements that they should look for in the text. Ask them to underline the part of the text which helped them decide and to compare their answers with a partner. Tell students that they should read the article carefully and check that the text matches the information in a sentence exactly before deciding if an answer is true. Ask

students to compare answers in pairs and to come to an agreement on their answers before checking in open class.

Answers

1 T
2 F The main reason the blogger writes the post is because she wants to change people's attitudes.
3 F The main character of the story is a man whose attitude to life was the same after he was attacked.
4 F The robber got into the shop intending to steal the money.
5 T
6 T
7 F The man made a joke and everyone found it funny.
8 T

5 **SPEAKING** Students discuss the questions in pairs or small groups. Encourage them to go into detail in their answers and refer to the blog to explain their opinions. Monitor to help with vocabulary, but do not interrupt to correct errors unless they impede communication. The aim here is to give students the opportunity to build their fluency.

▰▰ TRAIN TO THiNK ▰▰

Learning to see things from a different perspective

1 Books closed. To introduce this activity, draw a glass on the board with a line halfway up. Ask: *Is the glass half-full or half-empty?* Take a show of hands on this. Ask: *Does your answer to this question reflect your attitude to life in general?* Ask students to discuss the question in pairs and listen to some of their ideas in open class.

Books open. Give students time to read the two paragraphs. Students work in pairs to discuss what and who helped the people change their attitudes. Check answers in open class.

Answers

First speech bubble: A teacher helped them by telling them a useful saying.
Second speech bubble: Their best friend helped them by advising them to ignore the person making fun of them.

2 **SPEAKING** Give students some time to think of situations individually. Monitor and help with vocabulary and ideas, as necessary. Put students into pairs to discuss their ideas with a partner. Re-group students into small groups for students to report back on their discussions and share opinions.

Optional extension

Write the following situations on the board:

A young man in your street has bought a very expensive car.

Eaden passes exams easily and never seems to study.

George says: 'I'm not clever enough to go to university.'

Ask students to think of different ways people might react to the situations. What could be a positive reaction and what could be a negative reaction? For example: Positive: *What a lovely car – he must have worked really hard to get the money for that.* Negative: *He only has an expensive car to show other people how rich he is.*

It may help if students try to imagine the reactions of different members of their family. Would their reaction be different to their grandmother's, for example? After some individual thinking time, divide the class into small groups for students to compare and discuss. During feedback, ask: *What would you say to people to change negative perspectives?*

Student's Book pages 68–69

GRAMMAR

Ways of referring to the future (review)

1 At this level, students should have quite a good awareness of the four forms, so you could ask them to cover the rule box and divide the class into small groups for students to explain the uses of each one. Elicit some of their ideas in open class, but do not comment at this stage. Ask students to complete the rule. Did they manage to come up with all of the various uses for each form? Check answers in open class, referring to the example sentences and giving further examples for clarification, as necessary. Draw attention to the use of time expressions used in the sentences: *later today*; *two weeks from now*; *in five minutes*.

Rule

1 will   2 present simple   3 going to   4 will   5 going to
6 present continuous   7 present simple   8 will

Optional extension

Ask students to write two true and two false sentences about themselves using each of the tenses. In pairs, students read out their sentences for their partners to guess which are true. Students should take turns to quiz each other in order to work out which are the two false sentences before revealing them.

2 If you're short on time, set this exercise for homework. Consider doing number 1 in open class as an example. Students work individually to complete sentences 1–8. Allow them to compare answers with a partner before feedback in open class. Where more than one answer is possible, ask students to explain any subtle differences in meaning.

Mixed-ability

Weaker students could do this exercise in pairs.

Answers

1 arrives/is arriving/will arrive
2 are going to spill/will spill
3 will, rain
4 are seeing/are going to see
5 starts/is starting/is going to start
6 go
7 am going to buy/am buying/will buy
8 is/is going to be/will be

Fast finishers

As students tend to have more difficulty with present simple/continuous as future forms, ask them to write sentences showing the difference between the forms, e.g. *I'm playing football tomorrow. The game starts at 10.30.*

Optional extension

Do a teacher-student role play. Ask students to write sentences containing mistakes with future forms. Students pass their sentences to a partner. The partner has to act as the teacher, explain the problems wth the sentences and elicit the correct answer from the student.

Workbook page 64 and page 125

VOCABULARY

Phrases to talk about the future: *about to*, *off to*, *on the point of*

1 In pairs, students match sentences 1–3 to their uses. Check answers.

Answers

1 b   2 a   3 b

Look!

Refer to the Look! box to clarify the forms of the phrases. To check understanding, ask students to write a sentence about their future; one for each of the phrases. Monitor to check the phrases are being used correctly. Make a note of any repeated errors. Write them on the board and elicit corrections in open class.

LANGUAGE NOTE

Clarify that *about to* and *on the point of* are often used to describe actions in the near future, but these may not be very immediate; it all depends on context. For example:

We're about to buy a new house. (in the next few days or weeks)

They are on the point of splitting up. (It's going to happen soon.)

2 If you're short on time, set this exercise for homework.

Give students time to read sentences 1–6 and check understanding. Ask them to put their pens/pencils down before they start reading to dissuade them from answering straight away. Go through the first sentence in open class as an example. Once they've completed the exercise, ask students to compare answers with a partner before whole-class feedback.

Answers

1 about to 2 off to 3 about to 4 about to 5 off to
6 on the point of

Fast finishers

Ask students to write three sentences which are true for them using *about to*, *off to* and *on the point of*.

Workbook page 66

LISTENING

1 🔊2.03 Books closed. As a lead-in, ask students: *Which quiz shows have you watched on TV or listened to on the radio? What are the rules?* Students discuss the questions with a partner. To make the second question more challenging, ask them to imagine they are explaining the rules to a person who has never seen the show. Elicit a few examples of rules in open class as feedback and see if others in the class can guess the show.

Books open. Ask students to read question 1 before you play the audio. You could ask them to discuss possible meanings of the phrase (question 2) before they listen and check.

Allow them to compare answers with a partner before open-class feedback.

Answer

1 cloud

Audio Script Track 2.03

Presenter Hello and welcome to *Silver Linings*, the show where our guests try and find a little bit of good in everything. Well, we all know the expression: 'Every cloud has a silver lining' and that's exactly what my special guests Dan and Anna are here to do: find the silver lining. I'm going to give them some potentially disastrous situations and they're going to tell me why in fact it's actually a really good thing. A point goes to whoever gives the most imaginative answer. Dan, Anna, all clear? Great. So let's play Silver Linings. So Dan and Anna, round one. It's Monday morning, you arrive at school and the sports teacher tells you you've been dropped from the school football team.

Dan So the teacher is telling me I'm not good enough.

Presenter Exactly.

Dan Well that's easy. This is actually a really good thing because I've always wanted to learn to play basketball. So I'll do that now … and one day the teacher will regret it, and come back and ask me if I want to join the football team again … well, by then, I'll have become a big basketball star. I'll say: 'I'm so sorry, all I'm interested in is basketball these days …'

Presenter So, Anna. What about you? What would your silver lining be?

Anna OK, so this is on a Monday morning?

Presenter Yes.

Anna So tomorrow is Tuesday.

Presenter Er, yes. Very good.

Anna Well, on Tuesday afternoon my friends will be playing football. But I'll be sitting in the new ice cream shop near school, enjoying a delicious ice cream – strawberry, vanilla and chocolate. That's my silver lining.

Presenter OK, so now over to the audience. If you think Dan's answer is best, press the green button. If you think Anna should get the point, press the red button. And … the winner is Anna. Well done, Anna – one point for you. OK, round two. You and your family are off to Italy on a skiing holiday, but at the airport you find that your flight has been delayed for six hours because of bad weather. Six hours at Heathrow airport. What can possibly be good about that? Anna?

Ann Well, I don't want to sound like a stereotype of every girl but … but, erm … all those shops at big airports … I think I could easily spend six hours looking at things …

Presenter So while your parents try to entertain your little brother, you'll be walking around the shops?

Anna Yes, that's about it.

Presenter Poor parents! OK, Dan. What's your silver lining?

Dan Well this one's really quite easy, isn't it?

Presenter Is it?

Dan Yes. It's logical. Think about it. The plane is delayed because of bad weather. OK so I'm going to have this bad weather in Italy in the form of snow. Can I do that?

Presenter You can do whatever you want.

Dan OK. Snow in Italy. And I'm going on a skiing holiday. I'll just relax with a good book knowing that by the time the plane leaves London a lot of snow will have fallen on our ski resort in Italy. And I'll be happy knowing that in a couple of days we'll be skiing in perfect snow on a perfect Italian mountain.

Presenter Well, of course.

Dan Anna will still be shopping in Heathrow and she'll have missed her flight.

Presenter OK, audience, again please. Red for Anna, green for Dan. 3, 2, 1 and … It's Anna again. Dan, you have some catching up to do.

2 🔊2.03 Students may like to work in pairs and try to answer the questions from memory before listening to the audio again to check and complete their answers. After you've played the audio a second time, give students time to review and expand their notes before comparing with a partner. Check answers in open class.

Answers

Round 1:
Dan says it's a good thing because he's always wanted to play basketball and he'll become a big basketball star.
Anna says that instead of playing football she'll be eating a delicious ice cream at the ice cream shop near school.
Round 2:
Dan says that he can just relax with a good book and that it means that there'll be lots of snow to ski on when they get there.
Anna says she can spend the time shopping.

3 SPEAKING Divide the class into pairs for students to compare notes and decide who should get the points in each situation. Listen to some of their ideas in open class, insisting on students giving reasons for their answers.

GRAMMAR

Future continuous

1 Put students into pairs to complete the rule. Check answers in open class. Use the examples in Exercise 1 and a timeline like the one below to clarify the rule.

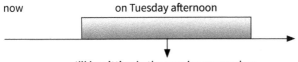

now   on Tuesday afternoon

I'll **be sitting** in the new ice cream shop.

| **Rule**

1 around   2 be   3 *-ing*

2 Before filling the gaps, ask students to quickly read the dialogue to answer the questions: *Is Jessie going to have a busy weekend? Why?* (Yes. She is going to London with her father.) This will ensure students have a gist understanding of the dialogue before they start focusing on form. Students work individually to complete the dialogues. Let them compare answers with a partner before checking in open class. During feedback, explain/elicit that we use the future continuous to talk about an action happening around a specific future time and the future simple to describe one particular action which takes place in the future. Check that students are contracting *will* to *'ll* and that they are placing the main stress on the principal verb rather than equally stressing all three words.

| **Answers**

1 will be sitting   2 will be walking   3 will phone
4 will be watching   5 will come   6 will be thinking
7 will put

Future perfect

3 Get students to complete the rule in pairs. During whole-class feedback, use the example sentences to clarify. Again use a timeline like the one below to show the difference between the future perfect and future continuous.

now   by the time we leave London

a lot of snow **will have fallen** in Italy

To check understanding at this point, elicit a few more examples of sentences with the future perfect and future continuous. Write some sentence stems on the board to get students started. For example:
By this next time next week ...,
At 7 o'clock tomorrow morning ... etc.

| **Rule**

1 will   2 have   3 past participle

4 If you're short on time, set this exercise for homework but perhaps do number 1 in open class. Students complete the exercise individually and check their answers with a partner before open-class

feedback. During feedback, ask students to explain why they chose their answers and why another form is not a possible answer in each case.

| **Answers**

1 have finished   2 have found   3 be sleeping
4 be flying   5 have spent   6 be teaching
7 have watched   8 be touring

> **Optional extension**
> Divide the class into pairs. Students take it in turns to say a time on a particular day. Their partner has to say what they will be doing at that time and what they will have done previously. For example:
> A: *8 o'clock on Monday morning.*
> B: *I will have had a shower and got dressed. I will be eating my breakfast.*

Workbook page 65 and page 125

 Be aware of common errors related to the future continuous. Go to Get it right! on Student's Book page 125.

SPEAKING

1 Write *Silver Linings* on the board. Divide the class into four groups (A, B, C and D). You might like to pair students within their groups (AA, BB, CC, etc.) for this preparation stage. Ask students to read the situation that corresponds to their letter and to discuss and make notes on their optimistic solutions. Point out that students should try to use the future perfect and continuous in their answers, where possible.

2 Form ABCD groups to play the game. Monitor and make a note of any future tenses being used correctly to highlight and praise during feedback. Also note down any examples where a future tense could have been used but wasn't for students to transform during feedback. Before focusing on future forms, ask students with the highest scores to give examples of their solutions.

Student's Book pages 70–71

READING

> **BACKGROUND INFORMATION**
> If students have access to the Internet in the classroom, you may like to divide the class into three groups and ask each group to research one of the three famous people quoted in the article. When they have made notes on their findings, regroup into groups of three for students to share information.
> **Charlie Chaplin** (16 April 1889–25 December 1977) was an English comic actor and director. His most famous films were *The Kid* (1921) in which he played his best-known character The Tramp, *Modern Times* (1936) and *The Great Dictator* (1940). Another famous quote from Chaplin is 'A day without laughter is a day wasted.'

Mahatma Gandhi (2 October 1869–30 January 1948) was the leader of the Indian Independence Movement from 1921 until India became independent from Great Britain in August 1947. He was a great advocator of non-violent revolution. He is widely described in India as the father of the nation. Another famous quote from Gandhi is 'Live as if you were to die tomorrow; learn as if you were to live forever.'

Winston Churchill (30 November 1874–24 January 1965) was a British politician. He was Prime Minister of the United Kingdom from 1940 to 1945 and from 1950 to 1955. His speeches inspired the United Kingdom to victory in the Second World War. He was named the Greatest Briton of all time in a 2002 poll. Another famous quote from Churchill is 'If you're going through hell, keep going.'

1 A recording of this text is available with your digital resources.

As a lead-in, show photos of worried-looking people of varying ages. Divide the class into pairs and ask: *Why do you think the people look worried?* Encourage students to use future forms in their answers where possible. Students discuss the question in pairs. Listen to some of their ideas in open class.

Students read the website and answer the questions. To encourage them to read quickly, set a three-minute time limit for the exercise. Students check answers with a partner before whole-class feedback.

> **Answers**
>
> It's for people who worry. The worries mentioned are about a decision to take a trip and being good enough to play drums in a band.

2 Students read the website page again to match each of the worries (A–B) with one of the answers 1–3. Before they read, check/clarify *inspirational, hang out with, audition.* Ask students to underline the parts of the text that helped them decide on their answers. Allow students to compare answers in pairs before checking in open class.

> **Answers**
>
> 1 – 2 B 3 A

3 Ask students to read the questions and then re-read the text to find the answers. Check answers in open class.

> **Answers**
>
> 1 The writer used to be a worrier too.
> 2 The writer can see the positive in their situations.
> 3 Worrier A is less pessimistic, seeing both positive and negative sides of the situation.
> 4 The Charlie Chaplin quote.

4 SPEAKING Give students time to read the questions. Clarify any difficult vocabulary. Divide the class into small groups for students to discuss the questions. Ask each group to appoint a secretary to note down their answers. When students have completed the exercise, you regroup students and ask them to repeat the exercise with new partners. As well as maximising speaking practice, this is often motivating for students as they are able to express themselves more fully on the second attempt. Ask individuals to report back to the class on their discussions.

VOCABULARY

Feelings about future events

1 To introduce this section and give students an example, elicit typical situations that make students worried.

Ask students to make a list in pairs. Monitor and help with vocabulary as required. To extend the discussion, ask students to rank their situations from most to least worrying. Regroup students and ask them to compare lists with different partners. Ask: *Which three situations would worry you most?* Listen to some examples in open class.

2 Ask students to read the extracts and decide which event each one refers to. Set a one-minute time limit to encourage students to read quickly and to focus on overall meaning rather than specific vocabulary. Allow students to compare answers with a partner before open-class feedback.

> **Answers**
>
> A a football or rugby match   B going back to college/university as a mature student   C an exam   D a visit to the dentist

3 Students complete the exercise in pairs. Allow them to use dictionaries if necessary. While students are working, re-create the two columns on the board for use during feedback. Check answers in open class, writing answers in the two columns. Ask students to copy the lists into their notebooks.

> **Answers**
>
> **expressing optimism:**
>
> I'm really looking forward to   I feel quite positive
> I've got a really good feeling about
>
> **expressing pessimism / worry:**
>
> I'm ... dreading   I'm feeling quite apprehensive
> I'm also a bit unsure   I just don't know where to start
> It's a nightmare – I'm really worried
> I'm getting so worked up   I've just got a bad feeling about

> **Optional extension**
>
> Ask stronger students to discuss which of the expressions are more or less optimistic.

4 Refer students back to the lists they created in Exercise 1 and ask them to complete the exercise in pairs. You may like to ask students to write answers so that you can monitor and check they are being used correctly.

> **Optional extension**
>
> To help students memorise the expressions, put students into pairs. Students take turns to close their books while their partner says the expressions for them to decide if they express optimism or pessimism.

Workbook page 66

FUNCTIONS

Cheering someone up

1 **2.04** As a lead-in, ask for volunteers to talk about one of their worries from Vocabulary Exercise 4. Encourage the other students to cheer them up and tell them not to worry. Write any interesting vocabulary on the board and try to elicit some of the expressions from the exercise.

Give students time to read sentences 1–5 and complete them with the words from the list. Play the audio for students to listen and check their answers. Allow them to compare answers with a partner before feedback in open class. Write answers on the board and ensure students are clear on what the full expressions are: *Cheer up! Things will seem better after/when …; Hang in there; Don't let it get you down; It's not the end of the world; Look on the bright side; There is light at the end of the tunnel.* Say each expression for students to repeat and check pronunciation. Ask them to cover the expressions to discourage them from reading and to ensure they repeat with feeling.

> **Answers**
>
> 1 Cheer   2 Hang   3 down   4 bright   5 light

2 Ask students to complete the exercise in pairs. Encourage them to give reasons for their answers rather than just using an expression to cheer them up. Listen to some of their ideas in open class.

PRONUNCIATION

For practice of appropriate intonation when encouraging someone, go to Student's Book page 121.

◼ THiNK SELF-ESTEEM ◼

What cheers me up

1 Ask students to think of two more things that cheer them up. Give an example of your own to get them started. If students mention a song or humorous video and you have access to digital technology in the classroom, make a note and choose some to show in the next lesson.

2 Students make notes on the reason why the things cheer them up. Monitor and help with vocabulary as necessary.

3 **SPEAKING** Divide the class into pairs or small groups for students to discuss. Monitor, but avoid error correction unless errors really hinder comprehension. The focus of this task is on fluency, not on practice of structures or lexis. Make a note of any nice expressions in English that students use during the activity and write them on the board at the end of the exercise for the whole class to copy. Praise the students who used the expressions, as giving positive feedback will encourage students to be more adventurous in similar communication tasks.

> **Optional extension**
>
> Ask students to refer back to the events they wrote down in Vocabulary Exercise 1 and ask: *Which of the events are you likely to face soon? Think about how you feel about each one and make notes.*
>
> As students make notes, monitor and help with vocabulary. Ask students to work in pairs or small groups and discuss their future events together, offering encouragement where they can. Students could suggest some of the things in Functions Exercise 1 when recommending ways to cheer each other up. For example:
>
> A: *I've got an important exam on Friday. I've got a bad feeling about it.*
>
> B: *It's normal to feel apprehensive when you've got an exam, but don't let it get you down. I'm sure you'll be fine. Why don't you go and buy some chocolate, that always cheers me up!*

WRITING

A short story

The planning for this exercise can be done in class and the writing set for homework.

Tell students they are going to write a story which finishes with the words *Every cloud has a silver lining.* Elicit the meaning in open class as a reminder. You could tell them a story of your own as an example.

Give students a short while to work individually to come up with an idea and make notes. Divide the class into pairs for students to take turns to tell their stories, expanding on the notes they made. When students have told their stories, ask them to give each other feedback. They should say how it could be made more interesting and point out any important elements that should be included. Give students time to revise their notes accordingly.

Ask students to write the story. If time allows, suggest they write a first draft, then exchange stories with a partner for students to read each other's stories and make comments and suggestions. Tell them not to correct every error, but to look for the following:

What further information would you like?
In what ways could vocabulary be improved?
What punctuation and spelling mistakes are there?

Finally, ask students to write a second draft incorporating their partner's suggestions and comments. Ask students to work in small groups and read each other's stories.

Student's Book pages 72–73

PHOTOSTORY: episode 3

The competition

1 If you're using an IWB, project the photos onto the board and ask students to close their books. Get students to try to recall what happened in previous episodes of the photostory. Next, ask them to guess answers to the questions, based on the photos. Write some of their ideas on the board.

2 🔊 2.07 Play the audio for students to listen as they read, and check their answers from Exercise 1. During whole-class feedback, refer to students' ideas on the board. Ask: *Who guessed correctly?*

> **Answers**
>
> 1 He wants to win a photo competition.
> 2 She thinks it's a bad idea.

DEVELOPING SPEAKING

3 Ask students: *What do you think happens next?* Ask them to brainstorm possible endings for the story. Students work in groups, with one student in each group acting as secretary and taking notes. During whole-class feedback, write students' ideas on the board to refer back to once they have watched the video. Don't give away answers at this stage.

4 📹 EP3 Play the video for students to watch and check their answers. During whole-class feedback, refer to students' ideas on the board. Ask: *Who guessed correctly?*

5 Give students time to read the statements. Students complete the exercise in pairs. Play the video again, pausing as required for clarification, for students to check their answers.

Check answers with the whole class. Ask students to correct any false statements.

> **Answers**
>
> 1 T   2 T   3 T   4 F   5 T   6 F

PHRASES FOR FLUENCY

1 Ask students to locate expressions 1–6 in the story on page 72 and underline them. To encourage speed-reading, you could do this as a race and ask students to find the expressions as quickly as possible. Ask students to compare their answers with a partner before feedback in open class.

> **Answers**
>
> 1 Liam   2 Emma   3 Justin   4 Emma   5 Emma
> 6 Nicole

2 Students work with a partner to complete the exercise. Check answers. Say each of the phrases for students to repeat and check pronunciation.

> **Answers**
>
> a 5   b 4   c 3   d 6   e 2   f 1

3 Ask students to complete the dialogues. Go through number 1 with them in open class as an example, if necessary. During feedback, say the sentences for students to repeat.

> **Answers**
>
> 1 for a start; Fair enough   2 go for it; get your hopes up
> 3 make a fool of myself; Anyway

> **Optional extension**
>
> Disappearing sentences: you'll need to write out the dialogues on the board or IWB for this one. Make AB pairs so that half of the class are A and half are B. Students practise the conversations from Exercise 3 in their pairs. Cover a small section of the dialogues, beginning from the right-hand side of the screen or board. Students repeat the dialogues in their same AB pairings trying to remember the whole thing, including the parts they can no longer see. Cover more and more of the dialogue, with students practising at each stage, until eventually nothing is left on the board. Ask for volunteers to perform for the class or have all As and all Bs perform in unison. This activity involving lots of repetition is a fun way for students to memorise useful chunks.

WordWise

Expressions with *so*

1 Books closed. As a lead-in, write *so* on the board and ask students to give different examples of its use in open class. Write any correct examples on the board.

Books open. Ask students to work with a partner and complete the exercise.

During whole-class feedback, elicit or explain the meaning of the five phrases and give further examples as necessary to clarify meaning.

> **Answers**
>
> 1 I told you so   2 So   3 I'm afraid so   4 I guess so
> 5 or so   6 so far

2 Students work individually to complete the sentences. Encourage them to refer to the sentences in Exercise 1 to help them choose the correct phrase. Students compare answers with a partner before whole-class feedback. During feedback, work on pronunciation and intonation of the sentences. Finally, ask students to work in pairs and practise the dialogues. You could adopt the 'disappearing sentences' approach here if you didn't do it earlier.

> **Answers**
>
> 1 So   2 I'm afraid so   3 or so   4 so far   5 I guess so
> 6 I told you so

Workbook page 66 ➤

8 MAKING LISTS

Objectives

FUNCTIONS	saying 'Yes' and adding conditions
GRAMMAR	conditionals (review); mixed conditionals
VOCABULARY	phrasal verbs (2); alternatives to *if*: *suppose*, *provided*, *as long as*, *otherwise*, *unless*

Student's Book pages 74–75

READING

1 SPEAKING Books closed. As a lead-in, ask students: *How do you organise your revision before exams? How do you make sure you don't forget to do any homework? What can you do to be more organised?* Give students time to discuss the questions in pairs or small groups. Invite students to report back to the class on their discussions in open class.

Books open. If there is an interactive whiteboard (IWB) available in the classroom, this activity would best be done as a heads-up activity. Focus on the photos. Ask students to work with a partner and note down their answers. Regroup students into small groups to compare ideas and expand on their notes. You may like to suggest that students use this as an opportunity to review and practise comparative forms.

2 Tell students they are going to read a book review. To encourage them to read the text quickly, give them three minutes to read the review to find the answer.

Answer

A checklist

3 2.08 Ask students to read the paragraph titles. Play the audio while students re-read the review and match the titles to the paragraphs. Ask them to underline the parts of the text that helped them choose their answers. Allow them to compare answers with a partner before whole-class feedback.

Answers

A 2   B 3   C extra title   D 1   E 4   F 5

4 Give students time to read the questions. Encourage them to underline the key information in the questions that they will be looking for in the text. Students then read the text in more detail to find the answers. Suggest that they underline the parts of the text that support their answers. Students compare answers with a partner before whole-class feedback. Ask individuals to refer to the parts of the text that support their answers at this stage.

Answers

1 The fact that no one was wearing a mask.
2 There were almost no infections over 27 months and it was estimated that around eight lives were saved.
3 A plane could crash; a skyscraper could fall down.
4 A lot of them weren't very enthusiastic because they thought it would be too difficult to use.
5 Because it's relevant for all people to avoid making mistakes.

5 SPEAKING Divide the class into pairs or small groups, roughly according to ability, to discuss the questions. Monitor but do not interrupt unless errors hinder comprehension. Make sure all students are speaking and encourage quieter students to give their opinions too. Nominate one or two students to report back to the class on their discussions.

TRAIN TO THINK

The 'goal setting' checklist

1 Ask: *What goals have you set yourself in the last year? Have your parents ever set goals for you? What goals have they set? Why is it important to set goals?* Students discuss the questions with a partner. Invite volunteers to report back to the class on their discussions and encourage reactions from the rest of the class.

Give students time to read through the ideas (a–h) and the checklist. Check/clarify: *approach*, *discipline*. Ask students to work individually to complete the exercise. Ask students to compare their answers in pairs, prompting them to justify their opinions and challenge each other's answers. Check answers in open class.

Answers

1 d   2 f,h   3 b,g   4 e   5 a,c,e

2 SPEAKING Working individually, students think of something they want to achieve. Perhaps elicit one or two ideas in open class to get them started. You could also give students time to work in pairs to brainstorm possible goals. Once they have something in mind, students make notes on points 1–5 in the checklist in order to define their goals. Monitor to help with vocabulary and ideas. As you monitor, make a note of some interesting checklists to come back to during feedback. Allow students to compare ideas in small groups and encourage them to give each other ideas on how to improve their checklist, for example, do they need to be more specific?

Student's Book pages 76–77

GRAMMAR

Conditionals (review)

1 Students complete the sentences individually and then look back at the book review on page 75 to check. Ask students to read through the table and work with a partner to complete it, using the sentences in Exercise 1 to help them.

It may be helpful to copy the table onto the board and to ask students to come out and complete it with their answers. During feedback, ask concept-check questions to help clarify meaning and usage of each type of conditional e.g. *What does sentence 1 refer to: the past, present, future? Or does it refer to an imaginary situation? Does sentence 2 refer to the past or present? Were they wearing masks?*

Answers

1 run, will be   2 had worn, wouldn't have been
3 use, don't … use   4 had, 'd want

Rule

1 present simple   2 1
3 present simple   4 future simple
5 4   6 past simple
7 2   8 *would(n't) have* + past participle

2 Do number 1 in open class as an example. Students work with a partner to complete the exercise. During feedback, refer to the rule in Exercise 1. Say sentences 1–4 for students to repeat. Check pronunciation and intonation.

Answers

1 b   2 d   3 c   4 a

3 If you're short on time, set this exercise for homework but go through the example in class, as necessary. Remind students to refer to the rule while they complete the exercise. Allow students to compare answers with a partner before whole-class feedback.

Answers

1 If you read books, you learn things about life.
2 You'll discover interesting things about pilots and doctors if you read it.
3 If Gawande wasn't a doctor, he wouldn't understand so much about this.
4 I wouldn't have found out about the importance of checklists if I hadn't read it.

Workbook page 72 and page 125

 Be aware of common errors related to the use of *would* in conditional sentences. Go to Get it right! on Student's Book page 125.

VOCABULARY

Phrasal verbs (2)

1 Ask students to read the sentences and work with a partner to try to complete them. Ask students to look back at the text to check their answers. This stage could be done as a class competition with students racing to be the first to find all eight phrasal verbs in the book review. Check answers in open class.

Answers

1 came down with   2 turned out   3 run through
4 carried out   5 points out   6 comes up with
7 look into   8 work out

2 SPEAKING Put students into pairs to discuss the meaning of the phrasal verbs. Encourage them to brainstorm other situations in which the verbs could be used. Monitor to get a sense of how well students understand their meaning. Nominate students to share their definitions in open class. Clarify/check understanding as necessary.

3 Give students time to read the sentences. Students work with a partner to complete the exercise. During whole-class feedback, ask: *What is different about the verbs work out and point out?* Elicit/point out that all the phrasal verbs are inseparable apart from *work out* and *point out*.

Answers

1 looking into   2 came down with   3 work out
4 carried out   5 point out   6 run through   7 turned out
8 come up with

Fast finishers

Ask students to look back at reading exercises in previous units in the book and find more examples of phrasal verbs. Get them to use the context of the reading to work out the meaning of the verbs. They can use a dictionary to check.

Optional extension

Divide the class into two groups. One group calls out a phrasal verb and the other group has 30 seconds to use it correctly in a sentence. In large classes, form four groups (ABCD) with A and B competing with each other, and C and D competing.

Workbook page 74

LISTENING

Why do we make lists?

1 SPEAKING Books closed. As a lead-in, write a list on the board outlining what you are going to do/have done in the lesson today. Ask: *Do you think this is a useful list? Who for? Why?* Students discuss in pairs or small groups. Listen to some of their ideas in open class. Ask: *Would you like me to write up a list like this at the beginning of every lesson?*

Books open. If there is an IWB available in the classroom, this activity would best be done as a heads-up activity. Focus on the lists. Ask students to discuss the questions in pairs. Regroup students into small groups to compare ideas. Nominate students to report back on their group's discussion in open class and note their answers on the board to refer to during feedback on Exercise 2.

2 2.09 Tell students they are going to listen to an interview with a social psychologist. Ask them to listen for which of the ideas on the board are mentioned.

Allow them to compare answers with a partner before feedback in open class.

Answer

People write lists for the following reasons: to organise information, to remember things, to focus their mind, to reduce stress by making them feel they're in control, to make them feel good about themselves

Audio Script Track 2.09

Brian The world is full of lists! Every time I turn on the TV there's a programme like 'the 50 best horror films of all time' or '100 great football moments'. The Internet is full of 'top ten' this and 'top ten' that sites. My guest today is Katy Spencer, a social psychologist. Katy, why are we so crazy about lists?

Katy Hi, Brian, and yes, you're right. List-making has become incredibly popular and you know, it's not a bad thing, because there are a number of reasons why making lists can be good for us. If I were more organised, I would have made a list of them, I suppose. But I'm not organised, so I haven't. But seriously, I can tell you, there are really five reasons. One reason why lists are so popular these days is because we're surrounded by new information all the time, lots of it. People make lists to try and organise this information. But I think the most obvious reason we make lists is to help us remember things. I don't know about you but I often find myself standing in the supermarket, and I'm thinking 'If I had made a list then I would know what to buy.'

Brian I know exactly what you mean. OK, so lists help our memory. What else?

Katy Well, lists are also a really good way of focusing our minds. For example, imagine you're planning a party. When you write down all the things you need to do, you're making sure that you won't forget anything essential.

Brian Oh, right.

Katy And here's another good thing. Making this kind of list can really help reduce stress.

Brian How exactly?

Katy Well let's take my party list as our example. Organising something like a party is often really quite stressful. Have I got enough food and drink? Where's everyone going to sit? What kind of music should I play?

Brian Absolutely.

Katy Well, when you sit down and make the list, it immediately relaxes you, because it gives you the feeling that now you've got some kind of control over things. Maybe you haven't got any control at all, but you feel like you have! The list shows you what needs to be done and now you can concentrate on doing it.

Brian Right! But what about those people who make lists like, all the airports in the world they've been to, or their 20 favourite songs?

Katy They're what I call 'me' lists, they're all about the person writing them. And I think people write them because it makes them feel good about themselves. They can see what they've done in their lives. They feel good because they've done things, been places, that sort of thing.

Brian So, making lists to help you feel important? Interesting … but I don't think anyone sensible does that, do they?

Katy Don't say that. I've made loads of lists like that!

Brian Oh, sorry! Anyway, Katy, thanks for coming in this morning. That was really interesting and you're now in my list of 'top five people I've interviewed'!

3 ◀)2.09 Students may like to work in pairs and try to answer the questions from memory before listening to the audio again. Where they can't remember, they can note down types of word appropriate to each space. Play the audio again for students to check and complete their answers. Allow them to compare answers with a partner before checking in open class.

> **Answers**
>
> 1 organise   2 memory   3 focus   4 stress   5 feel good

4 SPEAKING You may like to match the first list as a group, to clarify the exercise. Students work in pairs or small groups to discuss which list(s) corresponds to which reason(s). Nominate individuals to describe one of the lists as feedback.

> **Possible answers**
>
> The world's top five capital cities: to organise information
> The shopping list: to aid your memory, focus your mind
> Top five action films: to organise information
> Party list: to aid your memory, to reduce stress

5 SPEAKING Before starting the discussion, give students some time to work individually and think about their answers to the questions before they discuss in pairs. Monitor and encourage students to go into detail and give reasons for their answers. Avoid error correction unless errors really hinder comprehension. The focus of this task is on fluency, not on practice of structures or lexis. Listen to some of their ideas in open class.

GRAMMAR

Mixed conditionals

1 ◀)2.10 Ask students to complete the sentences with the words or phrases in the list. Let them compare answers with a partner before playing the audio to check answers.

> **Answers**
>
> 1 were, would have   2 had, would

2 Give students time to read the instructions and the rule. Students work in pairs to complete the rule. Check answers. Give further examples for clarification, as necessary. Remind students that it is possible to start conditional sentences with the *would* clause.

> **Rule**
>
> 1 2   2 1

3 If you're short on time, set this exercise for homework. Ask students to work individually to write sentences to describe situations 1–5. Get them to check in pairs prior to a whole-class check.

> **Answers**
>
> 1 If Anna and Dan hadn't had a big argument, they would be talking to each other.
> 2 If we'd left early, we wouldn't be late now.
> 3 If I had a good memory, I wouldn't have forgotten her birthday.
> 4 If I had eaten breakfast, I wouldn't be hungry now.
> 5 If he'd paid attention, he'd be able to do the homework.

> **Fast finishers**
>
> Ask students to write alternative *would* clauses for sentences 1–5.

4 Give an example of your own or elicit possible answers to number 1 in open class, to get students started. Divide the class into mixed-ability pairs. Adapt the time-limit according to the level of your class. To vary the pace and encourage an element of competition, tell students they should write as many sentences as possible in the time available. When the time is up, find out who has written the most sentences and ask the winning pair to share their sentences with the class.

Workbook page 73 and page 125 ▶

PRONUNCIATION

For pronunciation practice of weak forms with conditionals go to Student's Book page 121.

Student's Book pages 78–79

READING

1 SPEAKING A recording of this text is available with your digital resources.

Books closed. As a lead-in, elicit the names of ten school subjects studied by your students and write them on the board. Divide the class into pairs for students to agree on a ranking of their lists from most to least interesting, useful or difficult. You could start them off by tasking them to rank them by 'most interesting' and then assign 'most useful' and/or 'most difficult' to any fast finishers.

Books open. Students work with a partner to discuss the question. Ask students to make notes on any lists they've seen. Nominate one or two students to share their ideas with the class.

2 Set a three-minute time limit to encourage students to read the blog quickly for this initial reading-for-gist task. Allow students to compare answers with a partner before feedback in open class.

> **Answers**
>
> 1 Because no one sent him a list.
> 2 In the blog archive.
> 3 He wants them to send him lists.

3 Give students time to read the sentences. Check/clarify: *rub, warthog*. Point out that students need to decide which of the top ten lists the sentences *might* be found in. Students read the blog more carefully in order to complete this exercise. Ask them to compare answers in pairs before a whole-class check.

Answers

a 9   b 2   c 1   d 4   e 3

4 SPEAKING Ask students to work individually to decide which five lists they would like to read in full, and why, before they begin discussing in pairs. Listen to some of their choices in open class and have a show of hands to find out which lists were most popular.

> **Optional extension**
>
> If students have access to the Internet, ask them to do a search for one of the lists, in pairs. Give students time to make notes on the information they find. Put pairs together to make groups of four to share the most interesting information they found.

5 SPEAKING Students work in pairs to choose a category and make a list. Monitor and help with ideas. Encourage students to be as funny and imaginative as possible when choosing and creating their lists. Put three pairs together to form groups of six and ask students to feed back on their lists within their groups.

THiNK VALUES

Lists

1 Ask students to tick the sentences they agree with (they can choose more than one).

2 SPEAKING Divide the class into pairs or small groups for students to compare their choices. Monitor and help with vocabulary as necessary. Encourage students to give reasons for their choices and to try to use conditional sentences in their discussions where possible. Note down any repeated errors related to conditionals and elicit corrections during feedback. Also, invite students to share their opinions in open class.

3 Students complete the exercise individually. Ask them to compare answers in pairs. During feedback, nominate one or two students to share their ideas for list number 7.

> **Optional extension**
>
> Students work in pairs to write one of the top ten lists mentioned in Exercise 3. Monitor and help with vocabulary and ideas if necessary. If you have space, display the completed lists on the walls and ask pairs to circulate and discuss whether or not they agree with the choices.

VOCABULARY

Alternatives to *if: suppose, provided, as long as, otherwise, unless*

1 Books closed. To focus students on the vocabulary, write the five alternatives to *if* on the board and ask: *What do these words mean? What do they have in common?* (They are all alternatives to *if.*) Listen to some of their ideas but do not comment at this stage.

Books open. Ask students to read the Look! box and then to work in pairs and match the sentence halves from the blog. Check answers in open class.

Answers

1 c   2 b   3 e   4 a   5 d

2 Ask students to work in pairs, encouraging them to refer to the sentences in Exercise 1 to help them. Check answers in open class. Prepare to give example sentences of your own to clarify meaning, as necessary.

Answers

1 as long as/provided   2 suppose   3 unless
4 otherwise

3 Ask students to work individually to choose the correct option in each sentence. Let them compare answers with a partner before a whole-class check. During feedback, check understanding by asking students to rephrase the sentences using *if*.

Answers

1 provided   2 otherwise   3 provided   4 unless
5 as long as   6 Suppose

> **Fast finishers**
>
> Ask students to review Grammar Exercise 3 on page 77 and see which of the sentences could be rewritten using alternatives to *if*, and rewrite them.

Workbook page 74 ▶

FUNCTIONS

Saying 'Yes' and adding conditions

1 Give students time to read the sentences before they begin discussing who could be talking to whom in pairs. Do the first one in open class to demonstrate the activity. Tell them there is not one correct answer. Encourage strong students to think of various situations for each sentence. Listen to some of their ideas in open class.

2 Ask pairs to rewrite the sentences. Tell them to refer to the vocabulary section for help if necessary. Again, you could do the first one in open class as an example. Monitor to deal with any problems and to support weaker students. Check answers.

Answers

1 You can borrow it as long as you drive it really carefully.
2 Yes, you can go to the party, provided you promise to be home by 11 o'clock.
3 I'll get really bad marks unless you help me.
4 I'll fix it as long as you let me play games on it.
5 Close the door, otherwise it'll get cold in here.
6 Yes, you can practise, provided you don't make a lot of noise.
7 Suppose you could play the guitar – what kind of music would you play?

3 Students read the questions and make notes individually. Ask them to try to think of at least two conditions for each one.

4 Students work in pairs to create their own dialogues. Monitor to check they are adding conditions correctly. Invite volunteers to perform their dialogues in open class.

Mixed-ability

Weaker students can write their dialogues and practise them before trying to act out their dialogue without looking at their notes. Stronger students can be encouraged to be more spontaneous and perform dialogues on the spot.

Student's Book pages 80–81

CULTURE

BACKGROUND INFORMATION

The Seven Ancient Wonders of the World: the Great Pyramid of Giza (in modern-day Egypt); the Hanging Gardens of Babylon (whereabouts unknown); the Colossus of Rhodes (a 30m statue on the Greek island of Rhodes, destroyed by earthquake in 226 BCE); the Lighthouse of Alexandria (a 130m lighthouse in Egypt which survived until the 13th century); the Mausoleum at Halicarnassus (an ornate tomb in modern-day Turkey destroyed by earthquakes in the 12th–15th Centuries); the Temple of Artemis (a Greek temple in modern-day Turkey destroyed in 401 AD); and the Statue of Zeus (a 13m statue in Greece, destroyed in the 5th century AD. Only the Great Pyramid remains (mostly) intact today.

1 Put students into small groups to discuss the question. Elicit answers in open class and make a list on the board. If you have access to the Internet in the classroom, search for images of any 'wonders' mentioned by students and discuss why they might be on the list.

2 **2.13** First, ask students to look at the photos and guess the answers. Play the audio while students read and listen to the article to check their predictions. Ask students to check their answers with a partner before feedback in open class.

Answers

Petra is the oldest.
Christ the Redeemer is the newest.

3 Give students a minute or two to read the sentences and circle the key information that they need to look for. Students read the text again in order to answer the questions. Tell them to underline information in the text that helped them. Students check answers with a partner. During feedback, ask students to justify their answers by quoting the text they have underlined.

Answers

1 Petra 2 Taj Mahal 3 The Colosseum
4 Great Wall of China 5 Machu Picchu
6 Christ the Redeemer 7 Chichén Itzá

4 VOCABULARY Ask students to cover the definitions. Give them two minutes to find the highlighted words in the article and discuss their possible meanings

with a partner, using the context provided by the article to help them. Students uncover the definitions to check their ideas and complete the exercise. Check answers in open class.

Answers

1 abandoned 2 bury 3 flourished 4 hostile
5 icon 6 spectacles 7 succession 8 carved

SPEAKING

In pairs or small groups, students discuss the questions. Make a note of any nice expressions in English that students use during the activity. At the end write them on the board for the whole class to copy, and for you to praise the student who used them. Invite students to report back to the class on their discussions. Also focus on any recurring errors and elicit corrections during feedback.

WRITING

Essay

1 Draw students' attention to the photo. Ask: *What do you know about the Simplon Tunnel? Why do you think it is special? When and how do you think it was built?* Get students to speculate in pairs before they read and check. Set a two-minute time limit to encourage students to read the essay quickly to check predictions and answer the questions. Allow students to compare answers in pairs before whole-class feedback.

Answers

Because they were the longest tunnels in the world when they were built. / They were a big engineering achievement at the time.

2 Ask students to work in pairs and try to find the five mistakes. This can be done as a class competition with pairs competing to be first to find the mistakes. Check answers.

Answers

• a spelling mistake – 9
• a mistake with the verb tense – 4
• a mistake which is the wrong choice of connecting word – 6
• a preposition mistake – 1
• a mistake which is a missing word – 2

3 Students work in pairs to correct the mistakes. If you're using an IWB, project the text onto the board to refer to during feedback. Check corrections in open class.

Answers

1 in 2 the 4 took 6 during 9 than

4 This exercise is designed to get students thinking about the mistakes they make when writing. Ask students to work individually to note down their answers to each question. If available, ask students to refer to pieces of writing they have recently produced

to help them create a checklist. When students have completed the exercise, make small groups for students to compare ideas and checklists.

5 Ask students to choose a modern wonder and make notes on reasons for their choice. Monitor to help with vocabulary and ideas. Get them to share ideas in pairs or small groups. *Can they add any ideas or reasons for why it would be a good choice for a modern wonder of the world?*

6 Encourage students to make a plan before they begin writing their essays and to organise their writing as outlined in the instructions. They should also refer to their checklist of past mistakes once they've written it.

Alternatively, this could be done as a collaborative writing activity in class with pairs of students writing their essays together. On completion, ask students to exchange their essays with another pair for them to read and correct any grammatical errors, using the checklists they created earlier.

Optional extension

Ask students to work in pairs to create a peer feedback checklist and use it to comment on each other's writing so they're also feeding back on things like content and organisation, as well as accuracy.

Student's Book page 82–83

READING AND USE OF ENGLISH

1 Part 2: Open cloze

Answers

1 on 2 if/provided 3 by 4 have 5 out 6 an
7 long 8 will

Workbook page 71

TEST YOURSELF UNITS 7 & 8

VOCABULARY

1

Answers

1 down 2 about 3 up 4 unless 5 worried
6 flourishes 7 succession 8 through 9 forward
10 point

GRAMMAR

2

Answers

1 would be 2 will have 3 are going 4 will
5 would have 6 will be

3

Answers

1 It's Diana's birthday next Friday and she ~~will have~~ **is having** a party on Saturday.
2 I would have been happy if he ~~would have~~ **had come**.
3 If I hadn't made so many mistakes, I would ~~win~~ **have won** the tennis match.
4 This time tomorrow, ~~I'm lying~~ **I'll be lying** on a beach in the sun.
5 If I ~~had been~~ **were/was** taller, I wouldn't need the ladder.
6 We must finish cleaning the kitchen before our parents ~~are arriving~~ **arrive**.

FUNCTIONAL LANGUAGE

4

Answers

1 no, bright 2 provided, a good 3 unless, cheer
4 if, as long

9 BE YOUR OWN LIFE COACH

Objectives

FUNCTIONS	asking somone politely to change their behaviour
GRAMMAR	*I wish* and *if only*; *I would prefer to / it if, It's time, I'd rather / sooner*
VOCABULARY	life's ups and downs; work and education

Student's Book pages 84–85

READING

1 Books closed. As a lead-in, ask: *Other than your school teachers, who teaches you things?* Students discuss the question in pairs and make a list of the different types of people who teach them things. After a few minutes, elicit answers in open class and make a list on the board.

Books open. If there is an interactive whiteboard (IWB) available in the classroom, the lead-in to this activity would best be done as a heads-up activity. Display the photos on the IWB and get students to speculate about the relationship between the people in the photos, in pairs. Ask: *What might have happened before the photo? What might happen next?* Elicit one or two ideas in open class before students work individually to complete the exercise and match the thoughts to the people in the photos.

Answers

A 'She doesn't understand me.'
B 'I like it this way.'
C 'I hate doing this.'
D 'This is fun.' / 'Won't they just stop?'
E 'Why? Why? Why?'

2 SPEAKING Put students into pairs or small groups to compare their answers to Exercise 1 and to think of a piece of advice for each person. Nominate one or two students to share their ideas in open class.

3 Give students a three-minute time limit to encourage them to read the presentation quickly in order to choose a title. The focus here is on gist understanding. Also clarify that the question is about students' opinions. There are no right or wrong answers. Have a quick show of hands to see which titles students chose and invite one or two students to give reasons for their choice.

4 ◖⬤》2.14 Give students time to read the paragraph headings and check understanding. Also, check/clarify: *overdramatising, shame, simplistically, snap at, put things in perspective.* Students re-read the article

and complete the exercise. You may like to suggest that they read the first paragraph and then decide which is the most suitable heading, before moving on to the second paragraph. As they read, encourage them to underline the parts of the article that support their answers. During feedback, ask students to refer to the text to explain why they chose their answers.

Answers

A 2 B 5 C 6 D 1 E (extra heading) F 3
G (extra heading) H 4

5 SPEAKING Put students into pairs or small groups to discuss the questions. Monitor and encourage debate between students by tasking them with reaching consensus on their answers within their groups. During feedback, have a quick show of hands to find out which pieces of advice students chose for question 2 and nominate individuals to give reasons for their answers.

▮▮ TRAIN TO THiNK ▮▮

Jumping to a hasty conclusion

1 Do number 1 in open class as an example. Ask students to work with a partner to complete the exercise. Check answers.

Suggested answers

1 Many Brazilians love football.
2 A lot of teenagers get up late.
3 It often rains at the weekend.
4 People who live in big cities can be less caring than people who live in the countryside.
5 Almost everyone loves a box of chocolates for a present.
6 Maths is sometimes hard for people who are good at languages.

2 SPEAKING Before students begin their discussions, elicit one or two examples in open class. Put students into small groups to discuss hasty conclusions they've heard. Monitor to help with vocabulary and to ensure quieter students have an opportunity to speak. Avoid error correction unless errors really hinder comprehension. The focus of this task is on fluency, not on practice of structures or lexis. Ask each group to nominate a secretary to make notes of their answers (this could be one of the quieter students, to encourage participation). Do feedback in a more student-centred way by forming new groups within which students report back on their discussions.

Optional extension

Set up a role play. Divide the class into small groups. Half the group are adults who make hasty conclusions about teenagers. The other half are teenagers who must respond to the conclusions and say why they are not true. This can be done as a mingle with students changing partners every time you clap your hands. This gives the activity more spontaneity and encourages students to think on their feet.

Student's Book pages 86–87

GRAMMAR

I wish and *If only*

1 Ask students to try to complete sentences 1–4 before looking back at the presentation to check their answers. Confirm answers in open class. Ask students to work with a partner to complete the rule. Check answers.

> **Answers**
>
> 1 could   2 understood   3 had studied   4 hadn't said

> **Rule**
>
> 1 past simple   2 past perfect

LANGUAGE NOTE

Remind students that if you want somebody else to do something, we use *I wish* + subject + *would (not)* + infinitive.

For example: *I wish my brother would help me with my homework.*

---

2 If you're short on time, set this exercise for homework but do number 1 in open class to check that students fully understand the task. Students fill the gaps and then compare their answers in pairs before a whole-class check.

> **Answers**
>
> 1 didn't tell   2 hadn't told   3 hadn't stayed   4 won
> 5 hadn't given   6 hadn't lied   7 didn't eat   8 had invited

---

Fast finishers

Ask students to write sentences of their own using *I wish* and *if only* – one related to how they'd like things to be different in the present and one relating to the past.

---

3 **SPEAKING** Working individually, students imagine and write possible wishes for the people in the photos on pages 84 and 85. You may like to give an example to get them started. Monitor to help with any questions, to encourage creativity and to check students are using *I wish* and *if only* correctly. Make a note of any repeated errors and write them on the board, ensuring anonymity, for correction during feedback in open class. Prior to doing delayed error correction, put students into pairs and get them to take turns to read their sentences for their partner to guess the photo.

Optional extension

Put students into pairs. Ask them to take turns to make a statement to which their partner responds with *I wish …* For example:

A: *I haven't got any money.*

B: *I wish I hadn't spent all your money.*

Workbook page 82 and page 126

 Be aware of common errors related to *wish*.
Go to Get it right! on Student's Book page 125.

PRONUNCIATION

For practice of linking sounds, focusing on intrusive /w/ and /j/, go to Student's Book page 121.

VOCABULARY

Life's ups and downs

1 Books closed. Write *Life's ups and downs* on the board. Ask students: *What do you think this phrase means?* Elicit their ideas in open class.

Books open. Ask students to race to find expressions 1–8 in the article and to underline them. They could do this individually or in pairs. Ask them to try to explain the meaning of each expression to a partner, using the context provided by the presentation and without looking at the definitions on page 86. To check their answers, ask them to match expressions 1–8 with definitions a–h. Check answers.

> **Answers**
>
> 1 h   2 f   3 a   4 b   5 g   6 c   7 d   8 e

Fast finishers

Ask students to make notes on times or situations in which they've experienced ups and downs.

---

2 If you're short on time, you can set this exercise for homework. In order to encourage students to just focus on gist understanding the first time they read the text, ask them to read it quickly in order to answer these questions: *What did the writer decide to do to make his parents less angry about his mistake? Was it a success? Why (not)?* Check answers. Next, ask students to work in pairs to complete the text with expressions from Exercise 1. Check answers in open class.

Mixed-ability

Stronger students can try to complete the text without looking back at Exercise 1, and then refer to it to check their answers.

Weaker students can look back at Exercise 1 to complete the text from the outset.

> **Answers**
>
> 1 get in the way of   2 let … down   3 dwell on
> 4 tried … hardest   5 not worked out
> 6 lived up … expectations   7 blame   8 go … way

Workbook page 84 ▶

LISTENING

1 **SPEAKING** Books closed. As an introduction to the topic, ask: *Do all 19-year-olds go to university? If not, what do they do?* Give students time to discuss the questions in pairs, then listen to some of their ideas in open class, encouraging others in the class to react.

Books open. Students discuss the questions in pairs. Elicit/point out that the photo on the left refers to working as a life choice and the photo on the right refers to study. Monitor and encourage them to speculate and expand on their ideas. Nominate students to share their ideas in open class and write answers on the board to refer to after the audio.

2 ◀》2.17 Play the audio for students to listen and answer the question. Ask students to check answers with a partner before whole-class feedback.

Answer

Working in a coffee shop/restaurant

Audio Script Track 2.17

Chris   Hi, I'm Chris Williams and welcome to a special edition of Radio Helpline. Latest government figures show that of last July's school leavers one in every three is currently unemployed. Furthermore, nearly 25% of last year's university graduates are also without a job. And when you consider that university fees for the average student are nearly £30,000 for a three-year course, higher education is not as attractive an option as it used to be. Faced with such a depressing set of statistics it's no wonder that many of today's teenagers are worried about the future. I'm joined in the studio today by careers advisor Jo Harvey who is here to take some of your calls and help you with decisions about your future. Jo, welcome and thank you.

Jo   Thank you. First of all I'd like to say that it's true that the figures aren't great, but that there are still plenty of opportunities for young people out there and lots of reasons for them to get excited about their future.

Chris   Well, that's good to hear. Let's go straight to a caller. We've got Alex on the line. Hello, Alex, and what would you like to ask Jo?

Alex   Hi. Yes, I'm finishing school next July. My family and teachers are all expecting me to go to university, but I'm not so sure it's such a good idea.

Jo   Hi, Alex. Can I ask you what you're thinking of studying at uni?

Alex   Well, that's one of the problems. I'm not really sure.

Jo   Alex, I'm so glad you called. I think Alex is typical of so many school leavers these days. They feel pressure to go on to university straight after leaving school even

though they're not sure exactly what they want to do, and today's university students know that they've got to pay for it all themselves. Because it's so expensive there's a lot of pressure on making sure you choose the degree course that's right for you. But what happens when you're not sure what you want to study? How can you make the right decision? And this is why I'm recommending more and more young people who are in this position to take some time off before they go to university. And I'm not talking about a gap year to travel around the world. Realistically, how many of today's teenagers can afford that? I'm talking about getting a couple of years' experience of the working world. Try out a few jobs: work in a shop, an office, in a hospital or hotel. Or think about working abroad. Find out what you like and don't like. Then maybe you'll have a better idea of whether a university education is the right choice for you and if so, what you want to study.

Alex   But won't that put me at a disadvantage compared with all the students who go straight to university? I mean if I don't start until I'm 22 or something, I'll be 25 when I'm finished and …

Jo   … 25 is nothing. You're going to be working until you're at least 65 and probably longer. You won't be at any disadvantage if you start a few years after other people. In fact, if you use your time off wisely, go and work abroad for a while, get some useful work and life experience, then you're going to be much more attractive to most employers than your average 21-year-old fresh out of university. You really are.

---

3 ◀》2.17 This exercise is closely modelled on
✳ Listening Part 4 of the Cambridge English: First exam. Ask students to read the questions and answer as many as they can based on memory and/or general knowledge. Play the audio for students to check their answers. Get students to check answers in pairs before feedback in open class. During pair-checking and feedback stages, encourage students to explain why they chose their answers and why other answers are not possible.

Mixed-ability

To simplify this exercise for weaker students, for each question, tell them one option which isn't correct.

Answers

1 C   2 C   3 B   4 B   5 A   6 C

VOCABULARY

Work and education

1 Ask students to cover the eight definitions and read the words. Students work with a partner to try to define the words. They can then uncover the definitions and match them to the words. Check answers in open class. Ask students to mark where they think the main stress is on each word. Say the words for students to check and repeat.

Answers

1 b   2 d   3 h   4 e   5 g   6 f   7 a   8 c

2 Give students time to read the paragraph once in order to get a general understanding without trying

to complete the spaces. To encourage them to do this, ask them to answer this question, ignoring the spaces: *What would the writer like to do after leaving school?* Check answers before students read a second time and complete the exercise. Check answers in open class.

Answers

1 work experience   2 school leavers   3 higher education
4 graduate   5 degree course   6 careers advisor
7 degree   8 life experience

Fast finishers

Ask students to close their books and write as many of the collocations from Exercise 1 as they can remember before opening their books to check.

SPEAKING

Ask students to work individually to mark each sentence A or D. Put students into small groups to compare. Encourage students to justify their opinions and challenge each other's. You could tell them they should try to convince the rest of their group that their opinion is the right one as a way to generate maximum discussion. During feedback in open class, nominate one or two students to report back on their group's discussion and encourage further discussion.

Workbook page 84 ▶

Student's Book pages 88–89

READING

1 A recording of this text is available with your digital resources.

Books closed. Ask students to discuss these questions in pairs or small groups: *Which magazines do you read? Have you ever seen a multiple choice quiz in a magazine? What was it about? What are typical features of a magazine quiz? Who does them? How much do you believe the answers?* Nominate students to report back on their discussions in open class.

Books open. Tell students they are going to do a quiz to find out if they are in control. Before they begin the quiz, students should read the questions and underline any vocabulary they don't understand – they can then ask about these words or check in a dictionary. They should only check words that they need to know in order to be able to complete the quiz. Be strict on this.

2 Get students to compare their answers in pairs. Encourage them to give reasons for their choices. Ask: *How similar were your answers?*

3 In pairs, students read the key and discuss the questions. During feedback in open class, ask who agrees with the description, who doesn't and why.

4 SPEAKING Regroup students into new pairs or small groups so that they have different partners. Before students begin, elicit suggestions as to why or in what circumstances *c* might not be the best answer to number 1, in open class. Students then discuss

instances where *a* or *b* might be better responses to the remaining questions in their pairs or groups. They could also suggest alternative responses. Follow up with a class discussion on alternative best responses, encouraging students to give reasons to support their opinions.

GRAMMAR

I would prefer to / it if, It's time, I'd rather / sooner

1 Ask students to work with a partner to choose the correct option in each sentence before checking answers by referring back to the quiz. Students then complete the rule. Check answers in open class.

Answers

a didn't   b go   c got   d didn't   e take

Rule

1 c   2 b   3 e   4 a   5 d

2 If you're short on time, you can set this exercise for homework. Students work individually to complete the exercise. Let them compare answers with a partner before you do a whole-class check. During feedback, refer to the rule for clarification as necessary.

Answers

1 played   2 didn't tell   3 went   4 didn't invite
5 eat   6 leave   7 learned   8 to stay

Fast finishers

Ask students to rewrite sentences 1–8 using one of the other expressions. e.g *I'd prefer it if you listened to something else.*

Optional extension

Write the following pairs of phrases on the board. Ask students to work individually and choose which one from each pair they'd prefer to do, then think of a reason for their choice. They should express their choice using *I would prefer/rather/sooner*. Put students into pairs for them to compare preferences.

go to Paris   go to London
go swimming   play tennis
eat spaghetti   eat fish and chips
fly   drive
go to the beach   go skiing

Workbook page 83 and page 126 ▶

FUNCTIONS

Asking someone politely to change their behaviour

1 If there is an IWB available in the classroom, the lead-in to this activity would best be done as a heads-up activity with the whole class. Project the pictures and ask students to speculate as to what is happening in each one. Next, ask students to work with a partner to complete the conversation. Suggest they refer to the rule above if they are having difficulty

and/or to check their answers. Check answers in open class and say each phrase with suitably polite intonation for students to repeat.

Answers

1 didn't use   2 didn't eat   3 put

2 Working in pairs, students create a short conversation using expressions from Exercise 1. Monitor and make sure students are using the expressions correctly. Ask them to focus on using appropriate intonation and also encourage students to be polite in their responses. Invite one or two pairs to perform their conversations in open class.

■■ THiNK SELF-ESTEEM ■■

Being diplomatic

SPEAKING Books closed. As a lead-in, describe a situation in which you would need to be diplomatic. For example, your friend has had a bad haircut. Ask students: *What do you say to your friend?* Elicit ideas in open class.

Books open. Clarify *diplomatic* and *cause offence*. Give students time to read situations 1–4 and think about how they would respond. Students complete the exercise in pairs. Monitor to help with vocabulary. Make a note of any good responses to the different situations and ask those students to share them with the class during feedback.

> **Optional extension**
>
> Ask students to work in small groups and discuss the following questions:
>
> *Why is it important to be diplomatic?*
>
> *Can you remember any situations when you've had to be diplomatic? How did you do this?*
>
> *Do you know anybody you often have to be diplomatic with?*
>
> To give students intensive listening practice, dictate the questions instead of putting them on the board.
>
> Ask students to think of their own situation where they would have to be diplomatic and to create a role play. Listen to some examples in open class as feedback.

Student's Book pages 90–91

LITERATURE

> **BACKGROUND INFORMATION**
>
> Kazuo Ishiguro (b. 8 November 1954) was born in Japan to Japanese parents. His family moved to England in 1960. He became a British citizen in 1982. He has written seven novels. His second novel, *An Artist of the Floating World*, won the 1986 Whitbread Prize. He received the 1989 Man Booker prize for his third novel *The Remains of the Day*, which was made into a film starring Anthony Hopkins and Emma Thompson. Other notable books include *Never Let Me Go* (2005) and *The Buried Giant* (2015).
>
> **The Remains of the Day** was published in 1989 to wide critical acclaim. The novel recounts the memories of a butler who has spent most of his working life in the employment of an upper-class English family. The butler tells stories of his working life and of his unrequited love for a housekeeper who is now married with children. The film of the novel received eight Oscar nominations but won no awards.

1 Books closed. As a lead-in, ask students to make a list of five sad novels or films and to discuss what happens in them, in pairs or small groups. Elicit a few in open class.

Books open. Ask students to look at the photos and discuss: *Who might the people in the photo be? What's their relationship? Where do you think the book is set? What do you think it might be about?* Listen to some of their ideas in open class and then get students to read the introduction to check. Check/clarify: *butler*. Ask students to quickly discuss the question with a partner, encouraging them to give reasons for their answer.

2 Ask students to quickly read the extract and choose the best ending. You could set a three-minute time limit to encourage speed-reading. Allow students to check answers with a partner before whole-class feedback.

Answer

b

3 🔊 2.18 Play the audio for students to listen as they read the extract a second time. Allow students to check their answers with a partner. Nominate students to give reasons for their answers during whole-class feedback.

Answers

1 Lord Darlington died three years ago.
2 Stevens thinks that Lord Darlington made mistakes/his own decisions.
3 The stranger is an old man.
4 The people on the pier are happy when the lights come on.
5 Stevens thinks that it's pointless/not important to reflect on what he could have done better in his life.

4 VOCABULARY Students work individually to complete the exercise and then check their answers with a partner before feedback in open class.

> **Mixed-ability**
>
> Stronger students can look at the highlighted words in the extract and try to define them based on the context provided within the extract before referring to the definitions provided in the exercise.
>
> Weaker students go straight to the definitions in order to complete the exercise.

Answers

1 dignity   2 pleasure-seekers   3 youth   4 butler
5 contentment   6 misguided   7 aspirations
8 vouch for

5 SPEAKING Students discuss the questions in pairs or small groups. Monitor and make a note of any nice expressions in English that students use or any nice contributions they make during the activity. At the end write good expressions on the board to present to the whole class, and praise the student(s) who used them. Also, ask for volunteers to report back to the class on their discussions.

WRITING

A magazine article

1 As a lead-in, ask students to discuss the following questions with a partner: *Is it important to get work experience before going to university? What sort of work experience can you get when you are a teenager?* Listen to some of their answers in open class and encourage further class discussion.

Students read the article and answer the questions. Let them compare answers with a partner before a whole-class check. Also ask if any of the ideas they came up with during the lead-in discussion are mentioned.

> **Answers**
>
> 1 Yes
> 2 Graduates are feeling the pressure precisely because so many of them are looking for the same jobs at the same time and there's very little for an employer to choose between them; people who wait some years before they go to university will, as long as they have used their time well, be far more attractive as an employee; their extra experience of life will mean they can offer companies more than a 22-year-old graduate can; the fact they've taken time to decide exactly what it is they wanted to do shows that now they really want to do it.

2 Students complete the exercise with a partner, noting down reasons for their answers. Check answers in open class.

> **Answer**
>
> She questions/challenges the reader, which has the effect of making the reader think about their own life. She asks questions in the first paragraph and then uses the imperative in the final paragraph.

3 Students work with a partner to make notes on one of the topics. You might like to give students an example on the board based on the model text, using bullet points and note forms. Ask: *How would Eve's plan have looked?* During feedback, elicit examples of the type of things students have decided to include.

4 Students work with a partner to think about how they will start and finish their article and then compare with a partner, who could also give additional suggestions.

5 If you're short on time, you can set this exercise for homework.

Ask students to write their articles. This could be done as a collaborative writing activity in class with students writing one article as a pair. Encourage them to expand their notes and organise their writing in a similar style to the example on page 91. On completion, ask students to exchange their articles with another student/pair for them to read and comment on each other's first and last paragraphs and the overall organisation of the article.

10 | SPREADING THE NEWS

Objectives

FUNCTIONS	making a point; introducing news
GRAMMAR	reported speech (review); reported questions and requests
VOCABULARY	sharing news; reporting verbs

Student's Book pages 92–93

READING

1 Books closed. As a lead-in, tell students about an interesting piece of news you have heard recently and then ask: *What's the most interesting news you've received this week?* Make it clear that this could be news from a friend/family or from a newspaper/TV programme. Divide the class into pairs for students to discuss the question. Listen to some examples in open class. Ask: *Who heard the most interesting news?*

Books open. If there is an interactive whiteboard (IWB) available in the classroom, this activity would best be done as a heads-up activity. Ask students to discuss the questions in pairs or small groups. Elicit answers in open class and create a list on the board of other ways of giving or getting news.

Answers

A talking on the phone B texting C by mail
D talking in person/talking face-to-face
E reading a newspaper

2 If there is an IWB available in the classroom, this activity would best be done as a heads-up activity. Give students time to read the opinions. Nominate a student to point to the photo that corresponds to the first opinion on the board. Ask students to work in pairs to match the remaining opinions and discuss if each one is an advantage or disadvantage. Students will speak more if they disagree, so you could tell one of each pair to say that the opinions are advantages, while their partner says they are disadvantages. Have a quick show of hands to check answers and nominate one or two students to justify their opinions.

Answers

1 C 2 B,E 3 A 4 D 5 B,C 6 B

3 SPEAKING Students work in pairs to come up with more advantages and disadvantages. Make groups of four for pairs to compare their answers. Encourage them to think of any advantages or disadvantages of the other ways of sharing news that they came up with in Exercise 1. During feedback in open class, ask: *What do your parents/grandparents think about the different ways of sharing news?*

4 ◉ 2.19 Before students read the article, ask them to work with a partner and discuss these questions: *What do you know about Twitter and its uses? Do you use it? How?* Give pairs a couple of minutes to discuss and then elicit responses in open class. Tell students they are going to read and listen to a magazine article in order to find the three ways mentioned. Set a two-minute time limit to encourage them to read the text quickly and focus on gist understanding rather than on trying to understand every word. Students compare their answer with a partner before checking in open class.

Answer

Posting news, following celebrities, campaigning/sharing information

5 Give students time to read the sentences. Check/clarify: *cruelty, sources, protest.* Encourage students to underline the key information in the sentences that will help them match each of the tweets to the corresponding paragraphs in the article. Students read the article in more detail to complete the exercise. Suggest that they underline the parts of the text that helped them find their answers. Students should check their answers with a partner before whole-class feedback.

Answers

1 –2 2 –3 3 –1 4 –1 5 –2 6 –3

> **Optional extension**
>
> As a follow-up to working with a text, it can be useful to give students time to reflect on any new or unusual vocabulary they might be curious about. For example, this text includes phrases such as: *took on a life of its own; to get the attention of; they get to hear what …* etc. which you might like to draw your students' attention to. Or, you could ask them to choose five phrases (not single-word items) they would like to remember.

6 SPEAKING Put students into pairs or small groups to discuss the questions. To maximise communication, give students time to think about their answers prior to their discussions. Monitor to help with vocabulary and to prompt students to give reasons for their answers. Listen to some of their answers during feedback in open class.

▰ TRAIN TO THiNK ▰

Identifying the source of a piece of news

Ask students to read the introductory paragraph and answer these questions: *What is the doctor's agenda/ reason for his statement? What about the politician's?* Check/clarify: *impartial* (point out that we would normally use *biased* as the opposite rather than *partial*); *suit their own agenda.* Give students time to look at the jobs and the statements. Check/clarify: *abbreviations, helplessness, spread, effective.* Students work with a partner to match the statements to the people. Encourage them to give reasons for their choices. Check answers in open class, insisting on students qualifying their answers.

> ### Answers
>
> 1 b 2 d 3 a 4 c 5 e

> ### Optional extension
>
> Ask students to work in pairs to write a statement about Twitter that might be made by the following people. Tell them to think about what their opinion might be and how they might try and say it:
>
> 1 a teacher; 2 a teenager; 3 someone over 80; 4 a journalist

Student's Book pages 94–95

GRAMMAR

Reported speech (review)

1 Books closed. As this is a review, you may like to give students time to work in pairs to discuss what they remember about the rules of reported speech before starting the exercise. This helps prepare their minds for the review and encourages them to look for answers in the material. Listen to some of their thoughts in open class but do not comment at this stage.

Books open. Ask students to work in pairs to rewrite the sentences. Remind them to think carefully about the tenses they use. Let them check their answers on page 93, then discuss any changes between direct and indirect speech in open class. Students then read and complete the table with a partner. Check answers.

> ### Answers
>
> 1 I've just heard about Robin Williams – so sad.
> 2 I just saw Ariana Grande in town. Can't wait for the concert tonight.
> 3 (We should) save our cinema. Join us tonight 8 pm outside the mayor's house.

> ### Rule
>
> 1 past continuous   2 past perfect   3 past perfect
> 4 would   5 could   6 then   7 that   8 that day
> 9 the next day   10 the day before   11 that night

> ### LANGUAGE NOTE
>
> Point out that the past perfect and *would* do not change in reported speech. Also remind students that we do not change the other words in the list if the time or place of speaking remains the same. For example, 'I will finish it today' is reported as 'He said he would finish it today' if it is being reported on the same day as the original direct speech.

2 Ask students to work individually to report the tweets. Point out that they should look at the rule to check their answers. Allow students to compare answers with a partner before feedback in open class.

> ### Mixed-ability
>
> Support weaker students with more staging. Ask them to first circle the verb that will need to be changed, then note down the tense it will change to before finally rewriting the sentence in full.

> ### Answers
>
> 1 He said he'd be in town later that evening.
> 2 They said they'd had a great time at my house.
> 3 She said she was missing me and that she couldn't wait for the next day.
> 4 John's mum said John had missed his train and he was going to be late.
> 5 Becca said she was seeing Jan that night and would tell her when she saw her.
> 6 Jimmy said the baby was due that day.

3 **WRITING** Working individually, students write four tweets. Remind them that tweets cannot exceed 140 characters. Monitor and help with vocabulary and ideas and to encourage students to use a variety of tenses in their tweets. To make the activity more authentic, ask students to work in threes. They each write a tweet, and take it in turns to send their tweets to another student in their group of three who should then report what was said to the third student.

> ### Mixed-ability
>
> Stronger students can write four or more tweets. Weaker students can write two tweets.

> ### Optional extension
>
> For further practice, ask students to look back at the photostory on page 72. Working in threes, students take it in turns to report something that was said by one of the characters. The other two students should race to be first to find the direct speech.

> Workbook page 90 and page 126

 Be aware of common errors related to reported speech. Go to Get it right! on Student's Book page 126.

VOCABULARY

Sharing news

1 Match the first phrase to the definition in open class, as an example. Ask students to complete the exercise in pairs. Check answers in open class. During feedback, say the phrases for students to repeat. Pay particular attention to the linking of sounds between words such as *let you /letju:/, pass on, got in, keep in*. Clarify that the object pronouns (*you, me*, etc.) can be replaced by other objects or names and give some examples e.g. I'll let *him* know.

> **Answers**
>
> 1 f 2 a 3 g 4 b 5 h 6 c 7 d 8 e

> **LANGUAGE NOTE**
>
> *Break the news* is used when giving bad news. We use *get in touch* with people we haven't contacted for some time.

2 Working individually, students choose the correct option for each sentence. Students compare answers with a partner before feedback in open class.

> **Mixed-ability**
>
> Stronger students can cover Exercise 1 and complete the sentences before looking back to check their answers.

> **Answers**
>
> 1 let 2 break/pass on 3 keep 4 get 5 break
> 6 retweeted 7 dropped 8 give

> **Fast finishers**
>
> Ask students: *What do you use social media for?* Students write sentences to answer the question using phrases from Exercise 1.

3 **SPEAKING** Give some example answers of your own to get them started. Students discuss the questions in pairs or small groups. Monitor and answer any questions about vocabulary, but as this is a fluency practice activity, do not interrupt the conversations unless inaccuracy hinders comprehension. If you want to give students extended speaking practice, ask them to repeat the exercise with a different partner. They will then have an opportunity to improve their answers from the first attempt and should be motivated by their own sense of progress in being able to produce clearer, more fluent answers. Listen to some of their ideas in open class for feedback.

> **Mixed-ability**
>
> Divide the class into pairs roughly according to level. Allow weaker students some time to think about their answers before discussing them.

Workbook page 92

PRONUNCIATION

For practice of omitting the /h/ sound go to Student's Book page 121.

LISTENING

1 Books closed. As a lead-in, ask students to work in pairs. Ask half the class to make a list of sections of a newspaper and the other half a list of types of item on a news programme. You could start with a couple of examples: *business; sport*. Elicit answers in open class and create a list on the board. Make sure *international/foreign news* is on the list.

Books open. Students discuss the question in pairs. Write some of their answers on the board, but do not comment at this stage.

2 **◀))2.22** With weaker classes, play the audio for students to check which of the things they came up with in Exercise 1 are mentioned before setting up this exercise. Give students time to read the sentences. Ask them to underline the key information they will need to listen for. Play the audio while students decide if the sentences are true or false. Let students compare answers with a partner before feedback in open class. During feedback, ask students to explain the reasons for their answers.

> **Answers**
>
> 1 T   2 F (It's dangerous some of the time.)
> 3 F (She can't imagine working in an office.)
> 4 T 5 T 6 T

> **Audio Script Track 2.22**
>
> Janice   Hello, everyone. It's great to see so many of you here today. Well, I'm what's called a foreign correspondent. That means that I'm a reporter, for my newspaper, who reports on things that are happening abroad. So of course I spend a lot of time away from home, I travel around the world and I try to tell readers at home what's going on in other places. I'm here today to answer your questions so I hope you have lots of them. Where shall we start? The young man in the front row.
>
> Boy   Do you travel to dangerous places?
>
> Janice   Yes. Sometimes you go to a war zone, for example, because to get a really good story you have to get close to the action. And sometimes the action is in a place where there's fighting, and that's dangerous of course. But often, it's more dangerous for the local people who help me – drivers, translators, even the people who arrange interviews for me. I might stay in the country for a few days or weeks and then I come home, but they stay there because that's where they live, and it's not always easy for them. But you asked me if my job was dangerous. And, yes, it is some of the time.
>
> Girl   So why do you do it?
>
> Janice   Good question! Well, I do it because I think it's important and helpful. And of course it's exciting. It's very, very exciting and in a way you get hooked on it. I mean, I can't imagine working in an office, sitting behind a desk every day.
>
> Boy   How do you prepare for each story?
>
> Janice   Well you have to know quite a lot about the place you're going to. You have to spend time reading and talking to people and finding things out. And depending where you're going, sometimes you have to train physically, you know, you might be in a desert or up some mountains so you have to be fit. For one story I did, where I had to follow the army in the Sahara, I had two weeks of training with an army instructor.

> He asked me to run ten kilometres with a heavy pack on my back. I didn't like that much!
>
> **Girl** What is the most difficult part of your job?
>
> **Janice** Right. Well, I'd say the most difficult part is trying to be objective, you know, to write about what you see and not what you think you see or what you want to see. And sometimes people think your report isn't a fair representation of the facts. In one country – I'm not going to say which one – I sent a report to my newspaper and the government of that country didn't like it and they asked me to leave. And so I left, of course.
>
> **Boy** Would you recommend your job to other people?
>
> **Janice** Oh, yes, absolutely. I mean it isn't for everyone – just now, someone asked me why I do it and it's not the first time I've heard that question! But it's a fantastic job, I love it and feel very privileged to have the opportunity to do the work I do.

3 🔊2.22 Ask students to work with a partner to try to answer as many of the questions as they can from memory before you play the audio again for them to check. Get students to check answers in pairs before you do a whole-class check.

Answers

1 Be close to the action.
2 She's helped by drivers, translators and people who arrange interviews.
3 She has to train.
4 She was asked to leave a country.
5 Because the government of the country didn't like what she wrote.

4 SPEAKING Divide the class into pairs or small groups to discuss the questions. Monitor and help as necessary, encouraging students to expand on their ideas and to use any vocabulary they have learned from the text. Ask pairs or groups to feed back to the class and discuss any interesting points further. Ask: *Do you think foreign correspondents are necessary? Why?*

GRAMMAR

Reported questions and requests

1 Ask students to work in pairs to quickly decide which of the sentences are reported questions and which, requests. Check answers. Students then write the direct questions. Remind them that they may need to change pronouns and add auxiliaries when transforming sentences from indirect to direct speech. During feedback, draw attention to the differences between the reported questions and the direct questions. Ask students to read through the rule with a partner and fill the gaps. During whole-class feedback, refer to Exercise 1 and further examples of your own to clarify the answers.

Answers

1 question 2 request 3 question

a Is your job dangerous?
b Can you run with a heavy pack on your back, please?
c Why do you do that job?

Rule

1 yes/no questions 2 *wh-* questions 3 requests

2 Ask students to work individually to complete the exercise. Monitor and help with any questions. Allow students to compare answers with a partner before whole-class feedback.

Answers

1 One of the students asked her which newspaper she worked for.
2 One of the students asked her where she was going next.
3 One of the students asked her if she had ever been scared in her job.
4 One of the students asked her if her job was well-paid.
5 One of the students asked her who her boss was.

Fast finishers

Ask students to report the questions from Listening Exercise 4 on page 95, starting: *My partner asked me …*

Optional extension

Ask students to write three questions and two requests about next weekend. Students work in pairs and take it in turns to ask a question or make a request. Their partner has to put the question or statement into reported speech.

Workbook page 91 and page 126 ➤

SPEAKING

1 In open class, elicit names of famous people that students would like to meet. Divide the class into groups of four for students to agree on the best four and write questions to ask them. Monitor to help students with ideas for questions if necessary.

2 Students act out the interviews, noting down answers given. Encourage students to get into character and give detailed answers.

3 When the interviews are complete give students time to change the sentences into reported speech. Monitor to make sure students are reporting questions correctly and to make a note of any interesting questions to refer to during feedback.

Ask groups to decide which were the most interesting questions and responses from their interviews. Groups take turns to report back their highlights in open class.

WRITING

A magazine article

Students can do the preparation in class, and complete the writing at home. Clarify that students should use reported questions and statements. You could even establish a number and tell students to include at least three reported questions and statements. When they have finished, put students into small groups. Ask them to read each other's articles, count the number of reported statements and questions and check that all bullet points have been included.

READING

BACKGROUND INFORMATION

John Higgins (b. 18 May 1975) is a professional snooker player. He has won the UK championship three times and the world championship four times. After the sting operation in 2010, Higgins was cleared of match fixing, but fined £75,000 for not reporting the attempted cheating to the snooker authorities.

Jude Law (b. 29 December 1972) is an English actor, famous for films such as *The Talented Mr. Ripley* (1999), *Cold Mountain* (2003) and *The Grand Budapest Hotel* (2014).

Sienna Miller (b. 28 December 1981) is an English actress and model. Her most famous films are *Alfie* (2004), *Factory Girl* (2006) and *American Sniper* (2014). She was pursued by tabloid newspapers for many years after she became engaged to Jude Law in 2004. She has compared her life to a video game in which she is constantly chased by 10 to 15 men with cameras. In May 2011 she was paid £100,000 by the *News of the World* to settle her claims that her phone had been hacked.

Amy Winehouse (14 September 1983–23 July 2011) was an English singer. She released two albums: *Frank* (2003) and *Back to Black* (2006). Her most popular songs were *Rehab* and *Valerie*.

1 A recording of this text is available with your digital resources.

Books closed. As a lead-in, ask: *Which celebrities do you see most photos of? Where do you see the photos? What are the celebrities doing in the photos? Where do the photos come from?* Divide the class into pairs or small groups for students to discuss the questions. Listen to some of their ideas in open class as feedback.

Books open. Look at the title of the article with students and give them time to read the introduction. Ask students to work with a partner to read the titles of the sections (1–3) and predict what each section might contain. Students then read the article and match each section with a title. Tell them not to worry if they don't understand some of the vocabulary, they should just focus on the matching task. Allow students to check answers with a partner before feedback in open class.

Answers

A 2 B 3 C 1

2 Before re-reading the article, ask students to read the questions and underline the key information they should look for in the text. As they answer the questions, they should underline the part of the text which gave them their answers. Also get them to compare with a partner before checking in open class.

Answers

1 Journalists
2 He admitted being foolish but didn't think he had done anything wrong.
3 He used it in newspaper stories.
4 Because newspaper editors have to obey the law.
5 Because she was followed by photographers wherever she went.
6 He ordered the photographers to stay away from her home.

SPEAKING

Divide the class into pairs or small groups for students to discuss the questions. Check/clarify: *set someone up, cross the line, go too far*. Monitor, but avoid error correction unless errors really hinder comprehension. The focus of this task is on fluency and on reacting to the text, not on practice of specific structures or lexis.

VOCABULARY

Reporting verbs

1 Books closed. As a quick lead-in, write *say* and *tell* on the board and ask students when we might use these verbs (to report speech). Ask: *Do you know any other verbs we use to report speech?* Brainstorm verbs in open class and write them on the board.

Books open. Ask students to work with a partner to choose a verb to complete each sentence. Check answers in open class. Discuss the meaning of the verbs using the article to help if necessary.

If you're using an IWB, display the sentences in Exercise 1 and the rule box. Look at sentence 1 and elicit that the word that follows *accuse* is an object, and that the object is followed by a preposition (*of*) and a gerund (*taking*). Point out the position of *accuse* in the rule. Do the same for sentence 2, if necessary. If you're not using an IWB, write the sentences on the board and follow the same procedure. Ask students to work with a partner to complete the rule. Elicit answers in open class. Tell students that they should think about these structures when they learn any new reporting verbs to ensure they are using them correctly.

Answers

1 accused 2 agreed 3 admitted 4 denied
5 regretted 6 apologised 7 warned
8 criticised 9 ordered

Rule

1 apologise 2 agree 3 deny 4 order 5 criticise

2 If you're short on time, set this exercise for homework. Students work in pairs to complete sentences 1–6. Ask fast finishers to do 7–8 and/or set as homework. Check answers in open class.

Answers

1 He denied stealing the money.
2 She accused me of telling Jim her secret.
3 He warned me not to touch the dog.
4 She regretted saying those things.
5 He apologised for breaking my phone.
6 She criticised me for driving too fast.
7 He agreed to take me to the party.
8 She ordered me to tidy my room.

Optional extension

Ask students to work in pairs and test each other on the reporting verbs. e.g.

A: *Accuse*

B: *Accuse someone of doing*

Workbook page 92 ➤

FUNCTIONS

Making a point

1   **◁))2.23** Ask students to read the news story and answer this question: *Do you think this is an interesting story?* Ask students to discuss in pairs. Listen to some of their ideas in open class.

Play the audio once for students to listen and make notes on the editors' opinions. Repeat the audio for students to note down how the editors justify their opinions. Allow students to compare their answers before a whole-class check.

Answers

Editor 2   wants to run the story because their readers like controversy.
Editor 1   doesn't want to run it because the woman is not really famous now, so it's not news.

Audio Script Track 2.23

Editor 1   I'm sorry but there's no way this is a news story. I mean just because this woman was famous for a short while a few years ago doesn't mean that everything she says is news. I'm really against running this story. My mind's made up!

Editor 2   This is exactly the kind of story we want. This woman always causes controversy and that's what our readers like to read. She sells papers. We're definitely going with this story. And that's final.

---

2   **◁))2.23** Divide the class into pairs for students to order the words. Do number 1 in open class as an example if necessary. Once students have completed the exercise, play the audio again for them to check their answers. Confirm answers in open class, saying each of the sentences for students to repeat and for you to check their pronunciation. Point out the strong stress on *really*, *no way*, *exactly* and *definitely* to emphasise the speaker's opinion.

Answers

1   I'm really against running this story.
2   There's no way this is a news story.
3   My mind's made up.
4   This is exactly the kind of story we want.
5   We're definitely going with this story.
6   And that's final.

■■ THiNK VALUES ■■

News or not?

1   **SPEAKING** Give students time to read each of the five stories and deal with any comprehension issues. Discuss the first story in open class to demonstrate the amount of detail you expect from their discussions and the sorts of thing they should discuss. Students continue in pairs to agree on which stories they would publish and which not. Monitor to encourage students to expand on their answers and to make sure all students are giving their opinions.

2   **SPEAKING** Regroup students to discuss their choices. If they agree quickly, encourage them to discuss why they would not run the other stories.

For feedback, have a show of hands to decide on the most popular stories and ask students to give reasons for their choices.

Optional extension

If students have access to the Internet, ask them to work in pairs and search for some unusual additional stories to include on the front page of their newspaper. Ask them to make notes on their story and then describe it to a different pair. They should also give reasons as to why they chose the story.

Student's Book pages 98–99

PHOTOSTORY: episode 4

The news clip

1   If you're using an IWB, project the photos onto the board and ask students to close their books. Ask them to try to recall what happened in previous episodes of the photostory and to predict answers to the questions, based on the photos. Write some of their ideas on the board.

2   **◁))2.24** Play the audio for students to listen and check their answers from Exercise 1. During whole-class feedback, refer to students' ideas on the board. *Who guessed correctly?*

Answers

1   They're going to the skate park.
2   She was stopped by a news interviewer in the street.

DEVELOPING SPEAKING

3   Ask students: *What do you think happens next?* Ask them to brainstorm possible endings. Students should work in groups, with one student in each group acting as secretary and taking notes. During whole-class feedback, write students' ideas on the board to refer back to once they have watched the video. Don't give away answers at this stage.

4   **◀ EP4** Play the video for students to watch and check their answers. During whole-class feedback, refer to students' ideas on the board. *Who guessed correctly?*

5   Ask students to answer the questions in pairs. Monitor and help with any difficulties. Play the video again, pausing as required for clarification. Check answers with the whole class. Encourage students to use language from the photostory in their answers.

Answers

1   Because he didn't know the cinema was closing.
2   6.25
3   She tells her that she'd really miss the cinema, that she went there at least once a month with her friends and that she hoped someone would open up a new one soon.
4   Julia
5   Because she tripped over the camera after the interview.

PHRASES FOR FLUENCY

1 Ask students to locate expressions 1–6 in the story on page 98 and underline them. To encourage speed-reading, you could do this as a race and ask students to find the expressions as quickly as possible. Ask students to compare their answers with a partner before whole-class feedback.

> **Answers**
>
> 1 Emma 2 Liam 3 Liam 4 Liam 5 Emma
> 6 Emma

2 Students work with a partner to complete the exercise. Check answers. Say each of the phrases in Exercise 1 for students to repeat and check pronunciation.

> **Answers**
>
> 1 on earth 2 at least 3 don't bother 4 or something
> 5 in any case 6 It's none of your business

WordWise

Expressions with *way*

1 Books closed. To focus students on the topic, give them five minutes to look back through the unit to find examples of expressions with *way*. They could also include any other expressions they may know. Write their expressions on the board, but don't comment on meaning at this stage.

Books open. Ask students to work in pairs to complete the sentences with phrases from the list. Check answers.

> **Answers**
>
> 1 the same way 2 in my way 3 on my way 4 way too
> 5 the way 6 in a way

2 Students work individually to match the phrases from Exercise 1 with their meanings. During whole-class feedback, give further examples to outline the meaning of each of the phrases, as necessary.

> **Answers**
>
> 1 the same way 2 way too 3 on my way 4 in my way
> 5 the way 6 in a way

3 If you're short on time, set this exercise for homework. Students work with a partner to choose the correct option for each sentence. Check answers. For further practice and to personalise the language, you could ask students to write questions using the expressions in pairs. Put pairs together to make groups of four to ask and answer their questions. Monitor to check that students are using the target expressions appropriately.

> **Answers**
>
> 1 in my way 2 the same way 3 on his way 4 the way
> 5 in a way 6 way too

Workbook page 92 ▶

FUNCTIONS

Introducing news

1 As a lead-in, tell a story about something frustrating that happened to you (e.g. They are opening a late-night disco next to your house). Include some of the phrases to introduce news. In open class, elicit further examples of interesting news items (local, national or international) that students have heard recently.

Look at the two sentences. Students work with a partner to fill the gaps before checking answers in open class. Say the phrases for students to repeat and check pronunciation.

> **Answers**
>
> 1 guess 2 guess

2 Students work with a partner to complete the sentences. During whole-class feedback, drill the phrases, not being afraid to exaggerate slightly, and encourage students to use wide-ranging intonation as they say them.

> **Answers**
>
> 1 heard 2 about 3 know 4 Guess 5 believe

3 **SPEAKING** Put students into pairs to make notes on some interesting pieces of news. Monitor to help with vocabulary and ideas. Regroup into new pairs for students to give and react to their news and create short dialogues. Listen to some examples in open class as feedback.

Student's Book pages 100–101

THiNK EXAMS

LISTENING

1 ◀)) 2.25 **Part 4: Multiple choice**

> **Answers**
>
> 1 B 2 B 3 A 4 B 5 C 6 B 7 A

Workbook page 89 ▶

Audio Script Track 2.25

Narrator	You will hear an interview with a teenager called Diana Hollingsworth about the 'Good News Project'. For questions 1–7 choose the best answer (A, B or C).
Interviewer	We all like to complain that there seems to be nothing but bad news when we turn on the TV or open the newspaper but do we ever think of doing something about it? One person who has decided to do just that is 16-year-old Diana Hollingsworth who is here with me today to tell us all about her 'Good News Project'. Diana, welcome. Tell us, just what is the Good News Project?
Diana	The Good News Project is exactly what its name suggests. It's a project to hunt down and report stories that will make us feel happy about the world that we live in. We have links with the local newspaper and radio station and, if they like our

stories, they will make sure our story gets into the news. We're also hoping to get involved with local TV, but as of yet, that hasn't happened.

Interviewer And how did you come up with the idea?

Diana Well, as you said in your introduction, I was tired of seeing nothing but bad news on the telly but I was even more tired of hearing people complaining about this and I thought to myself, 'I can do something about this.' I was the editor of the school magazine so I decided that the next issue would contain nothing but good news. I also used the magazine to explain my idea to pupils. I was amazed by the response I got. Loads of them came forward with stories. That's when I thought I could do more.

Interviewer And what was the next step?

Diana My mum has a friend on the local newspaper and she arranged for me to meet her. I took along some of the stories that I'd been given by people at school and explained my idea to her. She loved the idea and said that each week they would publish one of our stories to see how the public responded to the idea. It was such a success that after a few months we were publishing around five stories in each edition and that's when the radio station got involved.

Interviewer The radio? Tell us more.

Diana The producer of the radio station had seen our stories in the newspaper and really liked the idea of doing something similar. I had a meeting with him and he asked if each morning we could produce one 'feel-good' story that they could broadcast at the end of their news bulletins. Of course, I said yes, even though it meant quite a bit of extra work. But the best thing is that he lets me read out the story. So every evening I have to record a story and send it in to the station.

Interviewer It sounds like you're quite busy.

Diana I am. I mean I don't do all the work myself. I have a team of reporters who find the stories but I'm the one who makes the final decision as to which stories we're going to pass on to the paper and the radio. It's actually quite a bit of responsibility because you need to be sure that the stories are 100% true, which can be difficult. It's probably the toughest part of the job.

Interviewer So tell us more about your reporters. Are they all young people like yourself?

Diana Most of them are. Most of them are pupils from our school but actually anyone can get in touch and send in a story. They can do it just once or they can contribute regularly. And they don't have to write the story. I'm happy to do that if I have all the facts. The only thing we ask any potential contributor is that they can prove their story is true and, of course, the story has to be uplifting. We can't forget that.

Interviewer And finally – can you give us some examples of the types of story you report on?

Diana Oh my goodness. Where do I start? Animals always make good stories. Animals doing funny things, people finding their lost cats, that sort of thing. We also have lots of stories about people doing amazing things to raise money for charities. Sport is also a good area. We had a story the other day about an 82-year-old man who still plays football every week. The stories can be about anything and everything. Well, that's not quite true. We avoid religion and politics completely. They're subjects that will always get you into trouble.

Interviewer Diana, it's been a pleasure. Thank you so much for telling us all about the 'Good News Project' and good luck for the future.

Diana You're welcome and thanks for having me.

TEST YOURSELF UNITS 9 & 10

VOCABULARY
1

Answers

1 degree 2 way 3 drop 4 apologise 5 regretted
6 careers 7 let 8 denied 9 live 10 blame

GRAMMAR
2

Answers

1 hadn't 2 had 3 would 4 didn't 5 was
6 wouldn't

3

Answers

1 I'd sooner ~~had~~ **have** a quick salad and then go back to work.
2 I wish he ~~didn't give~~ **hadn't given** me so many presents – it was so embarrassing.
3 Sheila said the film on TV the day before **was** ~~had been~~ excellent.
4 They announced that the president ~~will~~ **would** make a speech before tomorrow's ceremony.
5 I'd rather you ~~come~~ **came** round to my house, if that's possible.
6 He accused me ~~to break~~ **of breaking** his camera.

FUNCTIONAL LANGUAGE
4

Answers

1 guess, play 2 rather, prefer 3 didn't, to go
4 seen, know

11 | SPACE AND BEYOND

Objectives

FUNCTIONS	sympathising about past situations
GRAMMAR	speculating (past, present and future); cause and effect linkers
VOCABULARY	space idioms; adjectives commonly used to describe films

Student's Book pages 102–103

READING

> **BACKGROUND INFORMATION**
>
> Stephen Hawking (b. 8 January 1942) is an English physicist. He suffers from motor neurone disease, which has slowly paralysed him over the years to the point where he now communicates with a single muscle in his cheek attached to a speech-generating device. His book *A Brief History of Time* (1988), which explains theoretical physics in popular terms, has sold nearly ten million copies.

1 **SPEAKING** Books closed. As a lead-in, ask: *How many planets are there? What evidence is typically presented as evidence of alien or UFO sightings?* Divide the class into small groups to make a list of planets and typical evidence. If students have access to digital technology, encourage them to show each other photos illustrating their ideas. Listen to some examples in open class.

Books open. If there is an interactive whiteboard (IWB) available in the classroom, this would best be done as a heads-up activity. Display the picture on the IWB. Put students into pairs to answer the questions. Listen to some of their answers in open class.

2 **SPEAKING** Regroup students so that they are talking to different partners. Students discuss the questions. Encourage them to use comparative forms to compare life on other planets to life on Earth. Monitor and note down any errors related to comparatives and make a note of any interesting comments to refer to during feedback. Listen to some of their answers in open class and write them on the board to facilitate feedback on Exercise 3.

3 Tell students to focus their reading on checking which of the ideas on the board are mentioned, and not to worry if they don't understand every word. Set a three-minute time limit to encourage students to read quickly. Students compare answers with a partner before whole-class feedback. Refer back to the ideas on the IWB and compare with those in the article.

4 🔊2.26 Before students read the text again, ask them to work with a partner and underline the key information in the sentences that they will need to look for in the article. Check/clarify: *paid us a visit*; *abducted*; *resources*. Students listen to and read the article and complete the exercise. Encourage them to underline parts of the text that support their answers and to correct any false information. Allow them to check answers with a partner before whole-class feedback.

> **Answers**
>
> 1 T   2 F (He is almost certain.)   3 F (He thinks that some could be intelligent.)   4 T   5 F (He believes they may take what they want, destroy the rest and leave.)   6 T

5 **SPEAKING** Students work in pairs or small groups to discuss the questions. Elicit a couple of answers in open class to get them started. Also consider encouraging them to agree on just one thing for each question in order to maximise debate. Listen to some of their ideas during whole-class feedback.

> **Optional extension**
>
> Write the following statement on the board. Ask students to discuss it in pairs and make a list of the advantages and disadvantages of space exploration.
>
> *The world currently spends billions of dollars on space programmes every year. What are the advantages and disadvantages of this?*

▰▰▰ TRAIN TO THiNK ▰▰▰

Spotting flawed arguments

1 Explain/elicit the meaning of *flawed* (describes something which is not perfect or doesn't work properly). Ask students to read the introduction and invite comments. Divide the class into groups of three and ask each student to read one of the three paragraphs A–C, then summarise it for their partners.

To check understanding of the different types of flawed argument, ask students to match quotations 1–3 with the explanations A–C. Check answers.

> **Answers**
>
> 1 C   2 B   3 A

2 **SPEAKING** Look at the three statements with students and check understanding. Read through the example flawed arguments for the first statement and elicit which type of argument they are (A–C).

Students work in pairs to create arguments for the other statements. Listen to some examples in open class as feedback. Ask: *Which types of flawed argument are most convincing?*

Mixed-ability

Put students into pairs roughly according to level. Ask weaker students to focus on one statement and think of three flawed arguments to support it. Stronger students can create three flawed arguments for all three statements.

Optional extension

Make small groups. Ask students to take it in turns to expand on one of the flawed arguments and try to convince their groups that their argument is correct. They could then go on to discuss their own personal opinions on each statement.

Student's Book pages 104–105

GRAMMAR

Speculating (past, present and future)

1 Books open. Look at the eight forms and ask: *What do these have in common?* (They are all used to speculate or express different levels of probability.) Ask students to work in pairs to read sentences 1–8 and try to complete them with the words in the list before looking back at the article to check. Check answers in open class and then ask pairs to complete the rule. Elicit answers in open class, referring back to sentences 1–8 for clarification.

Answers

1 may have already   2 must have   3 very likely
4 can't be   5 certain to   6 might be   7 bound to
8 may

Rule

1 could   2 can't   3 must   4 have   5 base infinitive
6 certain

---

2 Working in pairs, students discuss the meaning of the various forms and match the sentence halves. During whole-class feedback, elicit the form/phrase for expressing uncertainty within each sentence and ask students to explain their answers by giving the meaning of the target forms.

Answers

1 f   2 h   3 a   4 b   5 c   6 d   7 e   8 g

Fast finishers

Ask students to speculate about life on other planets and the possibility of aliens coming to Earth, using some of the words from Exercise 1. Listen to some examples after feedback on Exercise 2.

LANGUAGE NOTE

Remind students that the opposite of *must be* when making deductions is **can't be**, not *mustn't be*.

Could/might/may have similar meanings when used to speculate. Point out that *may* is more formal and less commonly used than *could* or *might*.

---

3 SPEAKING Divide the class into pairs for students to discuss the statements and rank them in order of probability. Monitor as they are doing this and make a note of repeated errors, in relation to the target language. Write these up on the board, ensuring anonymity, and ask students to correct them as part of whole-class feedback. At the same time, make a note of any nice contributions to quote and praise at the end of the activity. Have a show of hands to decide on the order of probability as a class.

Optional extension

Students work in AB pairs. A claims to have seen a UFO and B is sceptical. A has to present pieces of evidence to try to convince B, as follows:

1 A large circle appeared in the field next to your house;
2 You heard the sound of a very large engine in the sky;
3 You saw a circle of light hovering in the sky;
4 You heard voices speaking in a strange language;
5 You found the map of another planet on the ground;
6 You saw a small man with long, green fingers in the distance. (Note: order of evidence from trivial to silly/ridiculous.)

B uses past modals to explain away each piece of evidence.

Workbook page 100 and page 127

PRONUNCIATION

For practice of stress on modal verbs for speculation go to Student's Book page 121.

FUNCTIONS

Sympathising about past situations

1 Books closed. To introduce the topic, tell students about something sad that happened to a friend of yours e.g. *my friend lost his wallet yesterday*. Elicit sympathetic responses from students and write all suitable examples on the board.

Books open. Give students time to read the sentences and replies. Students complete the exercise with a partner. Check answers in open class. Elicit/clarify that the phrases in italics are used to show sympathy. Ask students to underline the speculative language.

Answers

1 c   2 d   3 b   4 a

---

2 Look at the first sentence in the dialogue with students. Ask them to work with a partner to order the rest of the dialogue. Check answers in open class. Nominate students to read full sentences and pay attention to pronunciation and intonation. Ask students to practise the dialogue with a partner. Monitor to make sure students sound sympathetic when giving sympathy.

Answers

7, **1**, 9, 5, 11, 3, 4, 6, 10, 2, 8

Optional extension

Disappearing sentences: you'll need to write out the dialogue in the correct order on the board or IWB for this one. Make AB pairs so that half of the class are A and half are B. Students practise the dialogue in their pairs. Cover a small section of the dialogue, beginning from the right-hand side of the screen or board. Students repeat the dialogue in their same AB pairings trying to remember the whole thing, including the parts they can no longer see. Cover more and more of the dialogue, with students practising at each stage, until eventually nothing is left on the board. Ask for volunteers to perform for the class or have all As and all Bs perform in unison. This activity involves lots of repetition in a fun way for students to memorise useful chunks.

3 Working individually, students complete the exercise. Monitor to help with vocabulary and ideas.

4 SPEAKING Students work in pairs to tell each other their stories. Encourage them to refer to replies a–d in Exercise 1 and sympathise with speculative language. Listen to some examples in open class as feedback.

LISTENING

1 SPEAKING If there is an IWB available in the classroom, this would best be done as a heads-up activity. Display the pictures on the IWB and nominate a student to say what aliens might learn about humans from the first picture. Divide the class into pairs to talk about all of the pictures. Nominate students to share their ideas in open class during feedback.

2 ◀))2.29 As a lead-in ask: *Have you ever heard of the Voyager mission? What do you know about it?* Elicit answers in open class. Tell students they are going to listen to an extract from a radio show about the Voyager mission. Play the audio while students answer the questions. Tell them that they should just focus on answering the question and that they do not need to understand every word.

Allow them to compare answers with a partner before open-class feedback.

Answers

The mission was to explore Saturn and Jupiter. The spaceship took discs with recordings and photographs of life on Earth.

Audio Script Track 2.29

In 1977 two unmanned spaceships, *Voyager I* and *II*, were launched from Earth to explore the giant planets of Saturn and Jupiter. After they had successfully completed their mission, they continued their journey deeper into space to explore the outer planets of our solar system. From August 2012, *Voyager I* and *II* entered an area called interstellar space. No other object has ever travelled further from our planet.

Before the spaceships were launched into the sky, the scientists placed large metal discs in each one. On these discs were recordings and photographs of life on Earth. They were chosen by a special committee headed by the famous astronomer Carl Sagan. The idea behind them was that if the Voyagers should come across any alien life-forms, the data on the discs would educate them about the human race.

So what did the committee decide to put on the discs? What was it that they decided would best represent our planet?

The first thing you'd want to say to any extra-terrestrial life form would naturally be 'hello', so greetings in 55 languages were recorded and put on the disc from [sound clip of Akkadian language] which translates into English as 'may all be very well' in the ancient Akkadian language to [sound clip of Wu language] which means 'Best wishes to you all' in the Wu language of Shanghai.

After the greetings, Sagan decided to include audio clips of sounds from Earth. These included sounds like a crying baby being comforted by its mother, a train, footsteps, a heartbeat, and wild dogs.

Next to be recorded were extracts of music to show any extra-terrestrial life-forms the creative side of the human race. The selections were mainly classical with some traditional songs from different cultures and a little rock and roll.

Finally 115 photographs and diagrams were added to the disc to give aliens an idea of what we all look like and how our world works. The discs also include instructions on how to play them.

So what would any alien life form make of us if they should ever encounter either of the *Voyager* space-craft? What kind of message have we sent about ourselves? Well, it's estimated that it will be around 40,000 years before *Voyager* passes through the next planetary system so it could be quite a long wait until we find out.

3 ◀))2.29 Give students time to read the sentences and try to complete the exercise from memory. Where they cannot recall the answer, ask them to try to predict words or even the type of word (noun, verb, etc.) for each gap. Play the recording again for students to check and complete their answers. Do a whole-class check. If necessary, play the recording a third time to clarify answers.

Answers

1 Saturn, Jupiter   2 large metal discs   3 the human race
4 greetings/recorded greetings   5 dogs   6 classical
7 instructions   8 40,000

▮ THiNK SELF-ESTEEM ▮

Who we are

1 SPEAKING Ask students to read the instructions. You could give some ideas of your own or elicit one or two in open class to get them started. You could also input some expressions for negotiating before students begin. For example, *Why don't we include …? What about including … ? That's a great idea but I'm not sure about … Great idea! We should definitely include that on our list.* Write these on the board for students to refer to while speaking.

Students work in pairs to agree on what should be put on the disc. Ask pairs to choose one student to make notes on what they agree on. Monitor to prompt students to use the expressions you put on the board.

2 SPEAKING Ask students to compare their ideas with another pair. Make sure all students have the chance to speak when describing their list of objects. Encourage them to give detail on the reasons for their choices rather than simply reading through their lists. Ask each group to agree on a final list. For feedback, listen to some of their ideas and try to come to an agreement on a final list in open class.

Optional extension
Ask students to work in pairs to write a fifty-word message to send to aliens. How would they describe life on Earth? And how would they invite aliens to come and visit? Listen to some examples in open class and have a show of hands to decide on the best message.

VOCABULARY

Space idioms

1 Give students time to read the sentences. Ask them to work with a partner to match sentences 1–6 with sentences a–f and to use the context provided by each sentence to help them to deduce meaning and complete the exercise. Encourage students to guess answers if they are not sure, by elimination, if necessary. Check answers in open class.

Answers

1 e 2 f 3 a 4 b 5 c 6 d

Fast finishers
Ask students to discuss whether they have any similar space idioms in their own language.

2 If you're short on time, set this exercise for homework.

Students work with a partner to complete the exercise. Check answers in open class. Clarify that we use *over the moon* to describe somebody's reaction to a certain situation. It does not describe somebody's happiness over a long period of time.

Answers

1 over the moon   2 down to earth   3 out of this world
4 It's not rocket science.   5 once in a blue moon
6 starry-eyed

Optional extension
Put students into small groups to discuss the following questions:
1 *When did you last see or hear something out of this world?*
2 *Give an example of a situation when you might use the phrase 'It's not rocket science'.*
3 *Name something you do once in a blue moon.*
4 *Do you know anybody who is starry-eyed? How do they behave?*
5 *When did you last feel over the moon about something?*
6 *Do you know anybody who is down to earth?*

Workbook page 102

Student's Book pages 106–107

READING

1 A recording of this text is available with your digital resources. Books closed. As a lead-in, ask: *How many films about space can you think of?* Divide the class into small groups and ask them to list as many space films as possible in a three-minute period. When time is up, find out which group came up with the most

films and invite them to read out their list to the class while the rest of the class crosses off any of the films they hear that also appear on their lists, just to give them a reason to listen.

Books open. Tell students they are going to read a blog about space films. To encourage students to read quickly, set a two-minute time limit for them to read and answer the question. Tell them not to worry about any difficult language at this stage and to ignore the words in italics. Check answer.

Answer

The Martian

2 Check/clarify: *against all the odds* (something happened which seemed very unlikely to happen). Students re-read the blog in more detail to answer the questions. Ask them to underline the parts of the text that support their answers. Allow students to check their answers with a partner before feedback in open class.

Answers

1 WALL-E   2 Avatar   3 Apollo 13   4 The Martian
5 Avatar   6 WALL-E   7 The Martian   8 Apollo 13

3 SPEAKING Put students into small groups to discuss the questions. As they speak, ask them to discuss the merits of any films they mention and to describe the plots of any films other students have not seen. Monitor to help with vocabulary and ideas. During feedback, invite students to share their favourite space film with the class and perhaps hold a vote to find out the class's favourite space film.

Optional extension
If you feel your students need extra writing practice, ask them to write a blog entry describing a film of their choice. First, ask them to underline collocations and expressions that they like in the blog on page 106, and to try to incorporate them in their own blog. They should include information on the lead actors, a brief outline of the plot and their reasons for liking the film. This could either be done individually or as a collaborative writing activity with students working in pairs or small groups.

GRAMMAR

Cause and effect linkers

1 Ask students to complete sentences 1–4 with possible words that fit before locating the sentences in the blog to compare their answers. Ask students to work with a partner to complete the rule. Check answers in open class. Refer to the examples in Exercise 1 to clarify and add further examples if necessary.

Answers

1 Due to 2 as a result of 3 because of 4 consequently

Rule

1 because of 2 Consequently

2 If you're short on time, set this exercise for homework. This exercise is closely modelled on Reading and Use of English Part 4 of the Cambridge English: First exam. Ask students to read the instructions and example. Students work individually to complete the exercise and then check their answers with a partner before whole-class feedback. During feedback refer to the rule for clarification.

Answers

1 result of eating   2 due to the bad weather
3 because of a   4 as a result of   5 due to (a)

Fast finishers

Ask students to transform the sentences in different ways using the other linkers.

Workbook page 101 and page 127

 Be aware of common errors related to cause and effect linkers. Go to Get it right! on Student's Book page 126.

VOCABULARY

Adjectives commonly used to describe films

1 Ask students to look back at the blog for help in completing the exercise. Allow them to compare answers with a partner before checking with the whole class. Say the words for students to repeat and check pronunciation. Write the words on the board to elicit and mark the stress on each word. Point out the stress on *fetch* in *far-fetched*.

Mixed-ability

Stronger students can go to the text and try to deduce meaning of the words from the context, without looking at the definitions in Exercise 1. They then look at the definitions to check their answers.

Answers

1 delightful   2 stunning   3 thrilling   4 sentimental
5 far-fetched   6 breathtaking   7 memorable
8 action-packed

2 If you're short on time, you can set this exercise for homework. Give students time to read the sentences and deal with any queries. Check/clarify: *on the edge of my seat*; *car chases*; *dull*. Ask students to work with a partner to choose the correct word to complete each sentence. During feedback, ask students to say why the wrong answer is not suitable.

Answers

1 thrilling   2 sentimental   3 delightful
4 action-packed   5 far-fetched   6 stunning
7 memorable   8 breathtaking

Fast finishers

Ask students to try to rewrite the sentences so that they make sense with the other adjective. e.g *1. The ending of the film was really sentimental. I don't mind a happy ending but this was too much!*

---

3 Students work in pairs to come up with examples. Ask them to write them down in their notebooks. Monitor and help with vocabulary and ideas as necessary. For feedback, listen to some of their ideas in open class. Ask: *Which adjectives was it easier to think of example films for? Why?*

Workbook page 102

SPEAKING

Give some examples of your own or elicit some in open class to get students started. Put students into pairs to create their lists. Encourage them to go into detail when giving their reasons for choosing films and challenge them to use all of the adjectives in Exercise 2. When students have completed their lists, put pairs together to make groups of four. Ask them to compare and agree on a list of four for each category. Listen to some example lists in open class and decide on the best films in each category as a class.

Student's Book pages 108–109

CULTURE

1 If you have internet access in the classroom, introduce the topic with some film clips of rockets taking off or astronauts in zero gravity. As they watch, ask students to imagine what would be most difficult, frightening, fun about daily life in space. Get students to share their thoughts in pairs before inviting comments in open class.

Ask students to circle the key information in the questions that they will be looking for in the article. Tell students that they need to scan the text for specific information, so they do not need to read every word of the text in order to successfully complete the exercise. Set a two-minute time limit to encourage them to read quickly. Listen to some of their ideas in open class, but do not comment at this stage.

2 2.30 Play the audio while students read and listen to the article to check their answers to Exercise 1. Allow them to compare answers with a partner before feedback in open class.

Answers

1 The United States, Russia, China, Japan and India
2 Eating, washing and sleeping

3 Give students time to read through the questions. Ask students to re-read the article to complete the exercise. Ask them to underline parts of the text that support their answers. Students compare answers with a partner before whole-class feedback.

Answers

1 People who can afford them and are keen to have the experience.
2 It went everywhere because there's no gravity.
3 Because the water doesn't run down when there's no gravity.
4 It's comfortable and you don't need floor space, just an attachment to something.
5 In a sleeping bag floating in the module.
6 She meant the trip in the Soyuz spacecraft was as rough as she expected it to be.

4 VOCABULARY Ask students to look back at the text to find the highlighted words or phrases that match the descriptions. Check answers and during feedback, say the words for students to repeat and check pronunciation.

Mixed-ability

Stronger students may like to look at the eight words in the text and try to deduce meaning from context before referring back to the definitions, and checking and completing the exercise.

Answers

1 embark 2 profits 3 reputation 4 squeezed
5 drifting off 6 quest 7 bonus 8 portrayed

SPEAKING

Put students into pairs or small groups to discuss the questions. Ask one student in each group to act as an 'English police officer', giving one penalty point each time somebody speaks in L1. The winner is the group with the fewest points at the end of the exercise. Monitor and help as necessary, encouraging students to express themselves in English and to use any vocabulary they have learned from the text. Ask pairs or groups to feed back to the class and discuss any interesting points further.

WRITING

A report

1 Give students two minutes to quickly read the model report and answer the questions. Allow them to compare answers with a partner before a whole-class check. Ask students: *Is the language used formal or informal?* (formal); *What makes it formal?* (use of linking words to join sentences; repeated use of passive forms e.g. *can be done; being covered; is being prepared; can be introduced*).

Answers

Problem: computer malfunction due to food spillage
Solution: ban all liquid food

2 Give students time to read the functions. Ask them to re-read the report and complete the exercise before comparing answers with a partner. Encourage them to underline the parts of the report that support their answers and to refer to these during pair-checking and whole-class feedback.

Answers

1 A brief description of what the report is about
2 An outline of the problem
3 Suggestions for changes

3 You may like to approach this exercise with a test-teach-test approach. Ask students to work individually to rewrite sentences with the words in brackets. Do not offer any guidance at this stage. Monitor to gauge how well students are able to do this and to make a note of any repeated problems. During whole-class feedback, pay attention to the use of the words in brackets and elicit/clarify rules regarding punctuation and position in the sentence. If necessary, ask students to refer back to the grammar section on page 107 for further clarification and examples.

Answers

1 The computer had stopped working as a result of it being covered in a thick orange liquid.
2 The computer had stopped working because of it being covered in a thick orange liquid.
3 The crew were able to run the back-up computer. However, the incident has raised serious concerns about dining habits.
4 Despite the crew being able to run the back-up computer, the incident has raised serious concerns about dining habits.

4 Ask students to read the situation and to work in pairs to make notes on the problem and a possible solution. Monitor to help with vocabulary and to give ideas, as necessary.

5 This exercise can be set as homework or done as a collaborative writing activity in class with pairs of students writing together.

Before they begin writing, encourage students to underline collocations and expressions in the model report that they could use in their report. Remind them that they should also use linkers of cause and effect. When students have finished writing, ask them to exchange reports with another pair. Tell them not to worry about minor grammatical errors, but to make comments on the formality of the report and whether the problem and solution are clearly explained. Students can then return reports and incorporate comments to create a final draft.

12 MORE TO EXPLORE

Objectives

FUNCTIONS	speaking persuasively
GRAMMAR	passive report structures; the passive: verbs with two objects
VOCABULARY	geographical features; verb + noun collocations

Student's Book pages 110–111

READING

1 Books closed. As a lead-in, ask students: *Do you like visiting foreign countries? If you could go anywhere in the world, where would you go?* Elicit some answers in open class. Next, give students three minutes to agree on a list of the five most exciting places in the world, in pairs. Nominate students to share their lists in open class.

   Books open. If there is an interactive whiteboard (IWB) available in the classroom, this activity would best be done as a heads-up activity. Focus on the pictures and nominate students to describe them. Ask students to discuss the photos on pages 110–111 in pairs. Monitor and help with vocabulary as necessary. During whole-class feedback, write some of the students' answers on the board to refer to when they have read the article.

2 To encourage students to read the article quickly, set a four-minute time limit to read and check their answers to Exercise 1. Allow students to compare answers with a partner before a whole-class check. Refer back to students' ideas on the board to check if anyone guessed correctly.

   ### Answers

   Voronya Cave, Mariana Trench, Amazon rainforest, Greenland, deserts

3 **◀)2.31** Give students time to read the questions and deal with any questions about vocabulary. Play the audio while students re-read and listen to the article and answer the questions. Ask them to underline the parts of the text that gave them their answers. Allow them to compare answers with a partner before whole-class feedback.

Answers

1 Because it is so inaccessible and inhospitable to humans.
2 Because caving is very popular in those places.
3 Freezing temperatures and immense water pressure.
4 98%
5 Because of its climate, resources and biodiversity.
6 Understanding the history of the Earth's environment.
7 Explorers have died.
8 They have developed to survive in very high temperatures and with very little water.

Optional extension

To give students extra practice in scanning, write the following terms on the board and ask students to find them in the text and say what they refer to. To make the exercise more challenging, write the terms in random order for students.

Most of (the caves remain unexplored)
Thousands (of caves are thought to exist in China)
2% (of the ocean floor has been explored)
50% (of the world's rainforest is in the Amazon)
2,000 (species of bird and animal live in the Amazon)
2.5 million (insect species have been documented)
400,000 (plant species have been documented)
81% (of Greenland is covered in ice)
limited (the extent to which Greenland has been explored)
very few (desert explorations have been conducted)

4 **SPEAKING** Put students into small groups to discuss the questions. Monitor but do not interrupt unless errors hinder comprehension. Make sure all students are contributing to the discussion and encourage quieter students to voice their opinions too. To facilitate the involvement of quieter students, you could assign them the role of group secretary. They are then tasked with making detailed notes on the group's answers. Regroup students and ask them to share their ideas with their new groups. Nominate two or three students to report back on their discussions in open class.

TRAIN TO THINK

Exploring hidden messages

1 Ask students to read the introduction and to consider whether they do this. Ask: *Do you ever avoid saying what you really think? Can you give any examples?* Students discuss with a partner. Invite students to share their answers in open class.

   Give students time to read the statements and think about what the person might be hiding. Do the first one in open class as an example if necessary. Ask students to work in pairs to complete the exercise.

Tell them to think about who could have said each statement. Check answers in open class. Tell students that we sometimes use 'hidden message' language when we want to avoid being direct. For example, statement 4 might be used as a 'polite' way of accusing somebody of copying.

2 Students complete the exercise in pairs. Encourage them to practise responding in such a way that the true message is hidden. Listen to some of their responses in open class and ask the rest of the class to decide if the answers sound authentic.

Optional extension

Tell students that if two people do not particularly get on, they may have conversations which include a lot of hidden messages. This is commonly seen in comedy films where characters do it for comic effect. Students may enjoy creating dialogues containing a variety of hidden messages. For example:

(At Anne's party)

A: Hi, Anne. Great party! I like parties without too many people. (there's no atmosphere)

B: Hi! If I'd known you were coming I'd have invited John. (for you to speak to because I don't want to)

A: The music's good – I haven't heard this song since I was about 10. (you like children's music)

Ask students to create dialogues with a partner, then act them out for another pair, who have to guess the true meaning of the statements at the end of the dialogue.

Student's Book pages 112–113

GRAMMAR

Passive report structures

1 Before focussing on sentences 1–5, you may like to give students a brief review of the passive. Write the following sentences from the article on the board or project them if you have access to an IWB and ask students: *What do these sentences have in common?* (They are all in the passive.)

1 Only 2% of the ocean floor has been explored.
2 Research and development exhibitions are being carried out.
3 It's easy to think that everything that could be discovered already has been.

Ask students to work in pairs to name the passive forms. Check answers.

1 present perfect passive
2 present continuous passive
3 modal passive; present perfect passive

Ask students to look through the text and underline more examples of: the present simple passive; the present perfect passive; modal passives (e.g. *will/can/could*); and passive infinitives (*to be* + past participle).

Answers:

The present simple passive: *very little is known, is known about our solar system, studies are conducted, rainforest is said, are known to live there, more are believed to live there, is covered in ice*

The present perfect passive: *already has been, has been explored, has been almost impossible, species have been officially documented, has only been explored, have been drilled*

Modal passives (e.g. *will/can/could*): *could be discovered*

Passive infinitives: *to be revealed, to be opened up, to be determined, to be explored, to be learnt*

Next, ask students to read sentences 1–5 and ask: *Which of the sentences are facts and which are opinions?* (1 and 2 are opinions; 3–5 are facts.) Students work with a partner to find sentences in the article with the same meaning as sentences 1–5. Ask students to discuss the differences in the form of the sentences in pairs or groups. Check answers. Students work together to complete the rule. During whole-class feedback, elicit/give further examples to clarify the usage of each passive report structure, as necessary. Ask: *When and why do we use passive report structures?* (mostly in written language; to make language more formal and to avoid starting sentences with impersonal subjects such as *people* or *experts*).

Answers

1 tens of thousands more are believed to live there
2 thousands of caves are also thought to exist in China
3 The Amazon rainforest is said to comprise around 50% of all the rainforests in the world.
4 over 2,000 species of birds and mammals are known to live there
5 many people are known to have died on such expeditions

Rule

1 present 2 past 3 written

2 If you're short on time, you can set this exercise for homework but perhaps do number 1 in open class.

Students work individually to complete the exercise, then check their answers with a partner before whole-class feedback. During feedback refer to the rule for clarification.

Mixed-ability

Give weaker students the answers to the exercise showing the passive structures (you'll need to prepare this before the lesson) and ask them to write down the original (active) sentences. Stronger students can complete the exercise as it appears on the page.

Answers

1 is believed to be disappearing
2 is said to be 500 metres deep
3 in the deep ocean are thought to be blind
4 is known to have contained water only 5,000 years ago
5 are believed to have existed for millions of years

Workbook page 108 and page 127

 Be aware of common errors related to *been* and *being* when using the passive. Go to Get it right! on Student's Book page 126.

VOCABULARY

Geographical features

1 If you have access to an IWB, this would best be done as a heads-up activity with the images enlarged and projected onto the board. Ask students to cover the words and work with a partner to try to name each of the things. After two minutes, ask students to uncover the words and match the words to the pictures, in pairs. Check answers in open class and take the opportunity to say the words for students to repeat and check pronunciation. Pay attention to the long vowel sounds in *bay*; *volcano* and the short vowel sound in *glacier*.

Answers

1 D   2 F   3 G   4 B   5 E   6 A   7 H   8 C

2 Use the images to check/clarify: *surface*; *erupts*. Ask students to work individually to complete the sentences, then compare answers with a partner before feedback in open class.

Answers

1 mountain range   2 dune   3 waterfall   4 reef
5 volcano   6 glacier   7 bay   8 canyon

3 SPEAKING Divide the class into small groups to complete the exercise. Make the activity into a competition by setting a three-minute time limit and counting down every 30 seconds. When time is up, regroup students so that they can compare their lists.

This can also be turned into a quiz, with students asking each other where the geographical features are. Listen to some of their answers in open class.

Workbook page 110

LISTENING

Discovering new species

1 Books closed. As a lead-in, ask students: *How many different animal species can you name in English?* Elicit one or two in open class to make sure that students are clear on the meaning of *species*, and then ask them to make a list in pairs. Monitor and ask the pair with the longest list to share it with the class. Ask the class: *How many different animal species are there in the world?* (There were estimated to be 8.7 million different species in 2011.) Finally, give students three minutes to work in pairs and brainstorm things that animals have but humans do not, for example: *tusks*; *hooves*. Write all correct answers on the board.

Books open. If there is an IWB available in the classroom, this would best be done as a heads-up activity with the whole class. Project the pictures onto the board. Ask students to do the matching activity in pairs. During feedback, point to/elicit the following in the pictures: *fins*; *wings*; *antennae*; *feathers*; *beak*; *scales*.

2 Students discuss the questions in pairs. Ask them to rank the animals in order of beauty and danger. If students have access to the Internet, they could search for the animals to find out if they are poisonous or endangered.

Answers

Poisonous: tree frog; monitor lizard
All of them are endangered

3 ◀))2.32 Play the recording while students listen for the creatures mentioned. Students can check answers with a partner before whole-class feedback.

Answer

rainbow fish, monitor lizard, honeyeater

Erm, I'd like to give you just one example here and it's the island of Papua New Guinea. Papua New Guinea is a pretty big island just north of Australia. It's covered in rainforest and it's an incredibly, erm, an amazing place in terms of wildlife.

Now, here's something that might surprise you – in ten years between 1998 and 2008, just in Papua New Guinea alone, one thousand and sixty new species were found. One thousand and sixty, that's more than two species every week for ten years. Now, that includes plants and flowers, but lots of different kinds of animals and fish and things too. One example is a monitor lizard, a beautiful black lizard with blue markings that can grow to about a metre in length. They also found a bird called a honeyeater, with beautiful orange patches around its eyes. And this honeyeater is a very different bird because it's almost silent, makes no sounds at all, and that's why no one found it for so long, no one heard it!

And then there's fish, there's what's called the rainbow fish, and in fact seven different kinds of rainbow fish have been found over the last ten years or so.

So, the good news is that we're finding new species all the time. We don't know how many more species are still out there. What we do know is that more will be found – it's just inevitable, really, that we're going to find more species.

What's not so good, of course, is that all these animals and birds and fish are endangered. Their habitat, that is the places where they live, is being destroyed, and it's human beings who are doing it. Um, forests are being turned into fields to grow food, and trees are being cut down to get wood, and rivers are being used by more and more boats, and so these animals find it harder and harder to live. The consequences of this will be more and more animals becoming extinct– and that's a terrible thought. If we don't act now, to stop habitats being destroyed, many animals will disappear and future generations will only see them in books. I think it's vital for humans to find ways to live well and without harming other living creatures, don't you?

Anyway, back to discovering new species. There are other places, too, not just Papua New Guinea, where we …

4 ◀)) 2.32 Give students time to read the questions and underline the key information that they will be listening for. Play the audio again while students listen and answer the questions. Allow them to compare answers with a partner before a whole-class check.

Answers

1 an organisation called Species Specialists
2 1,060
3 Because it's a silent bird, so no one heard it.
4 That we're finding new species all the time.
5 Destroying animal habitats.

Optional extension

Ask students to work with a partner and discuss what they would do if they discovered a new species. Ask them to think about the procedure they would need to follow to get the new species recognised as a different species to those already listed. Ask them to imagine what the creature might be and what they would name it. More artistic students might also like to draw a picture of their creature.

FUNCTIONS

Speaking persuasively

1 ◀)) 2.33 Ask students to work with a partner to try to complete the extract from memory. Play the audio for them to check their answers. Check answers in open class.

Answers

1 consequences   2 terrible   3 don't act   4 vital
5 don't you

Audio Script Track 2.33

… and so these animals find it harder and harder to live. The consequences of this will be more and more animals becoming extinct – and that's a terrible thought. If we don't act now, to stop habitats being destroyed, many animals will disappear and future generations will only see them in books. I think it's vital for humans to find ways to live well and without harming other living creatures, don't you?

2 To check understanding of terminology (adjectives; adverbs; question tag; conditional clause) elicit examples of each in open class. Students work in pairs to complete the exercise. Check answers.

Answers

1 harder and harder, more and more   2 don't you?
3 If we don't act now

3 Refer students to the extract in Exercise 1 as an example of what is required. Students write persuasive sentences. Monitor and help with vocabulary and to check students are including examples of the structures in Exercise 2 to make their points strongly. Give students time to think about which words they will stress when giving their speeches. Put students into small groups to take turns to give their speeches. Students could vote on the most persuasive speech for each of 1–3 in their groups.

Mixed-ability

Stronger students can complete the exercise alone. Weaker students can work with a partner.

PRONUNCIATION

For practice of linking with the intrusive /r/ sound go to Student's Book page 121.

▋▋ THiNK VALUES ▋▋

Human activity and the natural world

1 Students work with a partner to discuss questions 1–3 and note down their ideas. Encourage students to use bullet points and to write down any interesting vocabulary they will need to use in their discussions. Monitor to help with vocabulary and ideas.

2 SPEAKING Tell students they are going to give a presentation. You could ask students to choose their own question from Exercise 1 to concentrate on, or you can assign questions if you want to make sure there is a balance of different presentations. Before students prepare their presentations, elicit/clarify that students should include a brief introduction before giving their opinions and ending with a strong conclusion. Remind students to use the kind of persuasive language used in the Functions exercise.

Monitor and help with any questions. When students have completed the exercise, divide the class into small groups for students to share their presentations (with smaller groups, this could be done in open class).

> **Optional extension**
>
> As students listen to their classmates' presentations, ask them to grade them from 1 (poor) to 5 (excellent) in the following areas: enthusiasm; eye contact/body language; subject knowledge; organisation. When the presentations have all been given, ask students to give each other feedback.

Student's Book pages 114–115

READING

1 **SPEAKING** A recording of this text is available with your digital resources. As a lead-in, ask students: *How would you travel to … (city near the school)?* Elicit answers from students in open class and make a note on the board. Ask: *How could you travel if there were no roads or railways? How long would it take?* Ask students to discuss with a partner before listening to some of their ideas in open class.

Students discuss the questions in pairs. If they have access to the Internet, give them time to research their answers to the questions before discussing them.

2 Ask students to work with a partner to discuss the pictures and title before checking their answers by reading the text quickly. Confirm answers in open class. Note: the highlighted state on the map is of Rondônia.

3 Before reading the text again, ask students to underline the key words in the statements that will help them decide if the sentence is true, false or not in the article. Students read the article again to complete the activity and correct the false statements. Check answers with the whole class. Ask students to refer to the parts of the article to explain their answers.

> **Answers**
>
> 1 DS   2 T   3 F   4 T   5 DS   6 T

> **Fast finishers**
>
> Ask students to write two more statements about the article for their partners/the class to decide if they are true, false or not in the article.

SPEAKING

Students discuss the questions in pairs or small groups. Monitor and help with vocabulary as necessary. Make sure all students get an opportunity to speak. Make a note of any interesting answers and refer to these during whole-class feedback.

> **Optional extension**
>
> Ask students to write five questions based on the article, in pairs. Put pairs together to form groups of four for them to ask each other their questions. Students score two points if they can answer correctly from memory and one point if they can find the answer after looking at the text for only 15 seconds.

GRAMMAR

The passive: verbs with two objects

1 Students find the sentence in the article. Ask students to complete the rule and then compare their answers with a partner. During whole-class feedback, give further examples of your own to clarify the rules, as necessary.

> **Answers**
>
> Sentence 3 is used in the text.
>
> **Rule**
>
> 1 indirect   2 direct   3 person

2 Ask students to look at the four pairs of sentences. Clarify that both are grammatically possible, but one of each pair is more usual. Students work with a partner to complete the exercise.

> **Answers**
>
> 1 B   2 A   3 A   4 A

> **Fast finishers**
>
> Ask students to find further examples of the passive in the article and think about why the passive is used in each case.

3 If you're short on time, you can set this exercise for homework. Students complete the exercise and then check their answers with a partner before whole-class feedback. During feedback elicit which is the indirect object in each sentence in order to clarify answers, as necessary.

> **Mixed-ability**
>
> Ask weaker students to underline the direct objects and circle the indirect objects before they rewrite the sentences taking the indirect object as subject.

> **Answers**
>
> 1 My mum was offered a job.
> 2 My dad was owed a lot of money.
> 3 He was given some medicine.
> 4 We were promised a week's holiday.
> 5 I was shown the right way to do it.

> **Optional extension**
>
> Write the following words on the board, randomly, for students to order into sentences. Stronger students/classes could follow up by writing example sentences of their own for their partners to order.
>
> 1 I was given a bicycle for my birthday.
> 2 She was told a story by her mother.
> 3 I was promised a big present if I passed my exams.
> 4 He was given some advice.

Workbook page 109 and page 127 ➤

VOCABULARY

Verb + noun collocations

1 Ask students to complete the exercise in pairs. Remind them to put the verbs into the correct form. During whole-class feedback, say the collocations for students to repeat and check pronunciation.

> **Answers**
>
> 1 made   2 made   3 take   4 play

2 Books closed. Display the five columns on the IWB and add the four noun collocates from Exercise 1.

Books open. Ask students to work with a partner to complete the exercise. If you are using an IWB, prepare a board with the words written in individual text boxes. Check answers. During feedback, ask individuals to come to the board and drag and drop words into the correct column. Elicit any further examples of noun collocates from students and add them to the table.

> **Answers**
>
> | make | take | play | do | give |
> |---|---|---|---|---|
> | friends | a photograph | a part | exercise | advice |
> | a deal | exercise | the fool | a deal | a speech |
> | a journey | advice | a joke | a favour | money |
> | a speech | a journey | a role | an exam | an example |
> | progress | an exam | | research | a test |
> | a wish | a decision | | good | |
> | an effort | revenge | | a test | |
> | a decision | a joke | | | |
> | money | advantage of | | | |
> | an example | a test | | | |
> | a joke | | | | |
> | a complaint | | | | |
> | amends | | | | |
> | fun of | | | | |

3 You could encourage students to first read the text in order to get a general understanding, before they read in detail to complete the exercise, by asking them to ignore the gaps and answer this question: *What preparations did the writer make before starting his journey up the river?* Students read again and fill the gaps. Allow students to compare answers with a partner before feedback in open class.

> **Answers**
>
> 1 take/make   2 gave   3 making   4 gave   5 made
> 6 done   7 taken   8 made   9 did/made   10 take
> 11 make   12 take

> **Fast finishers**
>
> Write the following questions on the board. Ask fast finishers to write answers.
>
> *What do you usually take photos of?*
> *How do you know when you are making progress with your English?*
> *How might you make amends when you do something wrong?*
> *Do you ever make fun of your friends?*

4 **WRITING** In pairs, students write the next paragraph of the story. Before they start to write, ask them to discuss what they are going to write,

and then note down some collocations to include. As they write, monitor to help with any questions and to check students are using collocations correctly. Ask students to exchange paragraphs with other pairs and to consider how similar or different their stories are, then take feedback on this in open class.

> **Optional extension**
>
> Divide the class into pairs for students to test each other on the collocations. For example:
>
> A: *a speech*
>
> B: *make a speech*

Workbook page 110 ➤

Student's Book pages 116–117

LITERATURE

The Lost World by Arthur Conan Doyle

1 Books closed. As a lead-in, ask: *Can you think of any novels or films about dinosaurs? What happens in them?* Students discuss the questions in pairs. Listen to some of their ideas in open class and write any repeated themes on the board.

Books open. Look at the photo and title and ask students to read the introduction. Check/clarify: *plateau.* Ask students to discuss the question with a partner. Nominate one or two students to share their ideas in open class.

2 Ask students to quickly read the extract and choose the best ending. You could set a three-minute time limit to encourage speed-reading. Allow students to check answers with a partner before whole-class feedback.

> **Answer**
>
> Ending 2

3 🔊2.36 Play the audio for students to listen to and read the extract. Tell them to concentrate on answering the questions in note form and not to worry about understanding every word or writing full sentences. Allow students to check their answers with a partner before feedback in open class. Nominate students to share their answers and to give reasons.

> **Answers**
>
> 1 To avoid any conflict.
> 2 They remained motionless and looked frightened.
> 3 Different groups of drummers were using the drums to communicate.
> 4 'We will kill you if we can.'
> 5 To avoid being attacked by native people. / So that they could escape more quickly. / So that they were more difficult to steal.

4 **VOCABULARY** Students work individually to complete the exercise and then check their answers with a partner before feedback in open class.

Answers

1 breaking out   2 clumsily   3 aware of   4 gazing
5 motionless   6 anchor   7 dawn   8 intently

5 SPEAKING In pairs or small groups, students discuss the questions. Monitor, encouraging students to fully develop and expand on their answers. Make a note of any nice expressions in English that students use during the activity. At the end write them on the board for the whole class to copy, and praise the student(s) who used them. During feedback, ask for volunteers to report back to the class on their discussion.

WRITING

A short biography

1 Ask students: *Have you ever read a biography of a famous person?* Elicit responses in open class. Ask students to read the short biography of O.R. Tambo and answer the questions. Allow them to compare answers with a partner before doing a whole-class check.

Answers

1 Education and law.   2 Zambia and London.
3 Because he had a stroke and could not work any longer.

2 Students work with a partner to complete the exercise. Check answers. Point out that the information is presented chronologically.

Answers

A Fourth paragraph   B Second paragraph
C First paragraph   D Third paragraph

3 Give students time to read the instructions. In open class, elicit the names of some places in students' cities which are named after famous people and write them on the board. Divide the class into pairs for students to choose a subject they are both familiar with and answer the questions. If students have access to the Internet, they can do the research in class. If not, this could be done at home. Students make notes, decide which information to include in their biography and then make a plan.

Students write their biography. Encourage them to use the structure of the text about O.R. Tambo as a template. In the next lesson, ask students to share their work with other students and decide which is the most interesting.

Student's Book pages 118–119

TEST YOURSELF UNITS 11 & 12

VOCABULARY

1

Answers

1 squeezing   2 solar   3 breathtaking   4 volcano
5 waterfall   6 reef   7 took   8 bonus   9 do
10 far-fetched

GRAMMAR

2

Answers

1 to have   2 consequently   3 can't have   4 to be
5 must be   6 was given

3

Answers

1 I'm sure a lot of people have met the new boy. Sue mustn't can't be the only one.
2 Only a few people are thought to have survive survived so long alone in the desert.
3 Oh dear, I'm bound to got have got this all wrong – I didn't understand the question.
4 My father was brought up by his aunt after his parents were died.
5 Kelly Jones is know known to have owned three houses, although she has always said that she's very poor.
6 I suppose it's possible – Carol might be have been at the party last night, but I didn't see her.

FUNCTIONAL LANGUAGE

4

Answers

1 must, dear   2 had been, terrible   3 believed, can't
4 thought, seen

PRONUNCIATION

UNIT 1

Diphthongs: alternative spellings

Aim: Students recognise and practise different spellings for the diphthongs /eɪ/ (e.g. aim), /aɪ/ (tie), /əʊ/ (toe), /aʊ/ (out) and /ɔɪ/ (boy). Diphthongs are made by merging two vowel sounds to create one long sound; the mouth changes shape when making the sound.

1 🔊 1.07 Ask students to listen and read the five tongue twisters. Students identify the long vowel sound in bold in each sentence.

> **Answers**
>
> 1 /aɪ/ (e.g. ice), 2 /əʊ/ (e.g. snow), 3 /eɪ/ (e.g. late),
> 4 /aʊ/ (e.g. out) and 5 /ɔɪ/ (e.g. boy).

Ask students to identify the different spellings of the same sound.

> **Answers**
>
> 1 igh, ie, i and i_e, 2 oe, o_e and ow, 3 ay, a_e, ai and aigh,
> 4 ou and ow, 5 oi and oy.

> **Optional extension**
>
> Write the following diphthongs on the board – *high*, *snow*, *late*, *town*, *boy*. Encourage students to say the diphthongs aloud, noticing how the shape of the mouth changes as they say the phonemes. (The mouth ends in a wider, stretched position when saying the /aɪ/ (high), /eɪ/ (late), and /ɔɪ/ (boy) sounds. It ends in a smaller, circular position when saying the /əʊ/ (snow) and /aʊ/ (town) sounds.)
>
> If you can, let students use a mirror or the camera on their mobile phones to see the way their mouths change.

2 🔊 1.08 Students listen again and repeat. They take turns saying the sentences with a partner.

> **EXTRA INFORMATION**
>
> - Recognising alternative and irregular spellings of the same phonemes is an important skill which will help students improve their pronunciation enormously. Encourage students to regularly look for and identify different spellings of the same sound as part of the language learning process.
> - Note that the phonemic script indicates the changes to the mouth when saying the diphthongs. The wider, stretched position in /aɪ/ (high), /eɪ/ (late), and /ɔɪ/ (boy) is shown by the /ɪ/ ending and the circular position when saying /əʊ/ (snow) and /aʊ/ (town) with the /ʊ/.
> - Note that the phonemic script symbols show how diphthongs are a merging of two short vowel sounds to create a long sound, for example /əʊ/ (e.g. toe) and /eɪ/ (e.g. late). Long vowel sounds where the mouth doesn't change shape are indicated by a double colon (they are monophthongs) e.g. /iː/ (e.g. see) and /ɑː/ (e.g. car).

UNIT 2

Phrasal verb stress

Aim: Students identify and practise primary and secondary stress in phrasal verbs.

1 🔊 1.13 Ask students to tell you what they think primary and secondary stress in the context of phrasal verbs could mean. Elicit that it involves two stressed syllables. The primary stress is the stronger one. To ensure that students are clear on the overall meaning of the text before looking at the pronunciation ask them to listen and read in order to answer this gist question: *What helped Gillian learn French?* (hanging around with her French friends).

2 Students listen and read while you play the recording again, paying attention to the two stresses indicated by the red (primary) and blue (secondary) colours. They practise saying the phrasal verbs from the dialogue in isolation before repeating the whole dialogue. Note that three-part phrasal verbs follow the same pattern (the final preposition isn't stressed).

> **Answers**
>
> 1 primary   2 secondary   3 particle   4 verb

3 🔊 1.14 Students listen to the recording and repeat. Then they practise with a partner.

> **EXTRA INFORMATION**
>
> - Some phrasal verbs only have one stress (*look at*, *care for*), in which case the stress always falls on the verb.
> - However, many more phrasal verbs have two stresses, including all those targeted in this unit (*put up with*, *bring about*, *run into*, *turn out*, *hang out with*, *pick up*, *go through* and *wear out*). In these phrasal verbs, the main (primary) stress falls on the particle, with the secondary stress placed on the verb.
> - Three-part phrasal verbs are practised in the WB. The pattern is the same, with the primary stress falling on the particle and the secondary stress on the verb. The final preposition is never stressed: ˌhang ˈout with; ˌput ˈup with

UNIT 3

Adding emphasis

Aim: To raise students' awareness of the increase in intonation range across a whole sentence when emphasisers are used.

1   ◀))1.18   Focus students on these gist questions before they listen and read the dialogue for the first time: *Did Hannah win or lose the match?* (She lost.) *Is she a good or bad player according to Rob and Millie?* (very good).

Play the audio again and tell students to pay attention to the stressed emphasisers, shown in bold. Ask: *Why do Millie and Rob sound so enthusiastic?* (Because they obviously love tennis and think that Hannah Smith is going to be a champion.)

2   ◀))1.18   Ask students to tell you whether they think the intonation in the sentences with emphasisers has a high range or not. (It does.)

Tell the students to say each line of the dialogue without using the words *such, so, did* and *do,* and then say them again with them. When saying the sentences without the emphasisers, they will notice that their voices are flatter. Encourage them to really stress the emphasisers. Explain that these words don't add meaning, but that they do make the meaning stronger.

3   ◀))1.19   Students listen to the recording and repeat. Then they practise the dialogue with a partner.

EXTRA INFORMATION

- When we use the words *so* and *such* or *do/does* and *did* in the ways shown in the dialogue, our intonation range increases across the whole sentence to show that we are making a strong point.

Optional extension

As an extension activity, you could ask students, in pairs, to write three or four sentences about their weekend. They then see which of the sentences they can add emphasisers to. Once they have some emphasisers in place, ask them to change their sentences into a dialogue to practise and then act out for the class.

UNIT 4

Pronouncing words with *gh*

Aim: Students recognise and practise the two pronunciations of the *gh* spelling in words found in this unit.

1   ◀))1.23   Ask students to listen and read the extracts, paying attention to the pronunciation of the words in bold. They will notice that they are pronounced in many different ways!

Elicit from the class that in the text there are two pronunciations of *gh.*

The letters *gh* are pronounced with the /f/ consonant sound in *laugh* and *enough.* The letters are silent in *thought, through, brought* and *right.*

2   ◀))1.24   Students listen to the recording and repeat. Then they take turns saying the extracts with a partner.

EXTRA INFORMATION

- Although words containing the digraph *gh* are often among those chosen to show how irregular the English spelling–pronunciation relationship is, there are only three possible pronunciations of this digraph: i) as silent letters (*through, high, straight*), ii) as /f/ (*laugh, enough*) and iii) most rarely /g/ (*ghost, ghastly* – there are only about five words in this category).

- Sometimes the digraph is part of a spelling pattern for a particular phoneme, for example *igh* is an alternative spelling for the /aɪ/ phoneme: *right, night, light, high*; and *augh* is an alternative spelling for the /ɔː/ phoneme in *daughter, caught* and *taught.*

- Pronunciation problems are mainly caused by the *ough* spelling, where pronunciation of words must be learned individually (compare *thought, through, enough* and *thorough*).

UNIT 5

The schwa sound

Aim: Students revise and extend their knowledge and practice of saying the schwa /ə/ in phrases, recognising the role of this short vowel sound in giving English its characteristic rhythm.

1   ◀))1.29   Students listen to the recording while reading the recorded message, paying special attention to the words in blue. Students may say that the small words are 'lost' or 'swallowed' or are hard to hear. Ask: *All the words in blue have the same sound. What is it?* (It's the schwa.)

2   ◀))1.30   Students listen to the recording and repeat. Then they practise with a partner.

UNIT 6

Linking words with /dʒ/ and /tʃ/

Aim: Students identify the voiced /dʒ/ and unvoiced /tʃ/ in connected speech. For example, these consonant sounds appear in *do you* (often pronounced /dʒə/), *did you* /ˈdɪdʒə/ and *don't you* /ˈdəʊntʃə/.

1 ◼️)1.33 Students read and listen to the dialogue. As a gist question, ask: *What does Sally choose; tea or coffee? Why?* (Sally chooses tea because they've both forgotten to get coffee.)

Explain that when the consonant sounds /d/ or /t/ are found at the end of joining words, the consonant sounds /dʒ/ and /tʃ/ often intrude. This is a natural effect of connected speech and students will need to be aware of it in order to understand fluent speakers in conversation. Note that in *do you* the two words can be joined to create the short /dʒə/ in order to maintain the rhythm.

Tell students to circle the linked words that have the /dʒ/ sound and underline the ones that have the /tʃ/ sound. Play the recording again for them to listen and check.

Answers

/dʒ/ sound: Would you, Do you, Did you, told you, Do you; /tʃ/ sound: Didn't you, Don't you.

2 ◼️)1.34 Students listen to the recording and repeat. Then they practise with a partner.

UNIT 7

Intonation: encouraging someone

Aim: Students identify and practise using a higher intonation range in phrases to show interest and encouragement.

1 ◼️)2.05 As a gist question students listen and read the dialogue and answer the question: *What's Becky trying to do in this conversation between her and Harry?* (Becky's trying to cheer Harry up and give him encouragement to try again.)

2 ◼️)2.05 Students listen again and draw arrows over the phrases in blue.

Answers

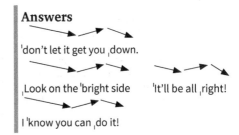

'don't let it get you ˌdown.

ˌLook on the 'bright side   'It'll be all ˌright!

I 'know you can ˌdo it!

Note the primary and secondary stress in the phrases as shown.

Students practise saying the phrases in blue using a rise-fall-rise-fall intonation pattern. Encourage students to exaggerate the range, explaining that they may come across as rude or uninterested if their voice is too flat.

3 ◼️)2.06 Students listen to the recording and repeat. Then they practise with a partner.

UNIT 8

Weak forms with conditionals

Aim: Students recognise that when spoken quickly modal contractions *would, could* and *should* + *have* are pronounced /ˈwʊdə, ˈkʊdə, ˈʃʊdə/. However, when the contraction is followed by a vowel sound, the /v/ is pronounced: *I could've asked* /ˈkʊdəˈvɑːskt/.

1 ◼️)2.11 Students listen and read. As a gist question ask students *What has Kim forgotten?* (Kim's forgotten her mother's birthday) and *Is her friend sympathetic?* (Nellie isn't sympathetic – she thinks Kim should have remembered.)

2 ▶️ 2.11 Explain that in fast speech the unstressed, contracted *have* is pronounced with the schwa /ə/ in most cases. However, sometimes we pronounce the /v/. Students listen again and circle the phrase where the /v/ is pronounced.

Answers

When the contraction is followed by a vowel sound, the /v/ is pronounced: *You should've asked your dad* /ˈʃʊdəˈvɑːskt/.

3 ▶️ 2.12 Students listen to the recording and repeat. Then they practise with a partner.

EXTRA INFORMATION

- Sometimes it can be difficult to understand English when it's spoken quickly because syllables and unstressed words are shortened to a schwa – or even lost. The pronunciation section in this unit aims to help students understand native speakers by focussing on the shortened contractions in modals + *have*. Students should enjoy practising these contractions, but explain to them that it's more important that they recognise what native speakers are saying. They will still be understood if they pronounce the contractions more carefully!

- An interesting and somewhat related fact that may interest your students is that native speakers sometimes write these words incorrectly, as *would of*, *could of* and *should of* because that is what they think they are saying.

UNIT 9

Linking: intrusive /w/ and /j/

Aim: Students recognise how vowel sounds at the end of a word and at the beginning of a word are connected in natural speech, using sound intrusions /w/ and /j/, e.g. *you /w/ always* and *tell me /j/ off*.

1 ▶️ 2.15 Students read and listen. As a gist question ask: *Why is Ellen annoyed with Evan?* (She's annoyed because she doesn't really want Evan's advice – she wants his sympathy.)

2 ▶️ 2.15 Explain that when a word in a sentence ending in a vowel sound is followed by a word starting with a vowel sound, we add a /j/ or a /w/ sound to join them together. Students listen again and write a letter *j* or a letter *w* above the gap between the words.

Answers

me (j) off / so (w) angry / you (w) ask / to (w) explain / be (j) able / you (w) always / to (w) everything / so (w) annoying / be (j) angry / be (j) annoying

Elicit the rule: when the first word has the /iː/ sound e.g. *me*, we join the two words with a /j/ sound. When the first word has the /əʊ/ or /uː/ sound e.g. *so* or *to*, we join the two words with a /w/ sound.

3 ▶️ 2.16 Students listen to the recording and repeat. Then they practise with a partner.

EXTRA INFORMATION

- These intrusive sounds are actually quite natural, since they're directly related to the vowel sound that ends the first word, that is, our mouth is already in the position to make the intrusive sound, e.g. *let's go (w) out* and *you may be (j) able to.* Therefore it shouldn't be difficult for students to understand and pronounce these intrusions, increasing the naturalness of their spoken English and making it easier for them to understand other features of connected speech.

- To reiterate the rule: when the first word has the /iː/ sound, we join the two words with a /j/ sound, e.g. *me off* /ˈmiːjɒf/. When the first word has the /əʊ/ or /uː/ sound, we join the two words with a /w/ sound e.g. *so angry* /səʊˈwæŋgri/.

UNIT 10

Linking: omission of the /h/ sound

Aim: Students recognise that the /h/ phoneme in unstressed words is often lost in natural speech e.g. *Did you ask her?* /ˈɑːskə/

1 ▶️ 2.20 Students listen to the recording and answer the gist question: *Why is Hilary upset with Harry?* (Harry told he didn't like her new haircut.)

2 ▶️ 2.20 Students listen to the recording again, underlining the silent letter /h/.

Answers

The letter h is silent in unstressed words *he* and *her*: He hurt her feelings. He said he didn't like her new haircut. Did he mean to upset her? Of course he didn't!

3 ▶️ 2.21 Students listen to the recording and repeat. Then they practise with a partner.

EXTRA INFORMATION

- The aim of this pronunciation focus is to help students understand native speakers. Although they may enjoy practising omitting the /h/ when speaking, it's not necessary for them to do so.

- When a word is stressed, which is often the case with verbs and nouns carrying meaning, the /h/ is pronounced.

- In a very formal setting we may pronounce the /h/ in all words – for example, when giving a speech. This is mainly due to speaking more slowly and carefully.

UNIT 11

Stress on modal verbs for speculation

Aim: When using modals to express degrees of probability, students recognise that placing stress on the modal or the verb is significant. It shows how likely we think something is, e.g. *she might be **coming*** (probable) as opposed to *she **might** be coming* (unlikely).

1 ▶️ 2.27 Students listen to the recording and answer these gist questions: *What does Ned think about the information in the TV show? What about Gina?* (Ned doesn't think that the information in the TV show is likely to be true whereas Gina tends to believe it.)

2 [2.27] Students listen and colour the squares black (primary stress) or leave them clear (secondary) to show the primary and secondary.

Elicit/explain that when we place the stress on the modal verb instead of the meaningful part of the phrase, it means we're not sure that something is true, or that it will happen. When we place the stress on the verb or noun we are more certain of something.

Notice how Gina puts the main stress on the information rather than *might* and *may*, which shows that she thinks the information is likely to be true. Ned is doubtful and therefore puts the main stress on *might* and *could* instead of the information itself.

> **Answers**
>
> (main stress shown in bold with secondary stress underlined):
> might have already **vis**ited us / **might** have, I sup**pose** / may have built the **py**ramids / **could** be true / may be in our **town**.

3 [2.28] Students listen to the recording and repeat. Then they practise with a partner.

> **EXTRA INFORMATION**
>
> • It is interesting to note the difference in stress in sentences containing a modal + verb + noun, e.g. *they may have built the pyramids.* If we think this is unlikely the main stress and secondary stress are as follows: *they **may** have built the pyramids.* However, if we think it's probable, the stress pattern is: *they may have built the **py**ramids.*

UNIT 12

Linking: /r/

Aim: Students recognise that two words can sometimes be linked with an /r/ sound, e.g. *your own car; more animals.*

1 [2.34] Students listen to the recording and find out the answer to this gist question: *How can you be part of this adventure?* (They can follow the blog.)

2 [2.34] Explain that in syllables with a vowel and the letter *r*, we often don't pronounce the /r/ sound. However, when these syllables end a word and the next word begins with a vowel sound, we do pronounce the /r/. Students say *We're off* and *We're coming* to hear the difference. Students listen again and circle the linked words where an /r/ is present.

> **Answers**
>
> 1 We're off on our adventure on Saturday.
> 2 We're going far away to explore amazing places.
> 3 We hope to learn more about our incredible Earth.
> 4 We'll remember our adventure for ever!
> 5 Join us on our adventure – follow our excellent blog!

3 [2.35] Students listen to the recording and repeat. Then they practise with a partner.

> **EXTRA INFORMATION**
>
> • Note that in American English the /r/ is often pronounced so that this is a more simple linking pattern as is found with other consonant sounds followed by a vowel, e.g. the carrying over of the /r/ phoneme in *for ever and ever* is comparable to carrying over the /m/ and /d/ sounds in *ham and eggs*.

GET IT RIGHT!

UNIT 1

Verb patterns

> **Focus:** Students at this level often use the wrong verb form after certain verbs, using the gerund instead of *to* + infinitive and vice versa.

Books closed. Write on the board: 1 *I _____ to go to the cinema with Sarah.* 2 *I _____ going to the cinema with Sarah.* Ask students to try and complete the sentences with suitable verbs. Tell them there are various possible answers and encourage them to discuss their answers in pairs before doing feedback. (Possible answers: 1 want / decided / managed / refuse / hope / chose / expected; 2 like / imagined / feel like / suggested / couldn't stand / enjoy / detest / didn't mind.)

Elicit/explain that some verbs are followed by *to* + infinitive while others are followed by the gerund, and that there is no rule for this – students will need to learn what follows each verb. Give students a minute to brainstorm other verbs which fall into one of the two categories. Take feedback and write all correct suggestions on the board. Books open. Students complete the exercise and check their answers in pairs before you check answers as a whole class.

> **Answers**
>
> 1 They wanted ~~going~~ **to go** sailing but the weather conditions were too extreme.   2 I enjoy ~~to wander~~ **wandering** around outdoor markets when I'm on holiday.   3 Correct   4 Do you think you'll manage ~~completing~~ **to complete** the mountain climb?
> 5 Correct   6 Kate had hoped ~~reaching~~ **to reach** the glacier by early afternoon but slipped on the ice and broke her leg.
> 7 The children learnt ~~building~~ **to build** a shelter during the survival course.   8 Megan was thrilled when she got her exam results as she'd expected ~~failing~~ **to fail**.

remember, *try*, *stop*, *regret* and *forget*

> **Focus:** Students at this level often use the wrong verb form after the verbs *remember*, *try*, *stop*, *regret* and *forget*. These can all be used with both the gerund and infinitive but with different meanings.

Books closed. Write on the board: 1 *Dave stopped to eat a sandwich.* 2 *Dave stopped eating sandwiches.* Ask students to discuss any differences in meaning between them in pairs. Ask them to add a new sentence to each one to try and show the difference in meaning. e.g. 1 *Dave stopped to eat a sandwich. He was starving.* 2 *Dave stopped eating sandwiches because he was putting on weight.*

Explain/elicit that the meaning changes depending on whether the verb *stop* is followed by *to* + infinitive or gerund. Ask the class for other verbs which behave similarly (*remember, try, regret, forget*) and give students a couple of minutes to work in pairs and think of example sentences which show the difference in meaning. Take feedback and write all correct suggestions on the board. Books open. Students work through the exercise individually before comparing answers in pairs. Then check answers as a whole class.

> **Answers**
>
> 1 to buy   2 to get a drink   3 climbing   4 to climb
> 5 studying   6 going   7 to complete   8 to inform

UNIT 2

that and *which* in relative clauses

> **Focus:** Students at this level often use *that* instead of *which* in non-defining relative clauses.

Focus students on the example sentences and ask them to discuss why the second sentence is wrong. Give them a minute for this. In open class elicit what type of relative clauses these are (non-defining) and therefore that the pronoun *that* cannot be used. Books open. Explain what the students have to do in the exercise and point out/elicit that a non-defining relative clause must always have a comma before the pronoun and that therefore if there is a comma they can't use the pronoun *that*. Do the example together as a class and then instruct students to continue the exercise by themselves. Allow them to check answers in pairs before doing a whole-class check.

> **Answers**
>
> 1c The grey whale is the animal that/which swims about 18,000 km every year. (defining)
> 2e Domenico Lucano had an idea that/which saved his village. (defining)
> 3a Our teacher always praises us when we've done well in a test, which helps give us confidence. (non-defining)
> 4f I spoke to him using Italian, which I had learnt while working there. (non-defining)
> 5d Elana has decided to live abroad, which I think is very brave of her. (non-defining)

Relative pronouns

> **Focus:** Students at this level often omit relative pronouns in defining relative clauses when it's incorrect to do so.

Books closed. Write on the board: 1 *She's the woman having the party.* 2 *She's the woman had the party last night.* 3 *She's the woman I met at the party last night.* Tell students that two of the sentences are correct and one is incorrect. Elicit which one is incorrect and why. (Answer: Sentence 2 is incorrect because the pronoun *who* is needed as it is the subject of the clause.) Elicit/ explain why sentences 1 and 3 are correct. (Answer: Sentence 1 contains a reduced relative clause as the words *who is* can be omitted; in sentence 3 the pronoun *who* can be omitted because it's the object not subject of the clause.) Books open. Do the example sentence in open class and ask students to complete the exercise in pairs.

Answers

1 ✓ 2 ✓ 3 They went through a bad time **which/that** lasted a few months. 4 ✓ 5 Those are the residents **who/that** live in that building over there. 6 The Tuareg are the people **who/that** regularly cross national borders.

UNIT 3

much vs. *many*

> **Focus:** Students at this level often confuse *much* and *many*.

Focus students on the example sentences and ask them to discuss in pairs why *much* and *many* are correct in the first sentences but wrong in the second ones. Elicit that *many* is used with plural countable nouns while *much* is used with uncountable nouns. Ask students to complete the exercise. Check answers with the whole class.

Answers

1 many 2 much 3 much 4 many 5 much 6 much

much and *most*

> **Focus:** Students at this level often make mistakes with *most* by preceding it with *the* or following it by *of* when this isn't necessary.

Books closed. Write on the board: 1 *The most of the students at school have lunch in the canteen.* 2 *Most of teachers give out homework once a week.* 3 *Most of them set an exam every term.* Ask students: *Which of these sentences are correct?* (Sentences 1 and 2 are not correct; sentence 3 is.) Elicit corrections of the sentences. (1 Most of the students at school have lunch in the canteen. 2 Most teachers give out homework once a week.) Explain/elicit that we never use *the* before the quantifier *most* unless it's followed by a superlative adjective. Books open. Do number 1 in open class and ask students to complete the rest of the exercise in pairs.

Answers

1 ~~The~~ Most of my teachers at school were quite strict. 2 Correct 3 Correct 4 Sally tried on a few outfits but ~~the~~ most of them were too big for her. 5 It would be interesting to know if most ~~of~~ people agreed with Amy Chua's parenting ideas. 6 Were ~~the~~ most of your old school friends at the reunion?

UNIT 4

used to

> **Focus:** Students at this level often make mistakes with *used to*, writing *use to* instead of *used to* and also using it to talk about present habits.

Books closed. Say to the class the following sentence: *I used to play tennis when I was a child.* Ask a student to write the sentence on the board. If the 'd' in *used* is omitted, add it in and then explain/elicit that although it is silent we always say *used to* when talking about past habits in positive statements, never *use to*.

Now write the sentence *Now I use to go running every day*. Elicit/explain that this sentence is incorrect as we cannot use *used to* to talk about present habits or routines. We use adverbs such as *usually* or *typically*. Books open. Do number 1 in open class and ask students to complete the rest of the exercise in pairs. Check answers as a whole class.

Answers

1 Liam ~~use~~ **used** to be very bad-tempered but he's nicer now.
2 There's a lot of planning involved in my job so I ~~use to be~~ **am usually** organised.
3 When I was at school we ~~use~~ **used** to sit in a row in some lessons.
4 They ~~use to~~ **usually** go to school by bus except for Tuesdays when they walk.
5 The man who ~~use~~ **used** to live there moved to Spain.
6 Sarah ~~used to watch~~ **usually watches** a lot of TV when she hasn't got much homework.

UNIT 5

should

> **Focus:** Students at this level often use *would*, *can* and *must* instead of *should*.

Focus students on the example sentences and elicit why the second sentence is incorrect. (When talking about opinions – saying that something is a good or bad idea – we usually use *should*. We use *must* to talk about obligation and necessity or to give very strong advice or recommendations.) Books open. Do number 1 in open class before students continue with the exercise. Ask them to compare and agree on their answers in pairs before you give feedback.

Answers

1 a 2 a 3 a 4 b

UNIT 6

Comparatives

> **Focus:** Students at this level often use the comparative instead of the superlative and vice versa.

Books closed. Write on the board:

Comparative	Superlative
better	the best
bad	the worst
funny	the funniest

and elicit full sentences using each of these words from the class. Books open. Focus students on the examples in the box and elicit why the two sentences are incorrect. (The first contains a comparative when a superlative is needed and the second contains a superlative when a comparative is needed.) Do number 1 in open class and ask students to complete the rest of the exercise in pairs.

> **Answers**
>
> 1 harder 2 best 3 happiest 4 higher 5 hardest
> 6 better 7 highest 8 happier

Linkers of contrast

> **Focus:** Students at this level often confuse linkers or make mistakes with form when using them.

Books closed. Write the following two sentences on the board and the list of linkers and tell the class that they must use each linker to join the two sentences (to create a total of five new sentences).

I studied really hard. I still failed the exam. (despite, although, nevertheless, in spite of, even though)

Elicit the answers making sure that the correct form is used with each linker. Write the correct sentences on the board. (Answers: *Despite studying really hard, I still failed the exam. Although I studied really hard, I still failed the exam. I studied really hard. Nevertheless, I still failed the exam. In spite of studying really hard, I still failed the exam. Even though I studied really hard, I still failed the exam.*) Books open. Look at the example in open class and ask students to complete the rest of the exercise in pairs. Then check as a class.

> **Answers**
>
> 1 **Despite** the fact she confessed to the crime, the police didn't arrest her. / **Even though** she confessed to the crime, police didn't arrest her.
> 2 We made an enquiry about the delivery. **However / Nevertheless**, no one got back to us. / **Despite this**, no one got back to us.
> 3 **In spite of / Despite** the fact that they made a complaint about the food, the chef didn't apologise.
> 4 The children took the move to the countryside in their stride, **despite the fact / in spite of the fact** they had been happy living in the town.

UNIT 7

Future continuous

> **Focus:** Students at this level often use the present continuous when the future continuous is more commonly used.

Books closed. Ask students: *What will you be doing at 7 o'clock this evening?* Elicit two or three responses and write them on the board, reformulating them if necessary to include the future continuous form. Then ask students: *What are you doing this weekend?* Again elicit two or three responses and write them on the board, again reformulating as necessary to include the present continuous. Remind students that we use the present continuous when we are talking or asking about general plans or arrangements and that we use the future continuous to talk about an action that will be in progress at a specified future time. Do number 1 in open class and ask students to complete the rest of the exercise in pairs.

> **Answers**
>
> 1 ✓ 2 I'**ll be seeing you** sometime over the weekend, so I'll show you then. 3 ✓ 4 I'll come to the airport to pick you up. I'**ll be waiting** for you at arrivals. 5 John **won't be coming** to the party on Saturday as he's busy. 6 This time next week they'**ll be lying** on a beach relaxing.

UNIT 8

would

> **Focus:** Students at this level often use *would* in the *if* clause of conditional sentences instead of using a present, past simple or past perfect form.

Focus students on the example sentences and elicit why the second sentence is incorrect. (We don't use *would* in the *if* clause.) Do number 1 in open class and ask students to complete the rest of the exercise in pairs.

> **Answers**
>
> 1 If they had run through the calculations they would have realised their mistake. (extra word: <u>would</u>)
> 2 The meal wouldn't have turned out so well if you hadn't lent me your cook book. (extra word: <u>wouldn't</u>)
> 3 She'll do it provided that we help her. (extra word: <u>would</u>)
> 4 If you don't wash your hands, you might get an infection. (extra word: <u>would</u>)
> 5 The cloth wouldn't have ripped if it had been stronger. (extra word: <u>would</u>)
> 6 It won't be a problem as long as you arrive on time. (extra word: <u>would</u>)

UNIT 9

wish

> **Focus:** Students at this level often use *wish* when *hope* or *want* are required and vice versa.

Books closed. Write on the board: *I want it … , I wish it … and I hope it …* . Elicit from students how the three sentences could be finished. (e.g. *I want it to be sunny tomorrow. I wish it wasn't so cold. I hope it doesn't rain during our picnic.*) Elicit from or explain to the class that all three verbs have a similar meaning but are all followed by different structures and that we use *wish* to talk about how we would like something to be different either in the present or the past:

want + object + *to* infinitive
hope + object + clause
wish + object + past simple/past perfect

Books open. Look at the first sentence in open class and ask students to complete the rest of the exercise in pairs. Then check as a class.

> **Answers**
>
> 1 wishes 2 hope 3 wants 4 wish 5 hopes
> 6 hope 7 hope

wish / if only

> **Focus:** Students at this level often use the past simple instead of the past perfect after *wish / if only* when talking about the past.

Books closed. Write on the board: *He wishes his parents weren't so strict. He wishes his parents hadn't been so strict.* Elicit the difference in meaning between the two sentences. (The first sentence is talking about a present situation – his parents are strict now; the second sentence is talking about a past situation – his parents were strict in the past.) Elicit that when talking about present situations we use the past simple after *wish* while we use the past perfect after *wish* when talking about past situations. Explain/elicit that we also use *if only* in the same way and with the same meaning. Books open. Students complete the exercise in pairs. Then check as a class. As an additional activity ask students to complete sentences 1–8 in their own words.

> **Answers**
>
> 1 c 2 f 3 g 4 a 5 d 6 h 7 e 8 b

UNIT 10

Reported speech

> **Focus:** Students at this level often omit *if* when reporting *yes/no* questions, or use the auxiliary *do* when it isn't needed in reported questions. Learners also need to be careful with word order.

Focus students on the example sentences and ask them to discuss why the second sentence is wrong. Give them a minute for this. In open class elicit that in reported *yes/no* questions we use either *if* or *whether* and that we don't use question word order. Look at the first sentence in open class and ask students to complete the rest of the exercise in pairs. Then check as a class.

> **Answers**
>
> 1 Simon asked me *if I had remembered* to pass on the message to the class.
> 2 ✓
> 3 Sandra asked how efficiently *the machine worked*.
> 4 She asked if any politician *could ever be* impartial.
> 5 The students asked the speaker how big *the impact of war had been*.
> 6 The chief editor asked the journalist *if he thought* the article was newsworthy.

UNIT 11

Cause and effect linkers

> **Focus:** Students at this level often make mistakes with cause and effect linkers: *so, consequently, because of, due to, as a result.*

Books closed. Write the linkers on the board and the following two sentences: *Josh didn't study very much for the exam. He failed the exam.* Ask students to make sentences using them. Correct as necessary. Books open. Focus students on the example sentences and ask them to discuss why the second sentence is wrong. (We do not use *for* with the meaning of *because.*) Look at the first sentence in open class and ask students to complete the rest of the exercise in pairs. Then check as a class.

> **Answers**
>
> 1 Due to 2 As a result 3 because of 4 consequently
> 5 so 6 because of

UNIT 12

been and *being*

> **Focus:** Students at this level often confuse *been* and *being*.

Books closed. Write on the board: *been* and *being* and ask students what these words are (*been* is the past participle of *be* and *being* is the gerund or *-ing* form). Then read out the example sentences in the Student's Book. Ask students which of the two words you are saying – *been* or *being*? Books open. Elicit from students why the second sentences are incorrect. (The first sentence requires the gerund as it is a present continuous passive while the second requires the past participle as it is a present perfect form.) Look at the first sentence in open class and ask students to complete the rest of the exercise in pairs. Then check as a class.

> **Answers**
>
> 1 being 2 being 3 been 4 being 5 being 6 been

WORKBOOK ANSWER KEY

WELCOME UNIT
A WHAT A STORY!

Descriptive verbs
Exercise 1
1 demolished 2 dived 3 fled 4 grab 5 raged
6 screamed 7 smashed 8 struck

Phrasal verbs
Exercise 1
1 take 2 ended 3 broke 4 give 5 carried
6 sort 7 looking 8 stands / stood

Elements of a story
Exercise 1
1 e 2 h 3 g 4 a 5 d 6 c 7 b 8 f

Exercise 2
1 plot 2 characters 3 hero 4 villain 5 dialogue
6 setting 7 opening 8 ending

Talking about past routines
Exercise 1
4, 2, 6, 1, 3, 5

SUMMING UP
Exercise 1
5, 1, 9, 3, 7, 8, 2, 6, 4

B AN UNCERTAIN FUTURE

Future plans
Exercise 1
1 e 2 f 3 a 4 b 5 c 6 d

Life plans
Exercise 1
4, 2, 3, 6, 1, 8, 7, 5

Future continuous
Exercise 1
1 'll be lying 2 won't be doing 3 'll be eating
4 won't be getting up 5 'll be staying 6 won't be taking

Being emphatic: *so* and *such*
Exercise 1
1 so 2 such 3 such 4 so 5 such 6 so 7 so
8 such

Exercise 2
1 such – C 2 such – F 3 so – D 4 so – E 5 such – B
6 so – A

Extreme adjectives
Exercise 1
1 fascinating 2 hilarious 3 freezing 4 terrified
5 enormous 6 tiny 7 boiling

Exercise 2
Suggested answers
1 fantastic 2 huge 3 amazing 4 hilarious 5 exciting
6 tiny 7 delighted 8 terrified

SUMMING UP
Exercise 1
1 retire 2 enormous 3 so 4 promote 5 amazing
6 such 7 travel 8 degree

C HOW PEOPLE BEHAVE

Personality
Exercise 1
1 selfish 2 polite 3 thoughtful 4 calm 5 lively
6 shy 7 generous 8 rude

Using *should*
Exercise 1
Suggested answers
1 You should buy him a present.
2 We should have got up earlier.
3 You should go to the dentist.
4 You should say sorry to her.
5 You should take up a hobby.

Exercise 2
1 should have brought 2 should've got up
3 should have set 4 should have put
5 shouldn't have stayed

Career paths
Exercise 1
1 street sweeper 2 engineer 3 lawyer 4 childminder
5 nurse 6 bus driver
Mystery profession: teacher

Exercise 2
1 healthcare 2 public service 3 education
4 qualifications 5 employees 6 employers
7 finance 8 law

Decisions

Exercise 1

1 c 2 e 3 a 4 b 5 d

Permission

Exercise 1

1 let 2 allowed 3 make 4 makes 5 let 6 allowed

Exercise 2

1 allowed 2 let 3 make 4 made 5 allow 6 let

SUMMING UP

Exercise 1

7, 1, 5, 9, 3, 4, 6, 10, 8, 2

D NEW THINGS

Reporting verbs

Exercise 1

1 explain 2 refuse 3 demand 4 invite 5 persuade
6 encourage 7 recommend 8 agree

Exercise 2

1 He explained how to get to the station by bus.
2 She refused to take Bella to the party.
3 He demanded that Ben get out of his house immediately.
4 She invited Jenny to the cinema.
5 He persuaded Jim to go to the party with him.
6 She encouraged Lucy to enter the talent show.
7 He recommended that Matt read this book.
8 She agreed to talk to Simon's dad.

Exercise 3

1 agreed 2 explained 3 invited 4 refused 5 persuade

Negative adjectives

Exercise 1

1 It's untrue.   2 It's an informal party.   3 They're impatient.
4 That was irresponsible of you.   5 Buy it. It's inexpensive.
6 They're impolite children.   7 I think that's impossible.

Changes

Exercise 1

1 f 2 h 3 e 4 g 5 d 6 a 7 b 8 c

Regrets: *I wish … | If only …*

Exercise 1

> ### Suggested answers
>
> 1 I wish/If only I could tell her I'm sorry. // I wish/If only I hadn't upset her.
> 2 I wish/If only I was at home. // I wish/If only I hadn't gone to bed so late.
> 3 I wish/If only I was in the school football team. // I wish/If only I had tried harder to get into the football team.
> 4 I wish/If only I had something to do. // I wish/If only I had organised something to do today.

SUMMING UP

Exercise 1

1 unhappy 2 take up 3 hadn't given it up 4 impossible
5 struggle 6 wasn't 7 encourage 8 refuse

UNIT 1 SURVIVAL

GRAMMAR

Exercise 1

to + infinitive	gerund
manage	*keep*
promise	suggest
ask	detest
decide	don't mind
want	miss
offer	can't stand
choose	enjoy

Exercise 2

1 to finish; to come; to give   2 taking; to carry; carrying
3 going; walking   4 playing; practising; to help   5 climbing

Exercise 3

1 climbing 2 to climb 3 to go 4 to stay 5 to get back
6 to reach 7 seeing 8 climbing

Exercise 4

KATE   I can't believe it. I managed ~~climbing~~ **to climb** Devil's Rock this weekend.
MATT   Did you? That's great.
KATE   I've watched you climb it a couple of times but I never imagined ~~to climb~~ **climbing** it myself. I'm hoping ~~doing~~ **to do** more climbing next weekend. I learnt ~~descending~~ **to descend** the rock face using the rope. That was scary! What did you do at the weekend?
MATT   I wanted ~~coming~~ **to come** climbing with you and the others but I had some homework to do.

Exercise 6

1 g 2 e 3 b 4 f 5 h 6 d 7 a 8 c

Exercise 7

1 to tell 2 to finish 3 not leaving 4 playing
5 lending 6 to pick it up

Exercise 8

1 to listen 2 listening 3 watching 4 to watch
5 eating 6 to eat 7 to tell 8 telling

GET IT RIGHT!

1 Jenny couldn't afford **to** do the survival course.
2 He started ~~feel~~ **to feel** a bit awkward as no one was talking to him.
3 Ethan suggested ~~have~~ **having** an early night before the exam.
4 I never promised **to** help you with your homework!
5 Do they practise ~~to sing~~ **singing** every evening?
6 We wanted **to** leave right away but we couldn't.

VOCABULARY

Exercise 1

O	C	L	I	M	B	T	T	T	H	P
D	S	S	A	Y	N	I	E	C	A	H
N	W	C	A	T	B	P	L	E	T	R
E	I	W	R	R	K	T	L	A	G	E
C	N	S	E	A	L	O	P	W	L	G
S	G	M	E	E	W	E	S	O	E	G
E	H	R	U	S	H	L	I	N	H	A
D	W	A	N	D	E	R	T	D	E	T
B	R	E	A	T	H	L	E	G	R	S

Exercise 2

1 swung   2 tiptoed   3 climbed   4 descended
5 rushed   6 hopped   7 wandered / staggered

Exercise 3

1 stuck   2 guilty   3 awkward   4 puzzled
5 ashamed   6 desperate

Exercise 5

1 right away   2 right up to   3 Too right   4 Right
5 right   6 All right

READING

Exercise 1

1 It was faster.   2 because of bad weather   3 his leg
4 Because he realised he couldn't save both his own life and
Joe's life.   5 three and a half days   6 Joe saved his own life.

Exercise 2

1 fingertips
2 914: the height in metres of El Capitan; 19: the number of
days it took the two climbers to make it to the top; 27: the date
in December that they began their climb

Exercise 3

1 T   2 F   3 F   4 T   5 F   6 F   7 T   8 F

DEVELOPING WRITING

Exercise 1

b

Exercise 2

a

Exercise 3

1 4,167 metres high; a challenge
2 exhausted
3 her mum, dad and older brother
4 more confident
5 take a hat, a water bottle and some water purification
tablets; prepare for a challenging walk

Exercise 4

	Adjective	Noun	New choice: suggested answers
1	tough	*trekking*	challenging
2	exhausted	I/Miriam	worn out
3	icy cold	nights	freezing
4	challenging	climb	tough
5	spectacular	views	breathtaking
6	fierce	sun	scorching

LISTENING

🔊04 **Exercise 1**

1 2   2 3   3 1

🔊04 **Exercise 2**

1 video   2 France   3 tunnel   4 snow   5 friendly
6 challenge

Audio Script Track 04

Dialogue 1

Sammy   Hey! Come and watch this video, James. You'll love it.
James   What's that, Sammy? Has it started yet?
Sammy   Not yet. I'm just downloading it.
James   When you've finished downloading it, give me a shout
and I'll come and watch it.
Sammy   OK. All right, James. Come and sit down. I'm ready to
start the video.
James   Wow! That's really cool. I don't know how they do it.
What do they call this sport?
Sammy   Passour or Parkour or something or other.
James   That's right, Parkour. I read about it. It started in
France. People jump, run, climb and swing over walls
and buildings.
Sammy   Wow! Did you see that? I bet you can't do that.
James   I bet you I can.
Sammy   All right. I challenge you to jump onto the kitchen
table.
James   But that's too easy.
Sammy   Yes, easy and safe. You need proper training to do
Parkour.

Dialogue 2

Chris   You go on ahead, Susie. I'll never manage to crawl
through that tunnel.
Susie   Of course you can, Chris. Come on. Keep going. You're
doing really well. I bet you can crawl through that
tunnel faster than I can.
Chris   You know what? I don't think I can continue. I'm too
tired and it's too difficult. We've still got that hill to
climb. And look! Now it's started to snow! I'll never
manage it.
Susie   You can't give up now. You're so close to the finish
line.

Dialogue 3

Louise   Hey, Jake, I'm so glad you joined this club. Are you
enjoying it?
Jake   Totally, Louise! Everyone's very friendly. I get on well
with everyone and it's good fun. And of course I love
the climbing. We've been on some great climbs.
Louise   Too right. I never thought I'd have the opportunity to
climb Ben Nevis. It's the best climb I've ever done.
Jake   It was a challenge but I'm glad I've done it.
Louise   Same here. What's our next challenge? I bet we can
climb Mount Everest one day.

Jake   No problem. It won't be for a few years though. I don't think we're ready for that yet.

Louise I think you're probably right. We need a bit more practice before we take on that challenge. Now, where were we? … I know. You were showing me how to do that knot.

DIALOGUE

Exercise 1

1 I bet you; I bet you I; I challenge you; that's too easy
2 I'll never manage to; Of course you can
3 No problem; I think you're probably right

PHRASES FOR FLUENCY

Exercise 1

1 e   2 f   3 a   4 b   5 d   6 c

Exercise 2

1 It's a deal.   2 Give me a shout   3 you know what?
4 where were we?   5 Same here.   6 something or other

CAMBRIDGE ENGLISH: FIRST

Exercise 1

1 would prefer not to see   2 refuse to leave him
3 don't have enough   4 didn't manage to complete
5 will never forget my

Exercise 2

1 haven't been swimming for   2 too late to go
3 wasn't able to see   4 has succeeded in climbing
5 stopped to buy   6 feel like having

UNIT 2 GOING PLACES

GRAMMAR

Exercise 1

1 who ND   2 which ND   3 who ND   4 who D   5 that D

Exercise 2

1 This is a photograph that/which I took in Italy.
2 The boy who/that bought my bike lives in this street.
3 My mother, who is a doctor, often has to work at weekends.
4 I've got a new phone that/which is far better than my old one.
5 The player who scored the winning goal in the 2014 World Cup final was Mario Götze.
6 I don't really like people who talk a lot.

Exercise 3

1 My father walks to work, which is good for his health.
2 My grandfather has three large dogs, which means he gets plenty of exercise.
3 Some blind people have guide dogs, which gives them more independence.
4 My sister spends hours working on the computer, which sometimes gives her a headache.

Exercise 4

1 I like watching films at home, which is cheaper than going to the cinema.
2 My friend is going to live in Colombia, which will be a big change in lifestyle.
3 My mother's car was stolen last week, which means she has to take the bus to work.
4 A famous band is playing in our town next week, which doesn't happen very often.

Exercise 5

1 –   2 who/that   3 –   4 –   5 that/which   6 who/that

Exercise 6

1 –   2 that/which   3 –   4 –   5 who/that   6 which
7 who/that   8 –   9 that/which   10 which   11 –

Exercise 7

1 Walter fell and hurt himself painting a wall.
2 We gave a lift to two students trying to get to London.
3 I met a French guy on the train going to the same place as me.
4 A scientist accidentally discovered Post-It notes trying to invent a strong glue.
5 The crew of the ship found a man hiding in the lifeboat.

GET IT RIGHT!

1 which   2 who   3 who   4 which   5 which   6 who
7 who   8 which

VOCABULARY

Exercise 1

1 employer   2 employees   3 pedestrian   4 residents
5 inhabitants   6 immigrants   7 crew   8 motorist
9 staff   10 audience   11 refugee   12 politician

Exercise 2

Suggested answers

1 motorists; pedestrians   2 employees; staff   3 politicians
4 immigrants; refugees   5 audience   6 residents; immigrants; refugees

Exercise 3

1 turned out   2 hang out with   3 put up with
4 brought about   5 picked up   6 run into
7 worn out   8 going through

Exercise 4

1 into   2 out   3 out   4 out with   5 through   6 up
7 about   8 up with

READING

Exercise 1

1 Many young people left Riace because there weren't enough jobs.
2 Domenico Lucano saw some people on the beach who had escaped their own country.
3 Lucano started an organisation called Città Futura.
4 The refugees had to work to earn their food and accommodation.
5 Lucano used empty buildings to house the refugees.
6 The male refugees renovated houses so they could be rented to tourists.
7 There are more children, which meant that the school could reopen.
8 Other politicians went and visited Riace to get ideas for their towns and cities.

Exercise 2

She usually feels strange, uncomfortable and scared. Now she feels being lost is something to enjoy.

Exercise 3

1 T   2 F   3 F   4 DS   5 F   6 F   7 T   8 DS

DEVELOPING WRITING

Exercise 1

1 Oakridge, Vancouver
2 understanding what people are saying; remembering to leave tips in restaurants, and that tax is added when you buy something

Exercise 2

1 b   2 c/f   3 a   4 c/f   5 d   6 e

Exercise 3

1 No worries, we can do this easily.   2 Having a good time?
3 See what I mean?

LISTENING

◀))06 Exercise 1

1 competition in   2 seven   3 pay for anything   4 the trip
5 a collection of   6 money   7 in the navy   8 Most of

◀))06 Exercise 2

1 the end   2 incredible   3 hardly believe
4 an unbelievable   5 over   6 quite a

Audio Script Track 06

Conversation One

Jill Hey, Max … Do you remember that competition we saw in that magazine? The one where the winner would get a trip to South Africa?

Max What's that, Jill? Oh yes, I remember. Why?

Jill Well, in the end, I entered it. I kind of thought I knew lots of the answers, most of them in fact. And so I thought 'OK, why not?'

Max And …? Hold on, you're not telling me …

Jill Yes. I won! I heard today. The magazine phoned me up and told me I'd won.

Max That's incredible! Wow. Well done. So – you've got a free trip to South Africa!

Jill That's right. I can hardly believe it myself. But it's true. It's three days in Cape Town and four days on a safari in the Kruger National Park, seven days all in. I've always wanted to go there! And everything's included – plane ticket, hotel, food, the lot! Nothing for me to pay for.

Max Brilliant. That's amazing. I'm really happy for you, Jill. But tell me – is the trip for one person or for two? Because, you know, I wouldn't mind …

Jill Sorry, Max – just one!

Conversation Two

Monika Thanks for bringing me here, Graham. This museum's so interesting.

Graham That's right. Wow, look at this collection of comic books! There must be well over a thousand. Do you collect anything, Monika?

Monika No – but my grandfather's got an unbelievable collection of money from all over the world. I think he's got coins and notes from over a hundred different countries.

Graham That's quite a collection! How did he get so many different kinds of money?

Monika Well he was in the navy as a young man and went to lots of different places, and he always brought back a coin and a banknote. Then he got other people to bring things for him when they travelled, and so his collection just grew and grew.

Graham That's amazing. I guess some of the money is old, too, right?

Monika Oh yes, most of it is. He's got things, for example, from countries in Europe before the Euro started – Italian lire, French francs, that kind of thing.

Graham It sounds fascinating. I'd love to see the collection one day.

Monika Sure, no problem. But now let's look at this one here!

DIALOGUE

Exercise 1

Dialogue 1

3, 1, 5, 4, 6, 2

Dialogue 2

3, 1, 5, 2, 6, 4

Dialogue 3

3, 1, 5, 4, 6, 2

CAMBRIDGE ENGLISH: FIRST

Exercise 1

1 Yes
2 a best; eleventh; white; usual; excited; fantastic; different; real; incredible; scary; fun; drenched; great
   b The best place I've ever visited? / And can you guess what it was? / what's not to like?

Exercise 2

Suggested answers

had always been my dream / I guess my real favourite / what's not to like?

CONSOLIDATION UNITS 1 & 2

◀))07 Exercise 1

1 the weather   2 the people   3 the food   4 transport

◀))07 Exercise 2

1 T   2 F   3 F   4 F   5 T

Audio Script Track 07

Tom Have you ever lived abroad, Amelia?

Amelia Yes, I spent a bit of time in Indonesia when I was about eight.

Tom Really? How come?

Amelia My dad worked for the British Council and they wanted him to go over there and help start up an office in a city called Surabaya. Originally it was only supposed to be for six months but he decided to take us all anyway. I'm glad he did because it ended up lasting for more than a year.

Tom So what was it like?

Amelia What I remember of it was brilliant. It was so different from the UK. I remember stepping out of the airport when we first arrived and feeling this wall of heat. It was always so warm there. Even in the rainy season. I mean that was really wet but it still felt hot.

Tom Did you find it difficult to get used to the heat?

Amelia At first, but after a while you soon get used to it. I must admit I found it more difficult to get used to the cold again when we returned to the UK.

Tom So what were the people like?

Amelia They were so friendly. I mean, it's obvious that you're not from the country and everyone wants to talk to you. They make you feel so welcome. I made loads of friends there and I'm still in touch with most of them.

> | Tom | So what is your biggest memory of the whole experience? |
> | Amelia | I've got to choose two. Firstly, the street food, especially a spicy rice dish called nasi goreng. It's fantastic. Every Thursday night this man used to walk around the house pushing his food cart and he rang this sort of bell and we all ran out to get our nasi goreng from him. Just thinking about it makes me want to get back on a plane to Surabaya. |
> | Tom | And the other thing? |
> | Amelia | The other thing was the bejaks, which are a kind of bike with a double seat at the front where you can sit and be cycled around the city. |
> | Tom | Like a taxi service. |
> | Amelia | Yes, only much more exciting than your regular taxi. I mean, the way they used to weave in and out of the traffic. I'm surprised I'm still alive. But it was so much fun. Just like all my time in the country. It was the best time ever! |

Exercise 3

1 helping 2 to take 3 eating 4 taking 5 telling
6 to have 7 to post 8 inviting

Exercise 4

1 My sister spends all day on her phone, which I find very annoying.
2 My favourite town is Brighton, which is on the south coast.
3 I thought that the film I watched last night was really boring.
4 My best friend is Al, who was born on the same day as me.

Exercise 5

1 f 2 g 3 a 4 e 5 h 6 c 7 b 8 d

Exercise 6

1 crawl 2 residents 3 crew 4 wandered 5 tiptoed
6 audience 7 employees 8 swung

Exercise 7

1 Of course I can 2 You know what? 3 I bet you can't
4 That's too easy 5 It's a deal 6 You'll never manage to do it

Exercise 8

1 bad weather; a great white shark 2 none 3 She was bitten by a black widow spider. 4 She brushed the spider away. 5 She used a golf tee to make a hole in her leg, and then squeezed the poison out. 6 She finished her game.

UNIT 3 THE NEXT GENERATION

GRAMMAR

Exercise 1

1 a, c, b, d 2 c, d, a, b
3 d, b, c, a

Exercise 2

1 majority 2 plenty 3 several 4 all of 5 most
6 almost 7 number 8 few 9 deal 10 hardly

Exercise 3

1 loads of 2 plenty 3 hardly any 4 loads
5 vast majority 6 All

Exercise 5

1 It's so hot today. 2 My uncle's such a rich man.
3 Dawn's got such a lot of problems. 4 I ate such a lot.

Exercise 7

Suggested answers

1 the queue is too long
2 this equation is too difficult
3 You don't spend enough time cleaning your room.

Exercise 8

1 d 2 f 3 a 4 b 5 c 6 e

Exercise 9

1 You do know Alan. You met him at Steve's party, remember?
2 We do spend a lot of our time talking about the same things. It's getting a bit boring.
3 My dad does embarrass me sometimes but I guess all dads do.
4 I don't know what May said but I did enjoy your party.
5 Miss Holloway's great but she does talk a lot.
6 I've hardly got any money left. We did buy a lot of things today.
7 I do miss my mum when she travels abroad for work.

GET IT RIGHT!

Bringing up children is not an easy job and some parents can be ~~such~~ **so** strict that their children sometimes rebel. There is ~~so~~ **such** a lot of advice out there about raising children that it's not always easy to make the right decisions. Amy Chua's book was ~~such~~ **so** interesting I read it twice and it contained so many useful pieces of advice. Childhood is ~~so~~ **such** a significant time in your life and it's so important to get things right.

VOCABULARY

Exercise 1

1 wig – C 2 belt – E 3 sunglasses – I 4 helmet – G
5 sword – D 6 mask – A 7 shield – D 8 cape – H
9 apron – B

Exercise 2

1 apron 2 sword 3 shield 4 helmet 5 mask 6 belt
7 cape 8 sunglasses 9 wig

Exercise 3

1 d 2 f 3 a 4 b 5 c 6 h 7 e 8 g

Exercise 4

1 get ahead in life 2 do your best 3 childhood 4 bringing
5 did 6 soft 7 growing 8 strict

READING

Exercise 1

1 Dale stood at the bus stop (outside his house) to wave Rain off.
2 Dale wore fancy dress to wave Rain off to school every day.
3 Rain could hear all of his school friends laughing at something as he was climbing onto the bus.
4 Dale waved Rain off come rain or shine.
5 Dale got a lot of his costumes from the family fancy dress collection.
6 Rochelle Price took photos of her husband to put on their website.
7 Rain was eventually able to see the funny side and realised that his dad was pretty cool after all.
8 Dale has no plans to wave Rain off to school next year.

Exercise 2

C

Exercise 3

A 5 B 3 C 6 D 1

DEVELOPING WRITING

Exercise 1

1 More parents are relying on their own mothers and fathers to look after their children so that they can go back to work.
2 Children are well cared for, and feel loved and secure. They can grow up to have a close bond with their grandparents, knowing they can turn to them for help with problems they don't want to share with their parents.
3 Parents should be careful not to forget their responsibility for their child's upbringing and happiness.

Exercise 2

1 far   2 Of course   3 always   4 indeed
These words add emphasis to the sentences.

Exercise 3

Suggested answers

1 You must always think of the child's safety.
2 It's far more difficult to spend all day looking after young children.
3 Grandparents love their grandchildren very much indeed. / Of course, grandparents love their grandchildren very much.
4 Grandparents always want to help their own children. / Of course, grandparents want to help their own children.

LISTENING

🔊08 **Exercise 1**

A Sue   B Dawn   C Jen

🔊08 **Exercise 2**

1 F   2 F   3 T   4 F   5 T   6 T

🔊08 **Exercise 3**

1 Dad does know how to embarrass me.
2 We're your parents, Jen, we do care about you.
3 It's such an inappropriate hairstyle for a man of his age.
4 Dad's so embarrassing.
5 I did like it when I was about eight.

Audio Script Track 08

Conversation 1 – Jen
Jen   Dad does know how to embarrass me.
Mum   What's he done this time, Jen?
Jen   Well, I was walking home from school with Chloe and Amelia and Dad pulls up in the car by the side of the road.
Mum   And?
Jen   Well, at first I didn't even know it was him but then he opened the window and called my name so I turned round and he asked me if I wanted a lift.
Mum   What's wrong with that?
Jen   I'm 16, Mum. I'm not a baby. When did I last need a lift home from Dad?
Mum   Um, last Saturday, when you needed to get back from Tom's party at midnight.
Jen   That's different, Mum.
Mum   Is it? He was probably just driving past and saw you and wondered if you wanted a lift. We're your parents, Jen, we do care about you.

Conversation 2 – Sue
Sue   Mum, you've got to have a word with Dad.
Mum   Why, Sue?
Sue   It's his hair, Mum. I mean, I don't mind him having long hair but does he have to tie it back in a ponytail? It's such an inappropriate hairstyle for a man of his age.
Mum   What do you mean? I quite like it.

Sue   You are joking, right? It's the sort of haircut that footballers used to have about ten years ago. No one wears their hair like that now.
Mum   Well your dad does. He likes it that way. And what difference does it make to you, anyway?
Sue   My friends think it looks silly.
Mum   Do they? Which friends exactly?
Sue   Well, no one's actually said anything but I know they're thinking it.
Mum   Sue, you need to worry less about what your friends might be thinking and more about hurting your dad's feelings.

Conversation 3 – Dawn
Dawn   Dad's so embarrassing.
Mum   Really, Dawn? What's he done now?
Dawn   Well, when my friends come round to our house, he tries to act really cool and join in our conversations.
Mum   What do you mean?
Dawn   For example, he tries to pretend he's really into music and mentions all the bands that he thinks we're listening to. Of course, he gets it all wrong. I mean he thinks we're into stuff like Avril Lavigne and Fall Out Boy.
Mum   I thought you liked that kind of stuff.
Dawn   Yes, I did like it when I was about eight. But now? Please …
Mum   Well, he's only trying to be friendly. Don't be too hard on him.
Dawn   I know, but to make it worse, he starts singing the songs. Mum, it's awful. You've got to make him stop.
Mum   Yes, that is embarrassing. I'll have a word with him.
Dawn   Thanks, Mum.

DIALOGUE

Exercise 1

5, 3, 11, 7, 1, 9, 12, 4, 10, 6, 2, 8

Exercise 2

1 But I did clean it, Mum.
2 Really? Last time I looked it was such a mess.
3 Well go and have a look now. It's so tidy. You won't believe it.

CAMBRIDGE ENGLISH: FIRST

🔊10 **Exercise 1**

Speaker 1 E   Speaker 2 A   Speaker 3 H   Speaker 4 C
Speaker 5 G

Audio Script Track 10

You will hear five short extracts in which people are talking about family holidays. For questions 1–5, choose from the list (A–H) what each speaker says about them. Use the letters only once. There are three extra letters which you do not need to use.

Speaker 1
We go on a family holiday for two weeks every July and we always go to the same place, a campsite by a beach in South Wales. I know some people might think this sounds a bit boring, but I really enjoy it. It's just me, my brother and Mum and Dad and we always have a great time. We don't really do anything special. We go for a few walks, swim in the sea and Dad makes the most amazing meals on the fire. We're all so busy in our day-to-day life, it's great just to hang out and spend some real time together – stress free. And amazingly, we never argue like we do all the time at home.

Speaker 2
I always like the idea of a family holiday. Mum and Dad take us to some amazing places, we're really lucky. But when we get back from them I always feel a bit let down. The problem is that Mum can never really switch off from work. We can be lying on a beach in the south of France and Mum will spend half the time talking on the phone while Dad just reads his book. It's a shame because it would be nice to have some quality time together but we just don't really get any chance to sit down and talk. Even when we're having an evening meal together you can bet that Mum's phone will ring. It's a shame.

Speaker 3
I quite enjoy our annual family holiday but as I get a bit older, I find I'm enjoying them less and less. The problem is that because I'm the oldest I get a bit bored with hanging out with my brother and sister. They're still happy messing around on the beach and swimming in the sea, but I don't really find that sort of thing much fun anymore. This year I spent most of the time playing games on my phone, which, of course, led to arguments with Mum. It was just like being at home. I'd really like to go on holiday with my friends next year but I'm not sure Mum will let me.

Speaker 4
I love family holidays. I'm an only child so Mum and Dad always let me invite a friend along to keep me company. It means that they don't have to worry so much about keeping me entertained. They can go off and do the sorts of things that adults enjoy doing, while my friend and I just have fun hanging out without having parents telling us what to do all the time. Everyone's happy and we all go home completely refreshed. My only problem is trying to choose which friend to invite. Maybe they'll let me take two this year.

Speaker 5
I don't really enjoy family holidays. It's just me, Dad and my sister and my dad only takes us to the places that he wants to go. That usually means some place of historical interest with a castle and lots of museums for him to drag us around. Why do we always have to do what he wants us to do? It would be much more fun if he let me and Jenny choose for a change. We'd take him to Disneyland and show him a really good time.

◀)) 11 Exercise 2

Speaker 1 G   Speaker 2 A   Speaker 3 H   Speaker 4 C
Speaker 5 F

Audio Script Track 11

You will hear five short extracts in which people are answering the question, 'What is the most important role of a parent?' For questions 1–5, choose from the list (A–H) what each speaker says about it. Use the letters only once. There are three extra letters which you do not need to use.

Speaker 1
There are so many roles that a parent has to play in a child's life that it's almost impossible to choose the most important. I mean they need to be teachers, friends, providers, protectors; they need to discipline us from time to time. I mean the list is endless. But I suppose that if I was forced to choose just one, then I would go for 'friend' because I guess in a way, a good friend is sort of all the other things too. The most important thing about a friend is knowing they will always be there for you, no matter what you do. And that's exactly what a good mum or dad should do too.

Speaker 2
Of the many roles that a parent plays in a child's life, the most important by far is that of being a provider. The first responsibility of any parent is to make sure that there is a roof over their children's heads and a meal on the table three times a day. Then they have to make sure that they get educated and are healthy. If you can ensure all these things then all children will

---

have the basic needs they require to have a chance in life. But of course, it's not just material things that a child needs. Parents also have the obligation to provide love. But then, it's almost impossible to be a parent and not do that.

Speaker 3
Children need to be disciplined. You see too many children these days who have absolutely no respect for older generations and think that the world revolves only around them. I blame the parents for letting them get away with doing whatever they want. You see it in the streets all the time, young children hanging out in large groups without a parent in sight. And if a policeman tries to move them on, they treat it as if it was just one big joke. They've no respect for anyone.

Speaker 4
It's very difficult to be a parent these days, that's for sure. The world is changing so quickly that it's hard to keep up with all the things that are going on. Having said that, some things will always be the same: love, respect, tolerance, living without prejudice. These are the things that are really important and these are the things that parents should pass on to their children. If they are successful in doing so then their children can pass them on to their children and so on. It means the world will always be a good place to live in.

Speaker 5
There's no one in the world who can love you like your mum and dad and this love is what makes a child feel safe and protected. Luckily it's probably the most natural thing a parent can do and something that they won't need to work too hard at. Of course, it's not easy bringing up children and there are many things you will need to do to make sure that they grow up into healthy, well-rounded individuals. But so long as you love them and give them a home where they feel safe, then you're giving them the best possible start to their lives.

UNIT 4 THINKING OUTSIDE THE BOX
GRAMMAR
Exercise 1

1 be   2 hearing   3 having   4 eating   5 wear
6 seeing   7 living   8 driving

Exercise 2

1 used to   2 was used to   3 got used to   4 used to
5 got used to   6 was used to   7 am used to   8 get used to

Exercise 3

1 is   2 get   3 get   4 got   5 is   6 was   7 get
8 are   9 get

Exercise 5

1 fast   2 beautifully   3 well   4 slowly   5 hard

Exercise 6

1 enjoyable   2 surprise   3 friendly   4 excitement
5 different   6 fear   7 strange   8 interest

Exercise 8

1 Jack approached the lion with fear.
2 Candy carried three suitcases with difficulty.
3 The boys ate their hamburgers with enthusiasm.
4 Jerry rode his horse in an awkward way.
5 Helen watched the football match with interest.

GET IT RIGHT!

1 I'll definitely finish the project by next Monday.
2 It's a good thing that you came immediately.
3 I totally understand your point of view.
4 Dan worked hard on his homework and got top marks.
5 Jo and Kate were speaking quietly so no one would hear them.
6 Do you always have to think creatively in your job?
7 I live locally so I can walk home.
8 This is probably the best pizza I've ever eaten.

VOCABULARY

Exercise 1

1 bright   2 imaginative   3 responsible   4 arrogant
5 cautious   6 confident   7 decisive   8 organised
9 practical
Mystery word: impatient

Exercise 2

1 bad-tempered   2 cautious   3 imaginative   4 practical
5 responsible   6 arrogant   7 impatient   8 dull

Exercise 3

1 in a hurry   2 by accident   3 in public   4 in a row
5 in private   6 in secret   7 in a panic   8 on purpose

Exercise 4

1 for good   2 not very good   3 It's a good thing
4 So far, so good   5 it's no good

READING

Exercise 1

1 F   2 F   3 T   4 T   5 F   6 T   7 T   8 F

Exercise 2

Possibility thinking: letting yourself imagine things that are often way outside reality, and pushing the limits of what you know.

Concentrated thinking: devoting a period of time every day to practise creative thinking.

Thinking about a problem for a long time and not giving up. (also possible: Thinking in images)

Exercise 3

1 c   2 d   3 g   4 f   5 a   6 h   7 e   8 b

DEVELOPING WRITING

Exercise 1

Marnie wants her sister Becca to give her some tips on how to revise.

Exercise 2

1 The thing is   2 you know that   3 Well   4 Now

Exercise 3

1 you know that   2 the thing is   3 Well   4 Now

Exercise 4

1 B   2 D   3 C   4 A

LISTENING

🔊 14 Exercise 1

A 2   B 3   C 1

🔊 14 Exercise 2

Conversation 1
1 to take off/undo   2 panic   3 undo it   4 pull it over
5 stuck

Conversation 2
6 as good as   7 it's not   8 give up   9 take up   10 see

Conversation 3
11 three new ideas   12 tomorrow   13 it's eight
14 stay up   15 possibility   16 leaves her

Audio Script Track 14

Conversation 1

Man   It's completely stuck. This is the third time it's happened. Now I can't take it off.

Woman   Do you want me to help you? I'm usually pretty good at things like this.

Man   No, just let me have another go, I think I can do it. Oh, no. This is hopeless! I'll never undo it. It just won't move! And now I'm soaking wet! Why can't people make …

Woman   Don't panic, calm down a bit, OK? You won't get anywhere if you lose your temper. Here. Let me have a look. Oh, no. I can't undo it, either.

Man   I think perhaps I'll just have to pull it over my head. It's the only way to get it off. Here goes. Oh no! Now it's stuck on my head.

Conversation 2

Boy   So, what do you think?

Girl   Let me have a look. Well, it's … interesting. I mean, I don't think it's quite as good as your last one.

Boy   Come on, admit it. It's not very good, is it?

Girl   Well, I'd have to say, no, it's not that good. Sorry, but you did ask me for my opinion.

Boy   No, it's OK. You're absolutely right. I give up. I'm useless at painting.

Girl   No, no, don't give up. Why don't you just start again? Maybe if you do that you'll get a better idea of what you want in the end.

Boy   No chance. I'm going to take up photography instead. I never want to see a paintbrush and a pot of paint ever again!

Conversation 3

Woman   Oh, this is pointless!

Man   What's the matter? Are you having trouble?

Woman   Trouble? Yes, I am having trouble. Big trouble. I'm supposed to have three new ideas for the company for tomorrow morning's meeting.

Man   And you're stuck?

Woman   Completely. I've been thinking for an hour – nothing! I'll never come up with any ideas. And it's eight o'clock already, I'm going to have to stay up the whole night if I don't get some ideas soon.

Man   Perhaps you're going about it the wrong way. Perhaps you need a different approach.

Woman   Like what?

Man   Well, I was reading something the other day about Einstein, and how he used 'possibility thinking'.

Woman   Einstein? Jack, I'm an editor at a gardening magazine, not a physicist. I don't think Einstein's going to help me get a good idea, thank you.

Man   Oh, OK then. I'll leave you to it. Good luck.

DIALOGUE

Exercise 1

Dialogue 1

3, 1, 7, 5, 4, 8, 2, 6

Dialogue 2

3, 5, 1, 7, 6, 2, 4, 8

PHRASES FOR FLUENCY

Exercise 1

1 just calm down   2 you're really out of order   3 That's just it
4 again   5 give it a rest   6 You can't be serious

CAMBRIDGE ENGLISH: FIRST

Exercise 1

1 Dear   2 Thank you so much   3 I'm writing now   4 two
5 great   6 I'm not very keen on   7 almost anything
8 Best wishes

Exercise 2

1 B   2 A   3 A   4 A   5 B

Exercise 3

Suggested answers

1 Explain to her why I am writing. / Tell her I'm easy-going.
2 Yes
3 I want to tell her what I can't eat/don't like. Yes, both.
4 Ask her if there is anything else she needs.

CONSOLIDATION UNITS 3 & 4

🔊 15 **Exercise 1**

1 B   2 B   3 C

🔊 15 **Exercise 2**

1 T   2 F   3 T   4 T   5 F

Audio Script Track 15

Lucy   Would you say you had a happy childhood, Paul?
Paul   Oh absolutely. I think my mum and dad did a really good job of bringing us all up.
Lucy   What do you remember most about it?
Paul   It was just a lot of fun. There was a lot of laughter. I can't remember my parents ever arguing. They just seemed to be really happy together and that meant we grew up in a really positive atmosphere.
Lucy   What! There weren't ever any fights in your house?
Paul   Not between my parents. Of course, I had a few with my brother and sister – just like all children I suppose.
Lucy   Would you say your mum and dad were quite soft?
Paul   No, they weren't soft at all but they weren't overly strict either. I think they were fair. They had their ideas on how to bring up children and they were always consistent with them, which was great because we always knew what they expected from us. Some of the decisions they made were quite tough for us but we learned to live with them.
Lucy   For example ...?
Paul   For example, we grew up with no TV. You've got to remember that this was back in the 1980s. Everyone had a TV. This was in days before the Internet so all the kids at school used to watch the same programmes and then discuss them the next day in the school playground. But I never could because I hadn't seen them. That was pretty tough for a while. But you know, I got used to it.

Lucy   Wow, no TV. That must have been hard. So what did you do?
Paul   I don't know, really. I mean, I used to read quite a bit and we used to play a lot of board games. I used to play a lot of sport. Dad taught me to play tennis. Mum taught me how to swim. I think we just spent a lot of time together as a family.
Lucy   What about friends? Were you allowed to invite friends over?
Paul   Absolutely. All the time. Our house was like an open house. It was always full of friends and Mum and Dad always made them feel very welcome. There was always homemade cake and biscuits for everyone. And they weren't embarrassing at all. My friends used to enjoy talking with my parents and my parents were always interested in getting to know them too.
Lucy   It sounds like it was a really happy time.
Paul   It was. I hope I can do the same for my kids when I have them.

Exercise 3

1 The vast majority of my friends have their own tablet.
2 We haven't got enough players for the board game tonight.
3 He is so practical that he can fix anything.
4 I do enjoy listening to music when I've got nothing to do.
5 I'll never get used to waking up so early.
6 Mr White teaches chemistry in an enjoyable way.

Exercise 4

1 mask   2 arrogant   3 shield   4 a helmet   5 decisive
6 wig   7 impatient   8 bright

Exercise 5

1 e   2 h   3 g   4 c   5 b   6 d   7 f   8 a

Exercise 6

9, 3, 5, 1, 11, 7, 4, 12, 8, 10, 6, 2

Exercise 7

1 She refused to do what he had asked.
2 She showed him a list of all the important occasions in her life that he had missed.
3 important phone calls, travel, urgent meetings, sudden problems at work
4 He realised that he had lost control of the balance between work and family, and that he had been neglecting his daughter.
5 He resigned from his job and now has more time to spend with his family.

UNIT 5   SCREEN TIME

GRAMMAR

Exercise 1

1 aren't supposed to   2 didn't need to   3 are not allowed to
4 don't let me   5 have to   6 shouldn't

Exercise 2

1 made   2 mustn't   3 aren't allowed to   4 had better
5 didn't let   6 didn't have to

Exercise 3

1 My mum made me leave it at home.
2 My parents didn't allow me to go.
3 You had better find it soon.
4 Sorry, I had to tidy my bedroom.
5 But you mustn't give your phone to anyone.
6 No, my parents didn't let me stay up for it.

Exercise 5

1 d 2 h 3 g 4 b 5 a 6 c 7 f 8 e

Exercise 6

1 Daniel didn't need to do his homework last night.
2 Sally didn't need to revise for her History exam.
3 I needn't have taken a thick jumper with me yesterday.
4 Lucy needn't have cooked Brian a birthday cake.
5 Liam didn't need to have dinner at home.
6 We needn't have taken a taxi to the hotel.
7 I didn't need to call Lara.

Exercise 7

1 James hasn't succeeded in passing his driving test yet.
2 I haven't been able to find my charger yet.
3 Sarah wasn't able to swim yesterday.
4 We succeeded in climbing Ben Nevis at the weekend.
5 They weren't able to access the Internet at the hotel last night.
6 He didn't have much time but he managed to finish the project.

GET IT RIGHT!

1 must 2 shouldn't 3 must 4 can't 5 must 6 Must
7 wouldn't 8 must

VOCABULARY

Exercise 1

1 protective case – C 2 webcam – E 3 charger – D
4 power lead – F 5 plug – B 6 headset – A

Exercise 2

1 c 2 d 3 a 4 b

Exercise 3

1 wireless router 2 protective case 3 power lead
4 headset 5 webcam

Exercise 4

1 stream 2 posts 3 zip 4 plug 5 upgrades 6 extract
7 save 8 sync 9 browse 10 connect

Exercise 5

1 posted 2 upgrade 3 was browsing 4 zip
5 connect 6 save

READING

Exercise 1

1 Children feel unfairly disadvantaged compared with their peers, which can lead to stressful family situations.
2 In the 1960s.
3 São Paulo in Brazil.
4 70%
5 Any three of the following: take photos; record videos; check emails and Facebook; surf the Internet; get directions; play games; shop; check in for a flight
6 To be unreachable and truly switch off.

Exercise 2

1 The number of known copies of Shakespeare's First Folio that still survive today.
2 The year from which the US Library of Congress have archived all public Tweets sent by Americans.
3 The number of articles on Wikipedia.

Exercise 3

1 1623 2 13th; Mesopotamia 3 special equipment
4 print 5 archive websites 6 printed copies

DEVELOPING WRITING

Exercise 1

B, D and E

Exercise 2

First Next Then After that Finally

LISTENING

🔊 17 **Exercise 1**

1 video games 2 texts 3 upset

🔊 17 **Exercise 2**

1 Write a video gaming guide for parents.
2 Because Alicia's mum is already worried that she spends too much time playing video games.
3 She should stop sitting around staring at screens all day.
4 He suggests that Alicia calls Jo. / He suggests that Alicia does some exercise.
5 Jo's skiing trip.
6 Because Alicia hadn't called her for weeks.

🔊 17 **Exercise 3**

1 is making us write; won't let me play; should go out
2 need to do 3 don't need to bring

Audio Script Track 17

Matt What do you think of the homework? I can't believe Mr Harrow is making us write this thing.

Alicia You mean the video gaming guide for parents? I think it's OK. Mind you, I'm not going to show it to my mum. She's already worried about me spending too much time playing video games. She won't let me play during the week at all.

Oscar You do spend a lot of time on the games console, Alicia. You should go out more.

Alicia Oh, no. Here we go. You're going to give me another lecture now, Oscar, aren't you? I don't always play games on the console. I stream movies and videos and I watch DVDs.

Oscar Yeah, but Alicia, you don't play tennis any more and you've stopped going to the swimming club. You just sit at home now.

Alicia What do you mean?

Matt You know what he means. You just sit around staring at screens all day.

Oscar You're turning into a couch potato. You need to do some exercise.

Alicia Do you really think that?

Oscar Yes. You don't see your friends any more. You just sit at home.

Alicia I text my friends all the time.

Matt That's not the same as seeing them. You should see your friends more often. You'll end up losing them otherwise. They'll all make new friends.

Alicia You're right. I haven't seen Jo for weeks. We used to do everything together.

Oscar She came back from her skiing trip yesterday. You should call her.

Alicia OK. I'll call her now and ask her to come and meet us at Bob's Café.

Jo Hi, Alicia. I haven't heard from you for ages.

Alicia I know, I'm sorry. Listen. Matt, Oscar and I are going to Bob's Café. Would you like to come along? We can't wait to hear about your skiing trip.

Jo I'd love to come. I'll meet you all there in an hour.

Alicia Great. We'll see you there. Oh, and you don't need to bring any money – it's on me!

Matt She's coming then?

Alicia	Yes.
Oscar	We already knew that.
Alicia	How come?
Matt	Jo rang me this morning. She was upset because you haven't called her for weeks. I told her not to worry. You'd call her today.

DIALOGUE

Exercise 1

1 made me   2 have to help me; need to finish; make me do it
3 had better get; should leave

CAMBRIDGE ENGLISH: FIRST

Exercise 1

1 D   2 B   3 A   4 C   5 B   6 A   7 D   8 C   9 B   10 A

UNIT 6 BRINGING PEOPLE TOGETHER

GRAMMAR

Exercise 1

1 F   2 F   3 T   4 T   5 F   6 T   7 T   8 T

Exercise 2

1 Euroair is much more expensive than Budgetline.
2 Budgetline is just as popular as Euroair.
3 Euroair is far quicker than Budgetline.
4 Budgetline is nowhere near as good as Euroair.
5 Euroair is just as frequent as Budgetline.
6 Euroair is not nearly as cheap as Budgetline.

Exercise 3

1 Every year the roads get busier and busier.
2 I love spring. Every day the sun stays up longer and longer.
3 Scientists say the temperature of the Earth is getting hotter and hotter.
4 The price of food is getting more and more expensive by the week.

Exercise 4

1 The hotter the weather is, the angrier I get.
2 The faster you drive, the more dangerous it is.
3 The hungrier you are, the better food tastes.
4 The older you are, the less sleep you need.

Exercise 5

1 e   2 f   3 a   4 b   5 c   6 d

Exercise 6

1 Although   2 In spite of   3 Even though   4 despite
5 Nevertheless   6 However

Exercise 7

1 Although I've got two bikes, I can't ride a bike.
2 My mother's French; however, I don't speak French.
3 Even though I love Italian food, I don't like pizza. / I don't like pizza, even though I love Italian food.
4 I always go to bed early; nevertheless, I'm always late for school.
5 In spite of the fact I'm only 14, I'm 1.75m tall. / I'm 1.75m tall, in spite of the fact I'm only 14.

GET IT RIGHT!

1 c – Ethan was offered the position of school counsellor. However, he turned it down.
2 f – Loom bands used to be a big craze. However, it seems to be over now.
3 b – The passengers were stuck on the train for two hours. However, nobody spoke to each other.
4 e – The Ice Bucket Challenge raised awareness about ALS. However, it also wasted a lot of water.
5 d – President Obama refused to do the challenge. However, he donated money instead.

VOCABULARY

Exercise 1

1 recommend; e   2 confess; b   3 introduce; f
4 enquire; a   5 announce; c   6 complain; d

Exercise 2

1 enquiry   2 complaint   3 announcement
4 recommendation   5 introduction   6 confession

Exercise 3

1 confessed   2 enquired   3 complained   4 recommended
5 introduced   6 announced

Exercise 4

1 in   2 split   3 married   4 engaged   5 out   6 going
7 on   8 start   9 over

Exercise 5

4, 9, 1, 6, 8, 2, 7, 3, 5

READING

Exercise 1

1 The amount people paid to the charity if they did the Ice Bucket Challenge.
2 The amount people paid to the charity if they refused to do the Ice Bucket Challenge.
3 The number of hours people had to post a video of their challenge online.
4 The number of people to be nominated for the challenge by each person who had done the challenge.
5 The number of videos posted on Facebook.
6 The number of countries where the videos were posted from.
7 The percentage of the British population who did the challenge.
8 The percentage of the British population who did the challenge and gave money to charity.

Exercise 2

Suggested answers

Using the Internet to communicate a message; stories going viral; being featured in the media; acts of kindness from strangers

Exercise 3

1 Glenn Buratti to Ashley Buratti
2 Alan Barnes to Katie Cutler
3 Ashley Buratti to Glenn Buratti
4 Katie Cutler to Alan Barnes or journalists
5 Alan Barnes to Katie Cutler
6 Alan Barnes to his attackers
7 Glenn Buratti to Ashley Buratti
8 Ashley Buratti/Glenn Buratti to Glenn's classmates

DEVELOPING WRITING

Exercise 1

She believes that all donations are welcome.

Exercise 2

Suggested answers
How people donate their time:
Driving elderly people to hospital
Doctors and rescue workers who help when earthquakes hit
How people donate their money:
Make online payments
Buy items from charity organisations

LISTENING

🔊 18 Exercise 1

A 2   B 3   C 1

🔊 18 Exercise 2

Conversation 1
1 £108   2 9.55

Conversation 2
3 a large orange juice, a chicken sandwich and a chocolate bar
4 30p

Conversation 3
5 one night   6 four days

🔊 18 Exercise 3

Conversation 1
whole lot; by far

Conversation 2
easily; even

Conversation 3
far and away; miles

Audio Script Track 18

Conversation 1

Ava   I'd like a single to Glasgow, please.
Man   What train are you thinking of catching?
Ava   I'm sorry?
Man   Do you want to catch the next one leaving at 8.55?
Ava   I think so. Is there a problem?
Man   It's just very expensive. If you can wait an hour and get the 9.55 it's a whole lot cheaper.
Man   Really?
Man   Yes, the 8.55 is £145 and the 9.55 is £37. If you're not in a hurry then you'd be much better off waiting.
Ava   No, there's no hurry. I'm going to spend the night at my friend's house so I can arrive an hour later, no problem.
Man   The 9.55 is actually half an hour quicker so you'll only be arriving 30 minutes later anyway.
Ava   Yes, that's a much better idea by far. Thanks!

Conversation 2

Woman   Hi there. What can I get you?
Ava   Umm, let me see. I'd like a regular orange juice and a chicken sandwich, please.
Woman   A regular orange juice and a chicken sandwich?
Ava   Oh, and a chocolate bar too.
Woman   Why don't you have a large juice then?
Ava   No, a regular one's fine.
Woman   It's just if you get a sandwich and a large drink, you get a free chocolate bar. It's part of our meal deal.
Ava   Really?

Woman   Yes, the difference between a regular and a large juice is only 30p and a chocolate bar is 70p so it's easily the best deal for you. It's usually best to go for one of our deals. And it's even cheaper if you've got a Trainclub card.
Ava   I don't have one of those but I would like to go for the meal deal please.

Conversation 3

Boy   So are you staying in Glasgow or are you going to have a look around the rest of Scotland?
Ava   No, it's just one night in Glasgow, then I'm off to Oban to catch the ferry to Mull.
Boy   Mull, you'll love it. It's beautiful.
Ava   Yes, I've seen photos. It seems a bit like the Lake District.
Boy   Mull's far and away more spectacular than the Lake District. It's amazing. Are you going to any other islands?
Ava   I don't think so. I've only got four days so I don't think I'll have enough time.
Boy   Well you must at least take a boat trip to Iona. It's just off the coast of Mull but it's smaller and miles less crowded.
Ava   Iona. OK, I'll keep it in mind. Thanks!

DIALOGUE

Exercise 1

12, 15, 7, 3, 1, 5, 10, 13, 2, 11, 4, 8, 9, 6, 14

CAMBRIDGE ENGLISH: FIRST

1 D   2 B   3 A   4 B   5 C   6 D   7 B   8 C   9 A   10 D

CONSOLIDATION UNITS 5 & 6

🔊 20 Exercise 1

1 the trumpet   2 (about) eight   3 at the theatre
4 on their wedding night

🔊 20 Exercise 2

1 T   2 F   3 F   4 F   5 T   6 T

Audio Script Track 20

Ollie   So Sam, how did you and Jim get together?
Sam   Well, it's a quite a story. How long have you got?
Ollie   Don't worry about me. I'm in no rush.
Sam   OK. So Jim was in a band. He played the trumpet.
Ollie   A rock band?
Sam   Yes, they were very cool. They had a trumpet player. Anyway, they weren't a very famous band but they were quite popular in the part of London where I lived and they were always playing shows in the area. A friend of mine took me to see one of their shows and I really liked the band.
Ollie   Especially the trumpet player.
Sam   Well actually it was quite a big band. I think there were about eight of them on stage and Jim always stood at the back so you couldn't really see him very well. But after a couple of shows I did start to notice him and I thought he was quite cute.
Ollie   So did you go up and introduce yourself to him?
Sam   No way. I mean they weren't a well-known band but they were still a band. I was far too shy to go and talk to anyone in a band. No, I just watched and daydreamed.
Ollie   So what happened?

> Sam Well after about year the band just broke up. That was it. No more shows. I'd never see my mysterious trumpet player again. I was heartbroken. Then one day about two years later I was at work. I should say here that I worked in a theatre. I was what they call 'front of house', which meant I was responsible for getting the audience in and out. Anyway, my manager called me into the office to introduce me to a new member of the team I was in charge of. And there he was …
>
> Ollie Jim?
>
> Sam Yes, although at that time I still didn't know his name. Anyway, he started working with me and after a few weeks he asked me out on a date. And that was it. Soon we were going out together.
>
> Ollie So did you tell him that you used to be secretly in love with him when he was in a band?
>
> Sam Well, that's the funny thing. I pretended that I never knew. He used to talk about the band all the time but I didn't say a thing. And then on our wedding night I finally confessed and told him the truth. You should have seen his face.

Exercise 3

1 g 2 e 3 a 4 b 5 h 6 c 7 f 8 d

Exercise 4

1 connect; wireless router   2 plug; power lead; adapter
3 webcam; headset   4 protective case   5 USB port
6 charger   7 browse; upgrade   8 sync

Exercise 5

1 announced; a family   2 recommended; on a date
3 enquired; out with   4 confessed; in love with

Exercise 6

5, 11, 7, 9, 3, 1, 4, 10, 2, 6, 8

Exercise 7

5, 9, 3, 1, 2, 8, 7, 6, 4

UNIT 7 ALWAYS LOOK ON THE BRIGHT SIDE

GRAMMAR

Exercise 1

1 My dad's going to Berlin on business next month.
2 The lesson starts in ten minutes.
3 As soon as Mum gets home we'll go to the cinema.
4 We won't have dinner until Dad comes home.
5 Tina and Tom will be staying with their aunt in Mexico in the summer holidays.

Exercise 2

1 'm going to ask   2 aren't planning   3 're travelling
4 're going to drive   5 're going to take
6 's Mr Jones going to hold   7 's organising

Exercise 3

1 are you doing; 'm going   2 will let; 'll ask   3 does the football match start; starts   4 'm going to look for; are joining
5 's; 're having; 'll rain   6 does the train leave; leaves

Exercise 4

1 Your computer will have a sense of smell. / Your computer won't have a sense of smell.
2 Facebook will still be the biggest social network. / Facebook won't still be the biggest social network.
3 Robots will do all the work on farms. / Robots won't do all the work on farms.
4 Planes will fly without pilots. / Planes won't fly without pilots.
5 We'll be able to upload the contents of our brains to our computers. / We won't be able to upload the contents of our brains to our computers.
6 People will be able to touch each other through their phones. / People won't be able to touch each other through their phones.

Exercise 5

1 I'll be swimming in the sea.   2 Sam will be looking for shells on the beach.   3 Mum will be exploring the town.
4 Dad will be buying food at the local market.

Exercise 6

1 'll have eaten; 'll have left   2 will have gone
3 'll have swum   4 'll have travelled

Exercise 7

1 will have landed   2 will be sailing   3 will have found
4 will be eating   5 will do

Exercise 8

1 'll be   2 'll be staying   3 'll send   4 'll be going
5 'll be having   6 'll have visited   7 'll have seen
8 'll have been shopping   9 'll text

GET IT RIGHT!

1 will   2 would   3 will   4 would   5 will   6 would

VOCABULARY

Exercise 1

1 point   2 off   3 about

Exercise 2

1 a – B   2 c – C   3 b – A

Exercise 4

1 b   2 d   3 a   4 c   5 f   6 e

Exercise 5

1 I told you so   2 so far   3 So   4 I guess so
5 I'm afraid so   6 or so

READING

Exercise 1

1 to be in a good mood   2 They thought he was going to die.
3 He said he was allergic to bullets.   4 playing the piano (OR her piano lessons)

Exercise 2

1 Jim Carrey was 14 years old when he took a factory job to help pay the family's bills.
2 Stephen King's first book, *Carrie*, was rejected 30 times by publishers.
3 Vincent Van Gogh painted more than 2,000 artworks in a decade.
4 Michael Jordan has lost almost 300 games in his career.

Exercise 3

1 c   2 e   3 f   4 d   5 a   6 b

DEVELOPING WRITING

Exercise 1

1 C   2 B   3 A   4 C

Exercise 2

1 kick off   2 upbeat   3 goodies   4 vintage
5 open-air   6 Thanks a million

Exercise 3

1 A big mug of creamy hot chocolate.
2 In her favourite sports car.
3 A barbecue in the castle grounds.
4 Darcy Night Carol
5 They will be toasting marshmallows on a campfire and looking at the stars.

LISTENING

◀) 21 Exercise 1

a 1   b 3   c 2

◀) 21 Exercise 2

Conversation 1
1 F   2 T

Conversation 2
1 T   2 F

Conversation 3
1 T   2 T

Audio Script Track 21

Conversation 1

May   Are you going to the rehearsal tomorrow night, Gina?
Gina   Yes, but I haven't practised all week. I'm feeling quite apprehensive.
May   You've got nothing to worry about. You always play beautifully.
Gina   Did you hear that Marcus is going to audition tonight?
May   Really? I didn't know he played a musical instrument.
Gina   He plays the violin but I don't think he's good enough for the orchestra.
May   Are you going to tell him?
Gina   No, I don't want to be the one to tell him.
May   Fair enough. I expect Mr Williams will. By the way, how are you getting on with your piano lessons?
Gina   I found playing the piano really difficult at first and I nearly gave up but my mum told me to hang in there. And now I'm starting to get quite good at it and I'm really enjoying playing.
May   There is light at the end of the tunnel then.
Gina   Yes, I suppose there is.
May   I'd love to be able to play the piano.
Gina   You could have lessons, May. My piano teacher's really good. You can come and practise with me.
May   Why not? I'll go for it!

Conversation 2

Harry   Hi, Matt. What's the matter with you? You look miserable. Cheer up. Things can't be that bad.
Matt   Can't they? Now be honest. Do you reckon I've got a chance of being in the team? I've got myself really worked up about it.
Harry   You shouldn't let it get you down like this. Now, I don't want to get your hopes up, but I think you've got a chance. Anyway, you should always look on the bright side. That's what my dad always says.
Matt   He's right. But do you really think I've got a chance?
Harry   Yes, you'd be good in the team. You're a great player. How tall are you?

Matt   I'm 1 metre 95.
Harry   That's tall! You should get in the team – no problem. However, I know Mike and Jake want to get in the team too.
Matt   Everyone wants to be in the basketball team and there's only one place. I don't want to make a fool of myself.

Conversation 3

Pia   Hey, did you hear? Jamie wants to join us.
Joe   Well, he can't, Pia.
Pia   Why not?
Joe   Well, for a start, he can't play any musical instruments.
Pia   I thought he could play the guitar.
Joe   Maybe a few notes. Anyway, I've already asked Amanda.
Pia   Asked her what?
Joe   I've asked her to be the new drummer in our band.
Pia   When did you decide that, Joe?
Joe   Yesterday. She's brilliant at the drums. And I've got a really good feeling about her being in the band.
Pia   But you could have discussed it with the rest of us first. You know Steve and Amanda don't get on.
Joe   But I want what's best for the band. Amanda's a brilliant drummer. You know she is and Steve knows that too. He's just jealous because she's a better musician than he is.
Pia   That's not fair, Joe. Steve's just as good a musician as Amanda.
Joe   Come on, Pia. Let's just give her a try. And if it doesn't work out, then we find someone else.
Pia   OK, but you tell Steve.

DIALOGUE

Exercise 1

3, 1, 7, 5, 2, 8, 6, 4

PHRASES FOR FLUENCY

Exercise 1

1 get my hopes up   2 make a fool of myself   3 go for it
4 Fair enough   5 Anyway   6 for a start

Exercise 2

1 Fair enough   2 go for it   3 get your hopes up
4 make a fool of myself   5 for a start   6 Anyway

CAMBRIDGE ENGLISH: FIRST

Exercise 1

1 because   2 when   3 with   4 much   5 lots/plenty
6 to   7 so   8 while

Exercise 2

1 up   2 are   3 but   4 like   5 been   6 of
7 compared   8 or

UNIT 8 MAKING LISTS
GRAMMAR

Exercise 1

1 f   2 d   3 i   4 a   5 h   6 b   7 c   8 e   9 g

Exercise 2

1 If Charles didn't work so much, he'd have (more) time to relax.
2 Mark would have taken part in the race if he hadn't broken his leg.
3 If people love cats, they often don't like dogs much.
4 Steve will buy a car if his father lends him the money.
5 Ed would ask Jenny out if he wasn't so shy.
6 Anne wouldn't have fallen if she had seen the ice on the path.

Exercise 3

1 had come; would have met   2 will put; goes on
3 own; don't use   4 would visit; lived   5 see; 'll tell
6 wouldn't have fallen; hadn't been riding
7 was; would be able   8 doesn't hurt; relax

Exercise 4

1 is   2 will   3 can't   4 won't   5 don't   6 can't   7 had
8 'd have   9 had   10 wouldn't have   11 'd have   12 hadn't

Exercise 5

1 If I had read his text carefully, I'd know where to meet him.
2 If Kim had seen the step, she wouldn't feel so silly.
3 If Len hadn't arrived so early, he wouldn't be waiting for his friends.
4 If I had studied Spanish at university, I could help you with your Spanish homework.
5 If I hadn't left the map at home, I'd know the way to their house.
6 If Monica liked opera, she would have accepted Oliver's invitation.
7 If Tessa had watched the last episode, she would know the ending.
8 If Tim hadn't lost control of his car, he wouldn't be in a hospital bed.

Exercise 7

Suggested answers

1 wouldn't have slipped on the banana skin if he looked where he was going.
2 wouldn't be so tired if they hadn't stayed up late last night.
3 hadn't spent all his money, he could buy the new game.

GET IT RIGHT!

1 If the police **hadn't looked** into the matter, the crime would never have been discovered.
2 Unless we come up with some new ideas, **we won't** have a chance of winning the competition.
3 Dave will get the answer as long as we **help** him.
4 Suppose I did go to the party, what **would** I wear?
5 Provided that the calculations were correct, the structure **will** be totally safe.
6 Come to my house by eight at the latest, otherwise we **will** miss the beginning of the film.

VOCABULARY

Exercise 1

1 turn out   2 come up with   3 come down with
4 carry out   5 look into   6 work out   7 point out
8 run through

Exercise 2

1 I didn't know where the shop was until Kate pointed out the store guide.
2 The instructions for the game were really long, so we just ran through them quickly.
3 The head teacher is looking into the disappearance of the school's pet snake.
4 We couldn't think of what to do until Sally came up with a brilliant idea.
5 Janet was having difficulty working out the clues in the crossword.
6 Some volunteers are carrying out repairs to old people's houses.
7 I think we ate something bad – we came down with a stomach bug.

Exercise 4

1 Otherwise   2 Suppose   3 as long as/provided   4 unless
5 provided/as long as

Exercise 5

1 Suppose you didn't live here, where would you like to live?
2 The teacher said I wouldn't do well unless I did my homework. / The teacher said I would do well as long as I did my homework. / The teacher said I would do well provided I did my homework.
3 OK, you can use my phone, as long as you don't make long-distance calls. / OK, you can use my phone, provided you don't make long-distance calls.
4 I have to go, otherwise I'll miss the bus.
5 Mum says we can go, as long as we promise to be back in time for dinner. / Mum says we can go, provided we promise to be back in time for dinner.

READING

Exercise 1

1 face masks   2 get things right   3 five-point
4 around two-thirds   5 too difficult   6 would

Exercise 2

well-known – a person who is invited onto the programme
eight – the number of pieces of music the guest is allowed to have on the island
luxury – a special item the guest is allowed to have with them on the island
imagination – something belonging to the people who come on the show

Exercise 3

1 A man called Roy Plomley had the idea for the programme, and wrote a letter to the BBC.
2 The guests are well-known people such as actors, singers, politicians and celebrities.
3 eight pieces of music, one book, one luxury item
4 four
5 Seven of her music choices were of herself singing.
6 Having to leave out pieces of music that you love.

DEVELOPING WRITING

Exercise 1

1 cold and wet   2 hat; sweaters; coats; waterproof shoes; gloves   3 sunglasses; sunscreen; lip balm; simple medicines

Exercise 2

1 one that covers your ears 2 several layers of thin clothing
3 the cold and wet 4 light and waterproof 5 to protect
your eyes from the bright reflection off the snow 6 with lip
balm 7 when you're going to be a long way from a town

Exercise 3

1 He repeats the information that Laura has given in her email.
2 He uses bullet points.
3 He uses full stops, commas and dashes to separate the
reasons from the things he suggests taking.

LISTENING

🔊 24 **Exercise 1**

Colin
1 phone 2 headphones 3 guitar

Beth
1 phone 2 bed 3 trainers

Alan
1 laptop 2 cat 3 bicycle

🔊 24 **Exercise 2**

1 T 2 DS 3 T 4 F 5 F 6 DS 7 T 8 F

Audio Script Track 24

Alan	Hey, guys. So Beth, why isn't Jacky here today? She's usually around on Fridays.
Beth	Well, Alan, believe it or not, she's gone on a special kind of weekend with her parents.
Colin	Special how?
Beth	Well I don't know the details, but it's some kind of camping place I think, where you spend three days living in the most basic way possible. And she told me that all you can take with you are some clothes – nothing else at all.
Alan	What? No books? No music?
Colin	No phone?
Beth	No, nothing at all. Just clothes. Nothing else.
Colin	Wow. I couldn't do that. I couldn't possibly not have my phone with me. It's one of the two things I couldn't live without.
Alan	So what's the other one, Colin?
Colin	OK – my phone's the first, and I'd have to have my MP3 player with me, otherwise I'd go crazy.
Beth	MP3 player? You don't need that. I mean, as long as you've got your phone, you've got music too, right?
Colin	Oh, yes, I suppose you're right. OK, so just the phone. But maybe headphones too – it's totally the best way to listen to music, right?
Alan	What about you, Beth? Are there any things you couldn't live without?
Beth	Oh absolutely. My top three things I couldn't live without – my phone, naturally; my lovely comfortable bed – you know how much I like sleeping, right? And then, third, these blue trainers.
Colin	Huh? Trainers? How come they're something you can't live without?
Beth	Because they're amazingly comfortable. I'd wear them all the time if I could. So they're in my list, for sure. And you, Alan?
Alan	Well, my list of three would be – my laptop WITH the computer games on it, erm, hold on let me think a bit … well, you know, I think the second's my cat and the third, well, I'm not so sure to be honest. I mean, do we actually have things that we absolutely couldn't live without? Because it's a bit sad if that's true, isn't it?
Beth	Oh, you're taking this too seriously!
Alan	Maybe. Anyway. My bicycle. That's my third thing.
Colin	Your bicycle? That's really in your top three?

Alan	Yes, really. When I'm cycling, I feel free. It's a great feeling and it keeps me fit too.
Colin	Fair enough.
Beth	But come on, Colin – we've come up with three each, but so far you've only got one.
Colin	Two – the phone and the headphones, remember?
Beth	Yes, sorry, I forgot the headphones. But anyway, what's it going to be? The third thing that would make your life miserable if you didn't have it?
Colin	Easy – you two!
Alan	Nice try, Colin, but no way – we're people, not things. You have to think of a third thing.
Colin	OK then. My guitar. If you heard me play it, you'd know how bad I am! But it's the best way I know to relax.

DIALOGUE

Exercise 1

Dialogue 1

5, 3, 1, 7, 4, 2, 8, 6

Dialogue 2

3, 5, 1, 7, 8, 4, 2, 6

CAMBRIDGE ENGLISH: FIRST

Exercise 1

Suggested answers

In picture A the people look unhappy and a bit fed up with
the weather. In picture B, the people look relaxed and happy,
enjoying the good weather.

🔊 25 **Exercise 2**

1 A 2 A 3 B 4 B 5 A 6 B

Audio Script Track 25

Examiner	Thank you. Now, Student B, I'd like you to compare your photographs, and say what you think the people in the photographs feel about being outside in these situations. Talk for about a minute, OK? You can start now.
Alexander	OK, well, in both of these two photographs, we can see some people in a town. And in Picture A, it doesn't look like they're enjoying it very much because it seems to be raining, some people have umbrellas. And apparently they've been shopping, because it looks like they are walking past some shops. OK. And in Picture B, it's really much nicer, there's some sunshine and the people look relaxed, it looks as though they're enjoying the nice weather. And I think perhaps it's somewhere in Europe, I don't know exactly where it is but it could be Sweden or Denmark? Anyway, maybe it's somewhere where the weather isn't always so nice, so they're happy because today the sun is shining and they can sit outside and meet their friends, so it's pleasant. And so, in Picture A, I'm not so sure, I don't think they are really very happy to be outside but in Picture B, yes, they seem to be having a good time.
Examiner	Thank you. Student A, what do you think?

Exercise 3

1 it doesn't look like; very much 3 it looks as though
4 exactly 5 really 6 seem to be

CONSOLIDATION UNITS 7 & 8

🔊 26 Exercise 1

Tick: A, C, D, E

🔊 26 Exercise 2

1 the cold; no proper bed or showers; the drinking water isn't very good
2 In case the water is really bad.
3 She might be a long way from a chemist's.
4 That she didn't sit around looking at it all the time.
5 He says there might not be a signal where she's going.
6 That Maggie will have had the best holiday of her life.

Audio Script Track 26

Dave   So you're off on holiday next week, right?
Maggie Yes, and to be honest with you, I'm dreading it.
Dave   Sorry? You're dreading it?
Maggie Yes. My parents have decided that we're going camping somewhere in the middle of nowhere for two weeks. Camping!
Dave   Yes, that doesn't sound like your thing really. Still, look on the bright side, eh? All that fresh air and nature …
Maggie … and the cold, and no proper bed, and no proper showers, and I've discovered that the drinking water there isn't very good either. That's why I'm making this list.
Dave   What list?
Maggie A list of things that I have to take with me.
Dave   And what's on your list so far?
Maggie Well, I've got … tablets for stomach ache in case the water really is bad, some cold and cough medicine since we're going to be outside so much of the time. I'm bound to catch a cold, I always come down with a cold as soon as the temperature drops a bit.
Dave   Well, always good to go prepared. And you might be a long way from a chemist's.
Maggie That's right. What else? Erm, a torch so I can see where I'm going and to read in bed. I mean, I have to be able to read my book in bed, otherwise I'll go crazy.
Dave   Hmm, yes. What else?
Maggie OK. Well, I asked my parents if I could take my tablet, and they said 'Yes' as long as I don't just sit around looking at it all the time, so of course that's on the list too.
Dave   Can I just point out that there might not be a signal where you're going?
Maggie Oh, Dave – don't say that! There will be a signal, surely? Dave, tell me there'll be a signal!
Dave   OK, Maggie, OK. Calm down. I don't know why I said that. I'm sure there will be a signal. There almost always is these days.
Maggie But suppose there isn't? Then what am I going to do?
Dave   Cheer up, Maggie! Stop being so pessimistic! There'll be a signal and you'll have a great time. By the time I see you again, you'll have had the best holiday of your life!
Maggie Well, I wish I could be so sure. But thanks anyway, Dave.
Dave   No problem, Maggie.

Exercise 3

1 get   2 'd be   3 don't   4 will have arrived   5 are going
6 wouldn't be   7 be watching   8 will have lived

Exercise 4

1 c   2 d   3 f   4 b   5 a   6 g   7 h   8 e

Exercise 5

1 point   2 forward   3 dreading   4 provided   5 worked
6 positive   7 turned   8 apprehensive

Exercise 6

1 I'm afraid so   2 for a start   3 I think so   4 Fair enough
5 Anyway   6 cheer up

Exercise 7

1 Elvis Presley   2 Claude Monet   3 Steven Spielberg
4 Elvis Presley   5 Charles Schultz   6 Claude Monet
7 Steven Spielberg

UNIT 9   BE YOUR OWN LIFE COACH

GRAMMAR

Exercise 1

1 PR   2 PA   3 PA   4 PR   5 PA   6 PR

Exercise 2

1 listen   2 understood   3 let   4 got   5 help
6 wouldn't get   7 been   8 worked

Exercise 3

1 If only; hadn't eaten   2 I wish; wasn't   3 I wish; knew
4 If only; had paid   5 I wish; hadn't gone   6 I wish; played
7 I wish; hadn't told   8 If only; could go

Exercise 5

1 didn't   2 to invite   3 started   4 took   5 spend
6 didn't   7 didn't   8 took

Exercise 6

1 had   2 to watch   3 talked   4 chat   5 watch

Exercise 7

1 'd prefer to play   2 time you learnt   3 only the film didn't
4 we ate   5 wish I hadn't told   6 'd prefer it if
7 time someone told

GET IT RIGHT!

1 would rather   2 would prefer   3 would rather
4 Would you rather   5 would prefer   6 would rather

VOCABULARY

Exercise 1

1 hardest   2 blame; way   3 get   4 dwell; work
5 let; expectations

Exercise 2

1 Rule 2   2 Rule 4   3 Rule 1   4 Rule 5   5 Rule 3

Exercise 3

1 degree   2 degree course   3 careers advisor
4 school leaver   5 work experience   6 life experience
7 graduate   8 higher education

Exercise 4

1 higher education   2 degree   3 work experience
4 graduates   5 school leavers   6 life experience
7 degree course   8 careers advisor

READING

Exercise 1

1 Question 5   2 Question 2   3 Question 3
4 Question 6   5 Question 1   6 Question 4

Exercise 2

The 'villains' are some of the obstacles that might get in the way of teenagers achieving their true potential. These villains need to be faced and defeated.

Exercise 3

1 robot   2 ghost   3 zombie   4 ninja   5 vampire
6 pirate

DEVELOPING WRITING

Exercise 1

a dedicated welfare officer; a careers office; a mentoring scheme

Exercise 2

Suggested answers

I expect this is true of most schools around the country. / There are many more important issues that young adults need to address other than just learning the facts. / This would certainly be useful in helping us make more informed decisions when we leave. / This would help make the transition from primary school to secondary school a lot smoother.

Exercise 3

1 someone   2 a place   3 a system

Exercise 4

Important teen issues (non-educational):
Learning how to deal with conflict at school and at home / Understanding how our emotions affect us / Knowing what opportunities are available after leaving school

Things school could offer:
Dedicated welfare officer / Careers office / Mentoring scheme

LISTENING

🔊28 Exercise 1

1 Alan   2 Rob   3 Steve

🔊28 Exercise 2

1 to check her email   2 she doesn't know where it is
3 if he wanted to play Playstation with her
4 because she's walked across his room in dirty trainers
5 he's trying to study   6 a sandwich and some juice

🔊28 Exercise 3

1 I'd rather you didn't take my tablet without asking.
2 I'd sooner you took your shoes off before you walked into my room.
3 I'd prefer it if you kept your door shut too.

Audio Script Track 28

Conversation 1

Steve Is that my tablet, Lucy?
Lucy Sorry, Steve?
Steve Let me see. Yes, it is. Here – give it to me.
Lucy I was only checking my email. What's the big deal?
Steve Well, it's mine. I'd rather you didn't take my tablet without asking.
Lucy Well you shouldn't leave it out on the kitchen table if it's so special.
Steve I didn't leave it on the kitchen table. I just put it down temporarily while I unpacked my schoolbag.
Lucy Rubbish. You're always leaving your tablet hanging about somewhere. You should be more careful with it.
Steve That's not true. I am careful with it. Anyway I don't know why you're arguing with me. You're in the wrong. Why aren't you using your own tablet anyway?
Lucy Because I don't know where it is. I haven't seen it for days.
Steve And I'm the one who's not careful? Sometimes I don't know why I even bother talking to you.

Conversation 2

Rob Lydia, you've done it again. I don't believe it.
Lydia Done what exactly, Rob?
Rob Your trainers. You've just walked across my room in your dirty, muddy trainers.
Lydia Really? They're not that muddy.
Rob So what's that then? I suppose that muddy footprint just appeared by magic.
Lydia Whoops. Sorry. But there's no need to be sarcastic. I only came to ask you if you wanted to play Playstation with me.
Rob Well I don't. I'm too busy studying for my maths exam tomorrow and next time I'd sooner you took your shoes off before you walked into my room.
Lydia So why are you in such a bad mood then?
Rob I'm not. I just don't like you messing up my room. I spent hours tidying it up. I don't really need you to come and spoil it all.
Lydia OK, if that's how you feel, I'm off. Bye.

Conversation 3

Alan Hey, Cindy. Any chance you could turn the music down a little?
Cindy Sorry, Alan. What did you say? I can't hear you.
Alan That's because your music's too loud. I said could you turn it …
Cindy Here, let me turn the music down.
Cindy Sorry, Alan. What did you want to ask me?
Alan To turn the music down.
Cindy Oh. Sorry.
Alan Yeah, and I'd prefer it if you kept your door shut too. I'm trying to study. I've got a really important English test tomorrow and I haven't looked at a thing yet.
Cindy OK, no problem. Will do. Anything else I can do for you?
Alan Well you could make me a sandwich and bring me some juice since you're asking.
Cindy Of course I will. For my favourite brother I'd do anything.

DIALOGUE

Exercise 1

7, 3, 9, 1, 5, 4, 8, 2, 10, 6

CAMBRIDGE ENGLISH: FIRST

🔊29 Exercise 1

1 B   2 B   3 C   4 A   5 C   6 A   7 C

Audio Script Track 29

You will hear an interview with Abby Jones talking about her gap year before going to university. For questions 1–7, choose the best answer (A, B or C).

Interviewer	More and more young people are going into further education and most of them are going straight from school but is it always a good idea? One girl who decided to take some time off before starting university is Abby Holmes and she's here today to tell us all about it. Abby, why did you decide to take some time off?
Abby	Well my original plan was to finish school and then try and get into the police force. I didn't even consider university. But then I did some research and found out that with a degree I could enter the police force at a higher level. Anyway, by the time I finally made up my mind it was too late to apply for university that year so I was going to have to wait 12 months.
Interviewer	How did you feel about that?
Abby	At first I felt really stupid. I couldn't believe I'd missed the opportunity to go straight to university. I was also a bit scared. All my friends were going and I know it sounds a bit silly but I thought all the good jobs would be gone by the time I'd finally graduated. It was then that I realised I had to do something useful with my year off.
Interviewer	So what did you do?
Abby	Well my dad suggested I get in contact with the police and see if there was any way I could work with them for a year as a volunteer. It seemed like a good idea but there was something troubling me. I already knew I wanted to be a police officer. I knew I was going to spend my life working for the police. This year off was going to be my only chance to do something different.
Interviewer	So what was that 'something different'?
Abby	Well that was the problem. Now I had to think of something else to do. I didn't want to waste the year. One of my friend's brothers had spent a year living at home while working in a local hotel. I didn't want to do anything like that. I wanted to do something more exciting. I wanted to see some of the world. Then my dad reminded me he had a cousin living in Thailand. He said maybe I could spend some time with her. I didn't even need to think about it. Thailand! I mean who wouldn't want to go there.
Interviewer	Wow, who wouldn't indeed!
Abby	So three weeks later I was in Bangkok staying with dad's cousin. My parents gave me the money for the flight. Dad's cousin was cool and said I could stay with her as long as I wanted for free. She even found me a job teaching English at a local school. Almost straight away I put the money I earned towards a mega holiday through Southeast Asia at the end of the year. So while all my friends were getting used to their new lives at university, I was thousands of miles away leading my new exotic life.
Interviewer	So what did you learn from your year in Thailand?
Abby	Oh where do I start? I learned how to be independent and look after myself. I learned how to live in a completely different culture and make friends with people who I could barely speak to. On a practical level I learned how to speak Thai quite well eventually just from chatting to people and I learned how to make Thai food. I did a course on that – it was great.
Interviewer	So would you recommend a year out for all school leavers who are planning on going to university?
Abby	Well, if you're the kind of person who likes adventure, then it really is a good opportunity to do something a bit different. Of course, you don't have to go travelling halfway around the world. You can do loads of cool things at home, but the important thing is to have a plan. I know I said that I didn't really have one but I was so lucky. My whole year off could easily have been a disaster. I wouldn't recommend leaving it to chance for others.

UNIT 10 SPREADING THE NEWS

GRAMMAR

Exercise 1

1 Matt said that he liked horror stories.
2 Ali said that he would see us at the concert on Saturday.
3 Helen said that she had been to Spain many times.
4 Elif said that she was looking forward to seeing me.

Exercise 2

1 he would see us all at Jake's birthday party on Saturday.
2 it was half-time and that their team had scored two goals.
3 he couldn't get tickets for the concert because it had sold out.
4 they weren't playing Sunnyhill School because they had cancelled the match.
5 his Maths teacher had quit yesterday and that he couldn't believe it.
6 he hadn't done enough revision for the History exam.

Exercise 3

1 that in 2013, it had taken one week for users to send a billion Tweets.
2 that 40% of registered Twitter users had never sent a Tweet.
3 that Twitter was available in 25 languages then.
4 that 75% of world leaders used Twitter.
5 that Barack Obama's victory Tweet had been the most retweeted Tweet in 2013.
6 that the country with the most Twitter users in 2014 had been China.
7 that Twitter had become the fastest way to break news.
8 that Twitter would become more like Facebook in the future.

Exercise 5

1 why I wanted to be a journalist.
2 to think of a name for the school online magazine.
3 to interview a foreign correspondent (for the school magazine).
4 to prepare some questions for the interview.
5 which countries he had reported from.
6 if he had reported from any war zones.
7 if I could get her a glass of water.

Exercise 6

1 e 2 f 3 a 4 b 5 h 6 c 7 d 8 g

Exercise 7

1 telling 2 of printing 3 for failing 4 for being
5 to speak 6 driving 7 that he had made
8 about entering

GET IT RIGHT!

1 ✗ 2 The teacher said to John that his essay was amazing.
3 ✗ 4 You need to tell them something to keep them quiet. / You need to tell them to keep quiet. 5 ✗

VOCABULARY

Exercise 1

1 d   2 f   3 a   4 e   5 b   6 c

Exercise 2

1 keep in touch   2 break the news gently   3 got in touch
4 retweeted   5 pass on the message   6 let you know
7 give me a call   8 drop you a line

Exercise 3

1 accused   2 admitted   3 apologised   4 ordered
5 regretted   6 criticised   7 agreed   8 warned

Exercise 4

1 the same way   2 one way or another   3 way too
4 the way   5 on her way   6 in my way

READING

Exercise 1

1 the co-founder of Twitter   2 breaking news   3 140
4 to follow their pop idols   5 campaigns   6 the power to
make a difference

Exercise 2

Suggested answers

A girl created an invitation to her party on Facebook, but the
post was open to the public and 3,000 people turned up.

A waitress complained about some customers and a tip they
gave on Facebook. Her company found out and fired her.

Thirteen crew members of an airline criticised customers and
complained about the cleanliness and safety of the planes on
Facebook. The airline found out and fired them.

Exercise 3

1 thirty thousand   2 had turned into   3 unhappy with a tip
4 an hour longer   5 their messages on Facebook
6 had replaced the   7 have issued warnings
8 to be more careful

DEVELOPING WRITING

Exercise 1

1 Paul Smith, a British blogger, writer and former radio
executive   2 March 2009   3 all around the world, from
Newcastle in the UK to Stewart Island in New Zealand
4 Paul travelled around the world.   5 using Twitter

Exercise 2

1 Lead sentence   2 Introduction   3 Main body
4 Closing paragraph and a quotation

LISTENING

🔊 31 Exercise 1

b

🔊 31 Exercise 2

1 T   2 T   3 F   4 T   5 T   6 F

Audio Script Track 31

Marcus	I'm really against running this story, Lucy.
Lucy	But why, Marcus? It's a great story. It's a story of success against all odds.
Marcus	Yes, and it's a story about ballet. Nobody at this school's interested in ballet. What do you think, Sarah?
Sarah	Marcus is right. Very few people are into ballet. And anyway, there's no way this is a news story. At least, it's not a news story for our school magazine. It's not about somebody at this school.
Lucy	You're right. It's not about our school or anybody at our school but it's an inspiring story. It's not just a story about ballet. It's a story that encourages you to follow your dreams.
Tom	I agree with Lucy. This is exactly the kind of story we want.
Lucy	Thank you, Tom.
Marcus	But why? You hate ballet.
Tom	I know, I know. But this is a story that says you can achieve anything. If you are determined, anything is possible.
Marcus	I'm sorry, guys. My mind's made up. We're not running this story in our school magazine.
Tom	But you haven't heard the whole story yet. When Michaela DePrince was three years old, her father was killed in the civil war in Sierra Leone. Then her mother died, and her uncle sent her to an orphanage. Whilst she was at the orphanage, she saw a picture of a ballerina in a pink ballet dress on the front cover of a magazine. She decided she wanted to be that ballerina and she kept the picture. And that's exactly what happened. She is now part of the Dutch National Ballet.
Marcus	So what happened? How did she become a ballerina in the Dutch National Ballet?
Lucy	You see. It is an interesting story. You want to know what happened. She was adopted by an American couple and she went to live in America. Her parents enrolled her at ballet school in Philadelphia.
Marcus	So after that it was all easy. What's the story?
Lucy	No it wasn't easy. She still had to work hard to achieve her dream.
Tom	Now with the help of her mother she's written a book about her life. It's called *Taking Flight: From War Orphan to Star Ballerina*.
Lucy	Yes, and she's going to use the money she earns from the book to open a free arts school in Sierra Leone. And she's going to teach ballet there. I think that's amazing.
Tom	We're definitely going with this story.
Lucy	And that's final.

DIALOGUE

Exercise 1

1 Have you heard   2 have you heard about   3 guess what
4 You'll never believe   5 did you know

PHRASES FOR FLUENCY

Exercise 1

1 d   2 e   3 a   4 c   5 f   6 b

Exercise 2

1 on earth; In any case   2 it's none of your business
3 or something   4 at least; don't bother

CAMBRIDGE ENGLISH: FIRST

Exercise 2

The Everest Files by Matt Dickinson

The Everest Files is **an** action adventure thriller for young adult readers. ~~Its~~ **It's** the first book in a series of three books and it was inspired by Matt Dickinson's own climb up Mount Everest.

Ryan, an eighteen-year-old American, is on a gap year adventure. He is working for a medical charity in ~~the~~ Nepal. A local girl asks him to find out why her sixteen-year-old Sherpa friend Kami never ~~have come~~ **came** back from an expedition up Mount Everest with a wealthy American politician. Some ~~says~~ **say** he's alive and others say he's dead. Ryan, who is determined and adventurous, can't resist the challenge. Kami's story takes place ~~at~~ **on** the magnificent and terrifying slopes of Mount Everest and it is very moving. The story was fast paced and there were some very tense moments.

One of the themes of the book is how climbers disturb the natural order of the Nepalese mountains and Mount Everest itself is one of the main characters of this dramatic mystery. Another theme of the book is the importance of showing respect for other cultures, and the author ~~is~~ **has** dedicated his book to the three Sherpas who he climbed up Everest with.

The Everest Files is very ~~much~~ **exciting** and the ending was unexpected. I really enjoyed ~~to read~~ **reading** it and I recommend it to both girls and boys who like ~~learn~~ **learning** about other cultures and love adventure. I'm looking forward to the second book in the series.

Exercise 3

determined, adventurous, exciting, fast-paced, magnificent, terrifying, unexpected

CONSOLIDATION UNITS 9 & 10

🔊 32 Exercise 1

b, c and e

🔊 32 Exercise 2

1 didn't have any regrets 2 hadn't gone his 3 consider 4 been suspended from work 5 damaged the reputation 6 will end 7 writing an essay 8 to Portugal for

---

Audio Script Track 32

And so here are our local news stories for today, here on radio AON news. First up, the manager of our local football team, Wenbridge United, Dave Godber, has decided to resign from his job with immediate effect. Mr Godber said that he didn't have any regrets about his three years at the club but he thought that perhaps it was time for someone else to take control and to try and improve the team's performance. He admitted that the situation hadn't always been easy at the club but he said he had always tried his hardest and that some things hadn't gone his way. When we asked him what he intended to do now, he said that he wanted to take a few months off with his family, to relax and to consider his future. The director of the club, Gordon Marsh, said that they would start looking for a replacement for Mr Godber as soon as possible. Let's hope they can find someone who can win a match now and again!

Now, a teacher at the local Wenbridge College of Art has been suspended from work after a Tweet that she sent last week, in which she said that she hated her job. Marjorie Green has been at the art college for twelve years. Ms Green admits that she sent the Tweet but says that it was not meant seriously and that it was intended only to be read by her closest friends. She also says that she now regrets sending the Tweet, that she's apologised to the college for sending it and she has closed her Twitter account. We asked the head of the college, Mr George

---

Brown, why such action had been taken and he replied that the Tweet had damaged the reputation of the college. Next Monday there'll be a meeting at the college to decide whether to end Ms Green's contract. Well, I don't know about you, but I think everyone hates their job sometimes, don't they? But perhaps it's better not to tweet about it, eh?

And last but not least … schoolgirl Annabel Lee from Longbury has won first prize in a magazine competition. Annabel wrote an essay entitled 'Living up to expectations' and her answer was chosen by a panel of judges as the best one. Her prize? A one-week trip to Portugal, all expenses paid. Well done, Annabel! Don't forget to send me a postcard, OK?

Exercise 3

1 to help 2 wasn't 3 got 4 if he wanted 5 had told 6 hadn't bought 7 I had left 8 didn't 9 left

Exercise 4

1 c 2 f 3 e 4 g 5 a 6 h 7 b 8 d 9 i 10 j

Exercise 5

1 way 2 deny 3 blame 4 touch 5 degree 6 hardest 7 experience 8 expectations 9 break 10 graduate

Exercise 6

1 never guess 2 at least 3 I'd rather 4 in any case 5 none of her business 6 don't bother

Exercise 7

1 It's believed that as primitive people cooked meat over fires, they began to stare at the flames and think in a different, more relaxed way.
2 Around the middle of the 20th Century.
3 sitting down in a cross-legged position with eyes closed
4 slowly and calmly
5 what you and your body are doing
6 outside, in an environment with nature
7 while going to school, work or the shops
8 It helps you deal with the stresses and strains of everyday life, and towards living more peacefully.

UNIT 11 SPACE AND BEYOND

GRAMMAR

Exercise 1

1 PA 2 PR 3 F 4 PR 5 F 6 PA

Exercise 2

1 have taken 2 be 3 have gone 4 know 5 're bound to 6 are likely to

Exercise 3

1 It's bound to rain 2 could be 3 must have spent all week 4 might have worked 5 Federer is certain to win 6 can't be inside 7 is likely to pass

Exercise 4

1 e 2 h 3 a 4 b 5 g 6 c 7 d 8 f

Exercise 5

1 As a result of my broken alarm clock, I overslept. / As a result of my alarm clock being broken, I overslept.
2 Due to my messy room, I couldn't find my tie. / Due to my room being a mess, I couldn't find my tie.
3 Because of my bike's flat tyre, I couldn't ride it to school.
4 I couldn't run to the bus stop as a result of my twisted ankle.
5 The bus journey was really slow due to an accident.
6 I couldn't get into school because of the locked school gate.

GET IT RIGHT!

1 must 2 might 3 can't 4 see 5 made 6 must

VOCABULARY

Exercise 1

1 d 2 f 3 a 4 e 5 b 6 c

Exercise 2

1 E 2 C 3 A 4 D 5 F 6 B

Exercise 3

G	D	E	L	I	G	H	T	F	U	L	E	A
N	S	P	Q	O	W	I	E	U	R	Y	J	C
I	Y	T	A	L	S	K	D	J	F	H	G	T
K	Z	M	U	X	N	C	B	V	R	G	R	I
A	L	A	T	N	E	M	I	T	N	E	S	O
T	Q	Z	A	W	N	X	S	I	E	C	R	N
H	V	F	T	B	G	I	L	Y	N	H	U	P
T	M	J	I	K	L	L	N	I	O	P	T	A
A	L	A	B	Y	I	K	S	G	E	I	S	C
E	L	B	A	R	O	M	E	M	A	E	L	K
R	U	E	H	A	C	R	A	C	S	O	G	E
B	U	T	F	A	R	F	E	T	C	H	E	D

Exercise 4

1 b 2 a 3 c 4 b 5 c 6 a

READING

Exercise 1

1 the pyramids; seeing strange spaceships in the sky
2 Because the universe is such a big place.
3 mainly simple single-celled organisms, but there could also be intelligent and dangerous life forms out there
4 He suggests they might take the Earth's valuable resources and then destroy the rest.
5 He suggests that if we make contact with other life forms, things might not turn out very well for us.
6 He suggests it could be so advanced that they might exist in forms that are too complicated for us to understand.

Exercise 2

District 9

Exercise 3

1 T 2 T 3 T 4 F 5 F 6 F 7 T 8 F

DEVELOPING WRITING

Exercise 1

1 a race of aliens from outer space   2 enemies of the Boov
3 the most unpopular Boov on the planet   4 the last free human on Earth

Exercise 2

1 The writer tells us what type of film it is, who it's made by, and whose famous voices it features.
2 Suggested answer: The Boov are aliens who come to Earth to make it their home and to hide from their enemies, the Gorg. But when one of them, called Oh, accidentally sends out a house-warming party invitation to the whole universe, he needs the help of Tip, the last free human on Earth, to save the planet.
3 The writer thought the film was enjoyable with plenty of hilarious moments, but that the story wasn't that memorable.
4 The writer recommends watching this film on a rainy day during the holidays.

LISTENING

◀))34 ## Exercise 1

A D   B T   C J

◀))34 ## Exercise 2

Conversation 1

1 David Smith
2 really badly

Conversation 2

3 She thought it would be cool to have another guitarist in the band.
4 She asked him to leave immediately.

Conversation 3

5 She thinks there must have already been some really good players in the team.
6 He plans to take up tennis.

◀))34 ## Exercise 3

1 Oh dear. 2 How terrible. 3 What a shame. 4 Poor him.

Audio Script Track 34

Conversation 1
Sara   Did you get a part in the school play, Hannah?
Hannah Yes, Sara. I'm going to be Juliet.
Sara   Juliet! That's the main part.
Hannah I know. Isn't it cool?
Sara   It's more than cool. You must be really excited. So who's going to be your Romeo? Don't tell me. Tim Lewis. I'm so jealous.
Hannah Actually no. It's going to be David Smith, which is cool because he's also really cute.
Sara   So didn't Tim audition for the part?
Hannah No, he did. He went for an audition but Miss Rose chose David.
Sara   He can't have been happy about that. How did he take it?
Hannah Really badly. I mean really badly. Miss Rose offered him another really big part but he just walked out and said he didn't want to be in the play.
Sara   Oh dear. Maybe I should go and talk to him to see if I can cheer him up.
Hannah Good luck.

Conversation 2
Liam   Hi, Liz. How's the band going?
Liz   Hey, Liam. It's going well. We're going to be playing at the end of the school party.
Liam   Cool. I'll look forward to it. By the way, is it true that Dan Ryan's playing guitar with you?
Liz   Um, no.
Liam   Oh, I heard that he was. Well, that's what he told me a few weeks ago.
Liz   Actually it's a bit of tricky situation.

Liam	What do you mean?
Liz	Well, he told me he played really well and asked if he could be in the band. I thought it would be cool to have another guitarist so I said he could.
Liam	So he is in the band.
Liz	Let me finish. So he came along to a practice and after about 30 seconds it was obvious that he really can't play guitar at all. Like, not at all. So it was really awkward. There was absolutely no way we could have him in the band so I had to ask him to leave, there and then.
Liam	How terrible. It must have been really embarrassing.
Liz	Tell me about it. It was awful and now he won't even speak to me.

Conversation 3

Amelia	Hey, Carl. What's up with Josh? I saw him earlier and he barely spoke to me.
Carl	Haven't you heard, Amelia? He didn't get into the football team.
Amelia	What! I thought he was almost guaranteed a place.
Carl	So did he. I think that's why he's feeling so bad. But the coach didn't want him apparently.
Amelia	What a shame. He really wanted to get it. He must be feeling awful.
Carl	He is. It's probably best not to talk to him about it for a while.
Amelia	OK, I'll keep that in mind. So there must have been some really good players.
Carl	Yes, I guess so. He didn't even make the second team.
Amelia	Poor him. So what's he going to do now? I suppose he could try for another team.
Carl	I think he's pretty much given up on football. He was talking about taking up tennis.
Amelia	He should. He'd be good.

DIALOGUE

Exercise 1

6, 3, 7, 4, 1

CAMBRIDGE ENGLISH: FIRST

⏵35 Exercise 1

1 They both agree that Wonders of the universe and Archery club would be popular, and that a Rock stars club wouldn't be popular. They disagree on the Film making club and the Baking club.
2 Which two clubs would be more popular?
3 Wonders of the universe and Archery

Audio Script Track 35

Part 1

Examiner	Now I'd like you to talk about something for two minutes. I'd like you to imagine your school is planning to start a new after-school club. Here are some ideas for the kind of club they could start and a question to discuss. First you have some time to look at the task. Now, talk to each other about why students might want to go to these clubs.
Tanya	Umm. Let's talk about the film making club. This is a good club for artistic people.
Alexander	Yes, and it's something different to other art clubs. Clubs for painting and drawing and that sort of thing.
Tanya	What about 'Wonders of the universe' – that sounds interesting. Lots of people are interested in space now so this is a popular club.
Alexander	It's good for science-y people.

Tanya	Yes, and we don't really learn very much about this in our school science lessons.
Alexander	I don't think archery is a good club. It's a very dangerous sport.
Tanya	Oh. Umm. OK archery. I don't think we are supposed to talk about what we like. The question says 'Why might students want to go to these clubs?'
Alexander	Oh. I think people who like dangerous sports will like this.
Tanya	OK, what do you think about 'Rock star'?
Alexander	What is it?
Tanya	I think it's a club for people who want to be in a band. It's for them to meet and get together and start to make music.
Alexander	So not for learning an instrument?
Tanya	Probably not. I think you need to play something already but this club will show you how to play with other people, umm write songs, ummm perform on stage, that sort of thing I guess.
Alexander	OK, and this one. Baking. I don't like cooking.
Tanya	Yes, but lots of students do. I think it would be popular. Students would go to this club to learn about interesting things to cook and how to do it.
Alexander	Yes, that's a good idea.

Part 2

Examiner	Thank you. Now you have about a minute to decide which two clubs would be the most popular.
Alexander	That's easy. I want a film making club and the space one. Film making is good because people like films.
Tanya	That's true – people like watching films but do they want to make them? I'm not sure.
Alexander	What clubs would you choose?
Tanya	Well, I agree with you about the space club. I think that lots of students would want to learn more about this.
Alexander	Me too. Let's choose it.
Tanya	OK.
Alexander	What is your second choice?
Tanya	Let's see. Umm I don't think Rock stars would be so popular. Not many students play instruments so there's a problem already.
Alexander	Yes, and if you want to be in a band then probably you are already in a band.
Tanya	So we agree. Not Rock stars. How about the baking club?
Alexander	No. Boys don't like cooking.
Tanya	What! Lots of boys like cooking.
Alexander	My friends don't like it.
Tanya	Well, OK. That leaves us with Archery.
Alexander	Yes, people like sports.
Alexander	OK, archery and …
Tanya	Wonders of the universe. Agreed.
Alexander	Yes. Agreed.

UNIT 12 MORE TO EXPLORE

GRAMMAR

Exercise 1

1 is known – C   2 are believed – D   3 is expected – A
4 is said – E   5 is thought – B   6 are known – F

Exercise 2

1 is   2 to have   3 are   4 to be   5 are   6 to have used
7 was   8 to be   9 is   10 to have suffered

Exercise 4

1 The newsagent showed <u>Penny</u> the new magazine.
2 They offered <u>the students</u> free books.
3 Someone promised a room with a view to <u>Kenneth</u>.
4 The police didn't give any information to <u>the reporters</u>.
5 Someone sent <u>me</u> a strange email.
6 The manager offered <u>her</u> a job.
7 They sold faulty goods to their <u>customers</u>.
8 The company gave excellent conditions to <u>their employees</u>.

Exercise 5

1 Jim was shown the photos.
2 Jackie was promised a part in the new play.
3 Film stars are asked a lot of questions.
4 Michael was given a horrible tie for his birthday.
5 The inventor is going to be paid a lot of money for her idea.
6 My grandmother was sent an advertisement for sports equipment.
7 My school was offered a new IT centre.
8 He wasn't told the truth.
9 The customers weren't given a refund.
10 The employees weren't offered good benefits.

Exercise 6

1 The new students were told the class rules. / The class rules were told to the new students.
2 My father was offered a job in London. / A job in London was offered to my father.
3 A large audience was shown the new film. / The new film was shown to a large audience.
4 The winner was presented with a trophy. / A trophy was presented to the winner.
5 Alice was sent some flowers for her birthday. / Some flowers were sent to Alice for her birthday.

GET IT RIGHT!

1 There are still many places on Earth that haven't been **explored** yet.
2 A research trip to the glacier **was taken/is being taken** this week.
3 He left the room after a joke **had** been made about him.
4 Every effort **was** made to find the missing man but to no avail.
5 A lot of progress **has** been made recently in Sam's work.
6 It's essential for good communication to be **established** between nations.

VOCABULARY

1 dunes   2 canyon   3 volcano   4 waterfalls
5 and 7 mountain range   6 bay   8 glacier   9 reef

Exercise 2

1 make   2 made   3 playing   4 make   5 done
6 taking   7 made   8 gave

Exercise 3

1 make   2 give   3 made   4 give   5 make   6 played

Exercise 5

1 I think that I am making progress with the piano.
2 Sally made an effort to reach the top shelf.
3 She made a complaint about the food.
4 Matthew took advantage of Kelly's offer of a lift home.
5 I forgot Jo's birthday, so to make amends, I took her out for dinner.

READING

Exercise 1

A 2;5   B 6;8   C 4   D 1;7   E 3

Exercise 2

3 Someone found money in an old house.

Exercise 3

1 tunnels underground; old ruined buildings; abandoned structures
2 to take photographs
3 He was taking photographs when he saw the bag of money sticking out from under the mattress of a bed.
4 Because one of the principles of urban exploration is: 'take nothing but pictures, leave nothing but footprints'.
5 He did some research into who had owned the house.
6 The money had come from a fruit stall that had been owned by the last owners of the house.
7 Because she was grateful that Dave had given her the money.
8 It can be dangerous and illegal.

DEVELOPING WRITING

Exercise 2

1 She says her family were risk-takers.
2 She was a PE teacher and then a wilderness instructor.
3 the first woman to get to the North Pole; the first woman ever to get to both the North Pole and the South Pole; the first woman to ski across Greenland
4 Most of her expeditions are done with all-women teams.
5 She aimed to bring attention to the world's water problems.

Exercise 3

1 C   2 D   3 A   4 B

LISTENING

🔊 36   Exercise 1

b and c

🔊 36   Exercise 2

1 an increasing population
2 incredible overcrowding
3 He thinks it would take too long to find other planets to live on.
4 finding other civilisations in space
5 She says the money could be used to find real solutions on Earth.
6 science fiction stuff
7 They initially disagree but then react positively.

Audio Script Track 36

Teacher   So, now, it's Mike's turn this week to give us a talk, and his topic is …?

Mike   It's 'Should we be doing more to explore space?'

Teacher   OK, then, it's over to you, Mike.

Mike   OK, thank you. Well, as I said, my topic is 'Should we be doing more to explore space?' and basically, my argument is that, yes, we should. What are my reasons for thinking this way? Well, I don't think anyone here can be in any doubt that there are problems here on Earth, and to my mind, one of the biggest is population. Now, I've heard arguments both ways about whether or not our planet can sustain our current population of over seven billion people. And by the way, it's getting bigger and bigger all the time. But if we don't do something soon – now, really – then the consequences could be very serious. I mean, incredible overcrowding. So, if we explore space more and find ways to let people go and live on other planets,

	like Mars, then we can help ease the pressure on Earth. And that's important, don't you think?
Steve	Excuse me, can I say something?
Mike	Sure, Steve.
Steve	Well, the way I see it, it will take far too long to find ways to let people live on Mars, and even if we did, then a billion people aren't going to be living there, right?
Mike	Well, you've got a point, Steve. But I think there are other good reasons for exploring space.
Teacher	OK, Mike, go on.
Mike	Well, if we explore space more, then we might find other civilisations that could help us develop more technology to solve some of our problems here. For example, find ways to grow more and better food very quickly and safely.
Hazel	Sorry, I have to interrupt here. I mean, sorry, Mike, but that's just never going to happen, is it?
Mike	Well I'm not so sure.
Angie	Hazel's right, Mike. We might never find another civilisation out there – in fact, there might not even be any. And the consequences of spending so much money in space exploration, with no definite result, I mean, it's crazy. All that money on sending space ships out there, when we could be using the money to find real solutions here on Earth.
Teacher	Mike?
Mike	Um, well, the thing is, we've been trying for a long time to do what Angie said, find solutions to the problems on Earth, and it hasn't worked yet, has it? I think it's vitally important for the human race to start looking outside our little world here – the answers are more likely to be out there.
Tom	Well, Mike, I just have to disagree with you there. If anything, I'd say that we need to solve our problems right here where we are, don't you agree?
Hazel	I think Tom's right. Perhaps you need to rethink some of those arguments, Mike. What do you think?
Mike	Yes, you could be right. Maybe I'm too influenced by science fiction stuff. I don't know.
Teacher	No, don't worry, Mike, your points are valid too. Thanks for your presentation. Seems like people don't really agree with you, but it's always good to have someone put their ideas out there, it makes us think. Right, everyone?
All	That's right / Way to go, Mike / Nice one, Mike.

DIALOGUE

Exercise 1

Dialogue 1
7, 1, 5, 3, 4, 2, 8, 6

Dialogue 2
5, 1, 7, 3, 2, 8, 6, 4

CAMBRIDGE ENGLISH: FIRST

🔊 38 Exercise 1

Suggested answers

1 Do you think that it's important for young people to have interests outside school?; Why?
2 It helps them to get into university.
3 To learn to be good at lots of different things.
4 She doesn't like art, but she's glad that she had the experience.
5 They should help them see what they like and what they want to do in the future.

Exercise 2

a G b G c B d B e G f B

Audio Script Track 38

Examiner	So now I'd like to ask you this question. Do you think that it's important for young people to have interests outside school? And if so, why? Student B, what do you think?
Tanya	Well, it's a good question. To my mind it's very important. That's because in my country, if you want to go to university, I mean to one of the really good universities, um, well you have to have an interview and you have to show that … um, you have to show a lot of things, not just that you are good at the subject you want to study, you know? The universities, they want people, young people, who can give more than just their knowledge and interest in science, for example. They want people who have lots of interests and abilities, it's important.
Examiner	Student A?
Alexander	Well, yes, I also think it's important. But I'm not sure I agree with Tanya. My own view is that, you know, we're people, and even if you want to go to university to study something … medicine, for example … well, what do I want to say? Sorry! Um, I mean, it's great to be really good at something like being a doctor, it's fantastic, but in our lives, we need lots of different things, so if you're a doctor but you can also do other things, for instance, um, you can play the guitar or you love football, well that's great. And it's great if a school makes sure that we don't only study but we learn lots of different things according to our interests. Actually, if a school doesn't do that, I think it's not a good school!
Tanya	Can I talk now?
Examiner	Yes, of course.
Tanya	OK, well, absolutely Alexander! I mean you're completely right. I agree with you.
Alexander	OK.
Examiner	OK, here's another question, it follows from what Alexander said. Should schools offer things like clubs for music, or sport, or art? Or should they just do school subjects like mathematics and history?
Alexander	Well, you know what I think, already! I think for a good life you have to have as many things in your life as possible. And I think that, well …
Tanya	That's right. I think that a school, the job of a school is to, um, to help people see what the possibilities are. I mean, I'm very lucky. In my school, there are lots of things. One example is that there are classes in art, in painting. Now, I'm really bad at it and I don't like it but it's good that we did painting classes, I had that experience. And you know, one time, a boy many years ago from our school became a very good artist and it started in our school, in the art lessons!
Alexander	It's a good story and I couldn't agree more that, um, well, a school, I mean, a school can help you see what you like, what your future … I mean, what you want to do in your future. And maybe that's mathematics, great, that's great, but maybe it's dancing or I don't know, looking after little children. Schools have to help us, I think.
Tanya	Yes, it's true. You're right.
Examiner	Well, that's great. Thank you. That's the end of our speaking test today. Thanks very much to both of you. And good luck!
Alexander / Tanya	Thank you / Thank you very much.

CONSOLIDATION UNITS 11 & 12

◄))39 Exercise 1

b, c and e

◄))39 Exercise 2

1 T   2 F   3 F   4 F   5 T   6 T   7 T   8 F

Audio Script Track 39

Mark   Hi, Josie. Have you got a moment? I want to show you something.

Josie   Sure, Mark. What is it?

Mark   Well, I was sent a link yesterday for an amazing website – it's a guy who puts up photos that he takes when he goes urban exploring. Some of them are just stunning!

Josie   Hang on. Urban exploring? I don't think I know what that is. Though I can kind of guess from the words.

Mark   Well, right, it's doing some exploration in towns and cities but to places where people don't usually go. So this guy, for example, he finds a way to get into places – I mean, he posted some photos that he took in the tunnel of an underground railway system, at night, just breathtaking.

Josie   Wow. What else?

Mark   Well he also found a way to climb up inside the tower of a bridge, and from right up at the top of the tower he took photos of the bridge down below and the traffic going past. And…

Josie   And?

Mark   Well, he got into an empty office building at night too, took photos there as well. This guy's amazing, he just goes everywhere. You know, I'm really excited and I think it might be something I'd like to do.

Josie   Really? I didn't think you were into stuff like that. And I mean, isn't it all a bit dangerous?

Mark   Well, yes, but that's why it's so exciting. And I'm pretty keen on photography, well you know that, so it'd be an opportunity to do some really different stuff.

Josie   Can we see the website?

Mark   Oh, yeah sure, of course. I've got my tablet with me here somewhere. Hang on a moment while I just … right, here we are. See the photos?

Josie   Yes, you're right, they are stunning. Do you think he does all this on his own?

Mark   Well I think so. Let's have a look if there's anything about it further down the page. Ummm … no, it doesn't say anything here about other people so I guess he does work alone then.

Josie   But it does say something else down here Mark … look.

Mark   Oh, right yes. I hadn't seen that before.

Josie   He says 'I realise that if I get caught doing this, I'm very likely to be arrested, and that's why I'm not using my real name here.'

Mark   Right. So maybe I'd better think again.

Josie   I think you should. But that doesn't stop us looking at these photos – look at this one, it's out of this world. I wonder where he was …

Exercise 3

1 e   2 h   3 a   4 b   5 g   6 c   7 d   8 f

Exercise 4

1 made   2 stunning   3 moon   4 take   5 give
6 far-fetched   7 science   8 make

Exercise 5

1 They might come.
2 He was absent from school due to a bad cold.
3 The house was destroyed by the earthquake.
4 He's bound to win.
5 You can't have tried your hardest.
6 It's likely there will be bad weather at the weekend.
7 I was given some money by my grandparents.
8 The president is thought to be doing a good job.

Exercise 6

1 terrible   2 Poor   3 the consequences   4 don't act
5 a shame   6 vitally important

Exercise 7

1 Because they thought old films wouldn't be all that good.
2 not very long
3 examples of Earth plant life
4 Lowell is helped by three people and three robots: Huey, Dewey and Louie.
5 to blow up all the domes
6 to make people on Earth think that all the domes have been destroyed
7 He sends it into space.
8 Dewey

WORKBOOK PRONUNCIATION KEY

UNIT 1

Diphthongs: alternative spellings

Exercise 1

/eɪ/: ate, straight, wait, weight
/aɪ/: climb, decide, height, high
/əʊ/: although, hole, know, tiptoe
/aʊ/: allow, how, loud, shout
/ɔɪ/: boil, enjoy, join, noise

UNIT 2

Phrasal verb stress

Exercise 1

The verb's always stressed when it isn't part of a phrasal verb. The phrasal verbs are:
1 picked **up**, 2 turned **out**, 3 ran **into**, 4 hang **out** with,
5 going **through**, 6 brings **about**, 7 put **up** with

UNIT 3

Adding emphasis

Exercise 1

1 John gets on <u>so</u> well with his parents.
2 We had <u>such</u> a fantastic holiday!
3 It may not seem like it, but he <u>does like</u> you.
4 I didn't pass the test – but I <u>did study</u> hard.
5 What a wonderful day – I <u>do love</u> it when the sun's shining!

UNIT 4

Pronouncing words with *gh*

Exercise 1

gh **silent**: although, brought, caught, daughter, fight, height, high, light, straight, thought, through, weigh
gh **pronounced /f/**: cough, enough, laugh, tough;
gh **pronounced /g/**: ghost

Exercise 3

a thought – sport; b laugh – half; c enough – stuff; d through – you; e ghost – toast; f high – buy; g straight – late; h height – white; i weigh – play; j brought – taught; k daughter – water; l cough – off.

UNIT 5

The schwa sound

Exercise 1

1 a 2 the 3 to 4 an 5 or 6 and / of

Exercise 3

2 There (are) no operators free (to) take your call (at) the moment.
3 Press 1 (to) leave a message.
4 Press 2 if* you wish (to) speak (to) an operator.
5 Please don't shout or scream (at the) operators.
6 Now please hang up <u>and</u> make yourself (a) cup of tea.

*NB: the other unstressed sound we use is the /ɪ/ phoneme (e.g. is, if)

UNIT 6

Linking words with /dʒ/ and /tʃ/

Exercise 1

1 don't 2 did 3 Would 4 Do 5 Could 6 Won't
7 just 8 can't

Words linked with a /dʒ/ sound:
0 should you; 2 did you; 3 Would you; 4 Do you; 5 Could you;
Words linked with a /tʃ/ sound:
1 don't you; 6 Won't you; 7 just you; 8 can't you.

UNIT 7

Intonation: encouraging someone

Exercise 1

Uninterested: 3, 5 and 6; Interested: 1, 2 and 4.

UNIT 8

Weak forms with conditionals

Exercise 1

In questions 1, 2, 4, 6, and 7 the contractions are pronounced /ˈkʊdə/, /ˈʃʊdə/ and /ˈwʊdə/.

UNIT 9

Linking: intrusive /w/ and /j/

Exercise 1

1 <u>Marie(j)always</u> has a solution <u>to(w)everything</u>.
2 Have <u>you(w)eaten yet</u>? Would you like some <u>tea(j)and</u> biscuits?
3 Do <u>you(w)understand</u> the question? If not, I might <u>be(j)able</u> to help you.
4 I'm <u>so(w)upset</u>! We've lost another match. Why do <u>we(j)always</u> lose?
5 If <u>she(j)ever</u> needs a lift she can come with us. We've got room for <u>two(w)in</u> the back.
6 I don't want to <u>see(j)another</u> film like that. It was <u>too(w)awful</u> for words!
7 <u>I(j)asked</u> Ashley <u>to(w)explain</u> her problem to me.

UNIT 10

Linking: omission of the /h/ sound

Exercise 1

Hugo was a hairdresser in a hotel. Harry went to ~~h~~im for a haircut. Hugo spent an ~~h~~our cutting Harry's hair. The haircut was horrible and Harry wasn't happy. He decided to be ~~h~~onest and tell Hugo how ~~h~~e felt. He didn't want to pay for ~~h~~is haircut. Hugo was upset because ~~h~~e liked the haircut and ~~h~~e also wanted ~~h~~is money. In the end, Harry paid ~~h~~im half.

Exercise 3

The two words in the story where the letter *h* is always silent are **hour** and **honest** (there are very few words like this; the others are *honour* and *heir*).

UNIT 11

Stress on modal verbs for speculation

Exercise 1

Likely: 1B, 2A, 3A, 4A, 5A. Unlikely: 1A, 2B, 3B, 4A, 5B.

UNIT 12

Linking and intrusive /r/

Exercise 1

1 I don't know why <u>they're(r)angry</u> with us. We didn't do anything wrong!
2 Some animals are finding it <u>harder(r)and</u> harder to live on our planet.
3 From <u>her(r)accent</u> I'd say Julie is French.
4 We're flying into <u>Atlanta(r)airport</u> on our trip to the USA.
5 It's <u>another(r)awful</u> day – I wish it wasn't raining again!
6 I'd like to go to <u>Australia(r)and</u> America when I'm older.
7 <u>Hannah(r)always</u> leaves her homework until the last minute.